The European Neighbourhood Policy – Values and Principles

The European Neighbourhood Policy is a key part of the foreign policy of the European Union (EU), through which the EU works with its southern and eastern neighbours with a view to furthering its interests and achieving the closest possible degree of political association and economic integration. The policy is underpinned by a set of values and principles that the EU seeks to promote.

The European Neighbourhood Policy – Values and Principles carries out a legal analysis of the values and principles that form the basis of the European Neighbourhood Policy – respect for human dignity, freedom, democracy, equality, the rule of law and respect for human rights (including the rights of minorities), plus the principles of conditionality, differentiation and coherence.

This collection explores the instruments that the EU has deployed under the European Neighbourhood Policy to spread its values and achieve its interests. It assesses to what extent the EU has been (and is) consistent in upholding its values in its relations with neighbouring countries, and examines how these values have been received by these countries. The book looks in particular at the nature of EU–Russia relations, seeking to identify areas of common interest as well as those of actual and potential disagreement.

Sara Poli is Associate Professor and Jean Monnet Chair of European Union Law at the University of Pisa, Italy.

The European Neighbourhood Policy – Values and Principles

Edited by
Sara Poli

Taylor & Francis Group

LONDON AND NEW YORK

First published 2016 by Routledge

2 Park Square, Milton Park, Abingdon, Oxfordshire OX14 4RN
711 Third Avenue, New York, NY 10017

Routledge is an imprint of the Taylor & Francis Group, an informa business

First issued in paperback 2018

Copyright © 2016 selection and editorial matter, Sara Poli; individual chapters, the contributors

The right of Sara Poli to be identified as editor of this work has been asserted by her in accordance with sections 77 and 78 of the Copyright, Designs and Patents Act 1988.

All rights reserved. No part of this book may be reprinted or reproduced or utilised in any form or by any electronic, mechanical, or other means, now known or hereafter invented, including photocopying and recording, or in any information storage or retrieval system, without permission in writing from the publishers.

Notice:
Product or corporate names may be trademarks or registered trademarks, and are used only for identification and explanation without intent to infringe.

British Library Cataloguing in Publication Data
A catalogue record for this book is available from the British Library

Library of Congress Cataloguing in Publication Data
Names: Poli, Sara, editor.
Title: The European Neighbourhood Policy : values and
principles / edited by Sara Poli.
Description: Abingdon, Oxon; New York, NY : Routledge, 2016. |
Includes bibliographical references and index.
Identifiers: LCCN 2015042420| ISBN 9781138943094 (hbk) |
ISBN 9781315672755 (ebk)
Subjects: LCSH: European Union countries–Foreign relations–Law and legislation |
European Neighbourhood Policy (Program)
Classification: LCC KJE5109.E936 2016 | DDC 341.242/209–dc23
LC record available at http://lccn.loc.gov/2015042420

ISBN: 978-1-138-94309-4 (hbk)
ISBN: 978-1-138-61430-7 (pbk)

Typeset in Baskerville
by Out of House Publishing

 Printed in the United Kingdom by Henry Ling Limited

Contents

Acknowledgements vii
Notes on contributors viii

Introduction 1

PART I
EU values and their contestation 9

1 The fluid concept of 'EU values' in the neighbourhood: a change of paradigm from East to South? 11
   NARINÉ GHAZARYAN

2 Promoting EU values in the neighbourhood through EU financial instruments and restrictive measures 33
   SARA POLI

3 The contestation of values in the European Neighbourhood Policy: challenges of capacity, consistency and competition 58
   SIEGLINDE GSTÖHL

PART II
Techniques to promote EU values 79

4 The ENP and multilateralism 81
   MARISE CREMONA

5 EU values in integration-oriented agreements with Ukraine, Moldova and Georgia 99
   ROMAN PETROV

PART III
The EU's values in EU–Russia relations 113

6 Shared values and interests in the conflictual relationship between the EU and Russia 115
PAUL KALINICHENKO

7 'New values' for a new 'Great Russia' 130
ELENA DUNDOVICH

PART IV
The ENP and the principle of coherence 143

8 The European Neighbourhood Policy's value conditionality: from enlargements to post-Crimea 145
DIMITRY KOCHENOV AND ELENA BASHESKA

9 Exporting the rule of law to the EU's eastern neighbours: reconciling coherence and differentiation 167
PETER VAN ELSUWEGE AND OLGA BURLYUK

Index 183

Acknowledgements

I would like to warmly thank Francesca Bianchini, Marise Cremona and Giuseppe Martinico for their support and advice.

With the support of the LLP programme of the European Union

Notes on contributors

Elena Basheska has her LLM and PhD in EU Law from the University of Groningen, the Netherlands. She has worked at the Law Faculty at the South East European University, Tetotovo, Macedonia, as Lecturer, Vice Dean for Postgraduate Studies, and Director of the Research Centre. Her research focuses on the enlargement of the EU and EU foreign relations. In particular, she has published extensively on the interpretation and application of the good neighbourliness principle in EU law. She has recently co-edited with Dimitry Kochenov *Good Neighbourliness in the European Legal Context* (Brill-Nijhoff, 2015).

Olga Burlyuk is Assistant Professor at the Centre for EU Studies, Ghent University, Belgium. Her research focuses on the EU's external relations, in particular its efforts to transform third states and societies through the promotion of democracy, the rule of law and human rights, as well as trade and development cooperation. The Eastern European Neighbourhood, specifically Ukraine, is her area of specialization.

Marise Cremona is Professor of European Law and Co-Director of the Academy of European Law at the European University Institute, Florence, Italy (EUI). Between November 2009 and June 2012 she was Head of the Department of Law at the EUI and between June 2012 and August 2013 she was President Ad Interim of the EUI. Her research interests are in the external relations law of the European Union. She is particularly interested in the constitutional basis for EU external relations law and the legal and institutional dimensions of the EU's foreign policy; the interaction between national, regional and international legal and policy regimes; and the EU as an exporter of values and norms. She has published extensively on the external relations law of the European Union, including *Developments in EU External Relations Law* (Oxford University Press, 2008); *EU Foreign Relations Law – Constitutional Fundamentals*, edited with B. de Witte (Hart Publishing, 2008); *The External Dimension of the Area of Freedom, Security and Justice*, edited with J. Monar and S. Poli (Peter Lang-P.I.E., 2011); and *The European Court of Justice and External Relations Law – Constitutional Challenges*, edited with A. Thies (Hart Publishing 2014).

Elena Dundovich is President of three departments' courses and President of the PhD programme in geopolitics at the University of Pisa, Italy (Department of Political Science). She is Professor of the History of Eastern Europe and the Soviet Union and History of International Relations. A PhD doctor from 2003 to 2007, she was a lecturer in the History of International Organizations at the School of Political Sciences, University of Florence, Italy, and in 2007 of East European History at the University of Padova, School of Political Science. From 2007 to 2010 she was lecturer of History of International Relations at University of Tuscia, School of Organisational and Management Sciences. She is a member of Memorial Italia, an association created in 2004 to study Soviet and Russian history and the destiny of Italian victims of the Gulag.

Nariné Ghazaryan is Assistant Professor at the University of Nottingham, UK. Previously, she has been a lecturer at Brunel University, West London. She specializes in EU external relations law, in particular the EU's neighbourhood policies. She is the author of the monograph *The European Neighbourhood Policy and the Democratic Values of the EU: A Legal Analysis* (Hart Publishing, 2014).

Sieglinde Gstöhl is Director of the Department of EU International Relations and Diplomacy Studies at the College of Europe, Bruges, Belgium. She has been full-time professor at the College since 2005. From 1999 to 2005 she was Assistant Professor of International Relations at Humboldt University, Berlin, Germany. She holds a PhD and an MA in International Relations from the Graduate Institute of International and Development Studies, Geneva, Switzerland, as well as a degree in Public Affairs from the University of St. Gallen, Switzerland. She was, inter alia, a research fellow at the Liechtenstein-Institut, Liechtenstein, and at the Center for International Affairs at Harvard University, Cambridge, Massachusetts, US.

Paul Kalinichenko holds a Doctor of Legal Science in International and European Law from Kutafin Moscow State Law University (MSLA) (2011). He joined the EU Law Chair of the MSLA in 2000. In 2012 he was appointed Professor of the EU Law Chair of the MSLA. He has been a Visiting Professor of the European Study Institute at the Moscow State Institute of International Relations (Moscow) since 2006. He has been Coordinator of the Research Center for European Law at the Immanuel Kant Baltic Federal University (Kaliningrad) since 2012, and Head of the European Law Department of the Diplomatic Academy at the Russian Foreign Ministry since 2013. His research activities focus on EU external relations law, EU environmental law and EU economic law. He devotes his attention to the legal aspects of Russia–EU relations. He has been engaged as a legal advisor in European affairs at the Ministry of Education and Science of Russia since 2010 and as a legal advisor in European law at the Eurasian Economic Commission since 2012.

Dimitry Kochenov is Visiting Professor and Martin and Kathleen Crane Fellow in Law and Public Affairs, Woodrow Wilson School, Princeton University, New Jersey, US (2015–2016); Chair in EU Constitutional Law, University of Groningen; and Visiting Professor, College of Europe, Natolin campus. He is mainly engaged with principles of EU law and the role of the individual in the evolution of the EU legal order. He has been the editor, most recently, of *EU*

Citizenship and Federalism: The Role of Rights (Cambridge: CUP, 2016); *Reinforcement of the Rule of Law Oversight in the European Union* (with C. Closa, Cambridge: CUP, 2016); *The Enforcement of EU Law and Values: Ensuring Member States' Compliance* (with A. Jakab, Oxford: OUP, 2016) and *Europe's Justice Deficit?* (with G. de Búrca and A. Williams, Oxford: Hart Publishing, 2015). At Princeton he is working on a monograph on EU citizenship for Hart Publishing, Oxford.

Roman Petrov holds an LLM in International and European Legal Studies from Durham University, UK (1998), a PhD in Law from the National Academy of Science of Ukraine (2000), a PhD in Law from Queen Mary University of London, UK (2005) and a Habilitation from the Institute of Legislation of the Parliament of Ukraine (2014). He conducted postdoctoral research as Max Weber Fellow at the European University Institute, Italy (2006–2008) and had visiting research fellowships at the University of Heidelberg, Germany, the University of Oxford, UK, and Ghent University, Belgium. He is founder and first elected President of the Ukrainian European Studies Association. Currently he is Jean Monnet Chair in EU Law and Head of the International Law Department and the Jean Monnet Centre of Excellence at the National University of Kyiv-Mohyla Academy, Ukraine. His areas of research and teaching include: EU law, EU external relations law, approximation and harmonization of legislation in the EU, the rights of third-country nationals in the EU and legal aspects of regional integration in the post-Soviet era.

Sara Poli has held a Jean Monnet Chair since 2013. She is Associate Professor of European Law at the University of Pisa, Italy. Previously she has worked for the University of Rome Tor Vergata, the University of Trieste, Italy, and for the University of Southampton, UK. She carried out research at the European University Institute, Florence, Italy, in 2002 and 2009. She was a teaching assistant in the European legal studies department of the College of Europe, Bruges, Belgium (1999–2001). She received her PhD from the Scuola Superiore Sant'Anna, Pisa, Italy. She has written on widely different topics of European law, including EU external relations law. She co-edited with I. Govaere *EU Management of Global Emergencies: Legal Framework for Combating Threats and Crises by the European Union* (Brill, External Relations Studies, 2014) and with M. Cremona and J. Monar *The External Dimension of the European Union's Area of Freedom, Security and Justice* (Peter Lang, 2011).

Peter Van Elsuwege is Professor in EU Law at the Ghent European Law Institute (GELI) of Ghent University, Belgium. He is also Visiting Professor at the College of Europe (Natolin Campus), Warsaw, Poland. His research activities focus on EU external relations law. He devotes his attention to the legal framework of relations between the EU and its East European neighbours. He is the author of *From Soviet Republics to EU Member States: A Legal and Political Assessment of the Baltic States' Accession to the EU* (Brill, 2008) and the editor (together with R. Petrov) of *Legislative Approximation and Application of EU Law in the Eastern Neighbourhood of the European Union: Towards a Common Regulatory Space?* (Routledge, 2014).

Introduction

The European Union (EU) is a 'community of values' and seeks to promote those values both inside and outside its borders. In order to establish an area of stability, security and well-being in its neighbourhood, the Union encourages third countries to adopt its economic and political model. Yet the European Neighbourhood Policy (ENP) is often criticized since there is an internal clash between the mentioned goals. In addition, the latter are subjugated to the EU's economic or security interests. These are some of the factors that have led to the ENP's multidimensional failures. Should the EU institutions introduce changes in this policy? Discussing these issues is particularly important at a time when reform of the EU's strategy is open. Indeed, High Representative Mogherini and Enlargement Commissioner Hahn launched the review process of the ENP with a consultation paper in March 2015.[1] The Council and the Parliament in the following months also took a position on the reform of the ENP, which is considered a 'strategic priority of EU's foreign policy.'[2] While calling for greater differentiation in the EU's relations with its partner countries, there seems to be a consensus that the ENP should remain a single policy – the alternative solution being the creation of a bundle of bilateral relations between the EU and each ENP country – and that its objectives and values-based approach should be kept.

The values upon which the EU is founded are respect for human dignity, freedom, democracy, equality, the rule of law and respect for human rights, including the rights of persons belonging to minorities. This list is included in Art. 2 of the Treaty of the European Union (TEU). The EU promotes these political values, broadly in the context of all its external relations. The specific purpose of the ENP is to inspire economic and political reforms in the partner countries providing 'a stake in the internal market' as an incentive.

---

[1] See joint consultation paper from the Commission and the High Representative of the European Union for Foreign Affairs and Security Policy 'Towards a New European Neighbourhood Policy', 4 March 2015.
[2] European Parliament Committee on Foreign Affairs, Report on the Review of the European Neighbourhood Policy, A8-0194/2015 of 18 June 2015, point H; Foreign Affairs Council meeting of 20 April 2015, doc 8084/15, p. 7.

The various contributions in this book critically examine the principles underpinning the ENP – such as those of conditionality, differentiation and coherence – and the way they have evolved. To what extent has the EU been consistent in upholding its values in its relations with individual ENP countries? How have EU values been received by partner countries? Should the EU values-based approach be changed? These are some of the questions that the contributors address. The techniques and instruments that the EU has deployed to diffuse its values and to promote its interests in its neighbourhood will also be illustrated.

There are four main ways for the EU to promote its values in its foreign affairs. The first is to consider them as 'essential elements' of legally binding agreements concluded with partner countries and to associate non-execution clauses in case of breach. Thus, the violation of these elements may lead to the suspension of the agreement itself. The second is to encourage third countries to ratify and effectively implement multilateral or regional agreements that are based on universal values. The third is to make respect for the mentioned values a prerequisite for receiving financial assistance from the EU. Finally, restrictive measures may also be used to sanction failure to respect democracy, human rights and international law.

The book is divided into four parts. Part I, entitled 'EU values and their contestation', comprises three chapters. The first, written by Nariné Ghazaryan, examines how the EU has shaped the values of Art. 2 TEU – in particular, democracy, the rule of law and human rights – in its relations with its eastern and southern neighbours. First, the author assesses whether there are any differences in the concept of 'EU values', as defined in soft law instruments (i.e. the foundational documents of the ENP and the Action Plans), depending on whether a country belongs to the group of southern or eastern neighbours. Ghazaryan's conclusion is that there is no East/South division. However, in the Action Plans of Armenia, Georgia and Azerbaijan the EU takes a more restrictive interpretation of EU values than in the case of other neighbours. The next issue is how the Arab Spring has impacted on the EU's values-based approach, both on soft law instruments and in practice. The ideal of 'deep and sustainable democracy' is shown to be inaugurated in the normative framework and is extended to the EU's relations with both southern and eastern neighbours. It is claimed that overall there are no significant variations between democracy and the understanding of this concept, following the 2011 uprisings. The only new elements in the ENP policy documents concern the emphasis on the need to establish democratic control over armed and security forces and the reference to the right to a fair trial. As to the implementation of this 'new approach', Ghazaryan notes that it is deficient in both the eastern and southern dimensions of this policy. Attention then shifts to the 'essential elements clauses' of the eastern Association Agreements and the Euro-Mediterranean Agreements. These clauses are paradigmatic of the values the EU wants to promote in its relations with ENP countries. Nariné Ghazaryan's detailed analysis leads to the conclusion that the clauses in the former group of agreements are wider in scope, and therefore much more onerous, not only in terms of the 'essential elements' themselves, but also for the normative internal framework underpinning them. This is understandable given that the European countries of the ENP may apply for the EU's membership.

Chapter 2 creates a bridge between Chapters 1 and 3. While the former focuses on the Action Plans and Association Agreements, the latter examines other instruments employed by the EU to promote its values abroad. These are the external financial instruments – in particular, the European Neighbourhood Instrument (ENI) but also the Decisions on macro-financial assistance based on Art. 212 (or 213) of the Treaty on the Functioning of the European Union (TFEU) – and restrictive measures, falling within the scope of the Common Foreign and Security Policy (CFSP). Sara Poli examines to what extent the way the EU promotes its values differs from the Instrument of Pre-Accession Assistance (IPA II), used within the framework of the enlargement policy. The conclusion is that the Regulation setting up the ENI in 2014 strengthens the importance of EU values compared to the previous regime (dating from 2006) and is similar in content to the IPA II. Decisions on macro-financial assistance are scrutinized to examine to what extent they are based on political conditionality. Does respect of EU values matter to receive the EU's financial assistance? A further question is whether the EU has specifically used this form of financial support to the benefit of ENP partners or has also extended its assistance to other third countries (i.e. the 'near neighbours'). The Chapter highlights that after 2013 Decisions on macro-financial assistance have been adopted to support the transition of third countries to democracy. However, they are not reserved for ENP countries.

Turning to restrictive measures, the analysis is aimed at examining whether there are distinctive features in the sanctions adopted against the governmental leadership and/or nationals and entities of ENP countries. The term of comparison is restrictive measures enacted against other third countries and/or legal and natural persons in situations in which human rights or democratic rules were breached. It is argued that there are categories of sanctions concerning the ENP countries with distinctive elements. The EU's judicial assistance to democracies in transition, such as Tunisia and Egypt, in fighting the misappropriation of funds is specific to the ENP. Restrictive measures adopted against the secessionist Ukrainian Republics, in reaction to their breach of the principle of territorial integrity and sovereignty, and also against Russia are also unique and worth highlighting. This denotes that the EU is more committed to supporting the establishment of its values in its relations with its neighbours than with other third countries.

In Chapter 2 Sara Poli also dwells on the rationale for an EU values-based approach and the criticism that it has attracted. This contribution thus introduces the debate on the contestation of EU values presented by Chapter 3.

Sieglinde Gstöhl's chapter focuses on the reasons that weaken the EU values-based approach. These are on the one hand, endogenous factors: the ambiguous nature of these values and the potential conflicts between them, which have resulted not only in policy incoherence but also in the selective application of the principle of conditionality. It is argued that the EU's assumptions at the root of the ENP and the techniques used to export the EU's values are also flawed. For example, the EU mistakenly took it for granted that all partner countries would try to emulate the European model. In addition, the principle of conditionality, used to enforce these values was not entirely suitable; indeed, the EU values need to be internalized for their effective implementation. The EU can be also criticized for basing the ENP on the principle of joint ownership, which is at odds with the principle of political conditionality. On the other hand, there are exogenous factors that ultimately undermine the adherence of some ENP partners to these values; for example, neighbours have in some cases been incapable and in others unwilling to absorb them. As the author states, the export of EU values in the neighbourhood is characterized by a lack of capacity to absorb EU values, consistency problems, and an unwelcome normative rivalry with Russia and its Eurasian integration projects.

Part II focuses on techniques to promote EU values. On the one hand, the EU seeks to support universal values as a result of its commitment to *multilateralism*. Chapter 4 considers how EU's policy of *multilateralism* is translated in the ENP context. On the other, the EU concludes *bilateral* agreements with ENP countries that are instrumental to promoting values, as noted in Chapter 1. The EU agrees with the ENP country the changes to be introduced in their domestic legal orders to implement common values. In Chapter 5, Roman Petrov looks at the latest generation of European integration agreements with eastern neighbours. Although there are variations amongst the agreements, it may be said that this set of agreements is the most open to EU values.

In Chapter 4 Marise Cremona shows how the EU lives up to its commitment to promote multilateralism within the context of the ENP. First, neighbour countries are invited to ratify and effectively implement basic human rights conventions and other key international agreements; to support international institutions (i.e. International Criminal Court/International Atomic Energy Agency) as well as the EU's position in international forums on key security issues. Second, the EU also asks ENP countries to assist in the promotion of negotiations regarding new international agreements. Third, the EU sponsors regional multilateralism by favouring regionally-oriented technical assistance projects and collaboration with the Council of Europe. The EU has thus set up joint programmes for both eastern and southern neighbours, focusing on judicial reform, electoral standards and the fight against corruption. Fourth, a technique worthy of mention concerns the use of the EU sanction measures to enforce the UN and Council of Europe Conventions against corruption. Fifth, the EU seeks the support of its 'rings of friends' within the context of its Common Foreign and Security's initiatives. For example, ENP partners are invited to join the EU in adopting restrictive measures or to align to the EU's public statements. However, the degree of commitment of the ENP countries varies depending on their own positions and interests. The last example of commitment in this area concerns the invitation to ENP partners to participate in EU-led crisis missions. In the case of Moldova, Georgia and Ukraine, the terms of this participation are formalized in a legally binding agreement.

Chapter 5 examines the Association Agreements with Ukraine, Moldova and Georgia of 2014. These instruments are different both from other Association

Agreements with southern countries and also from those with (candidate) countries with a European perspective. According to Roman Petrov, the Agreements with eastern European countries are 'integration-oriented', which means that they include principles, concepts and provisions which are to be interpreted and applied as if the third country concerned were part of the EU. There are many novel aspects in these agreements: EU values and the principle of conditionality play a prominent role. For example, the objective of setting up Deep and Comprehensive Free Trade Areas (DCFTAs), leading to gradual and partial integration of Ukraine, Moldova and Georgia into the EU Internal Market, is something new. In addition, the scope of the cooperation in these complex agreements is wide, ranging from the fields of trade to Common Foreign and Security Policy and Justice and Home Affairs. There is a strong emphasis on regulatory convergence between the parties and the possibility to apply and implement most of the EU *acquis* within the Ukrainian, Moldovan and Georgian legal orders. The author of the chapter notes that two different forms of conditionality can be distinguished in these agreements. The classic 'common values' conditionality is accompanied by an explicit 'market access' conditionality. The decision to grant additional access to a section of the EU Internal Market can be taken only if these countries have successfully implemented their legislative approximation commitments, which are subject to a strict monitoring procedure.

This collection of essays also looks at EU-Russia relations in order to investigate the reasons why they have deteriorated over time and have ultimately transformed Russia from a 'strategic' to a 'distant neighbour'. Part III is devoted to this topic. The two chapters highlight, on the one hand, the EU and Russia's shared values and interests but also the reasons for their conflictual relationship and, on the other, the values behind Putin's idea of a great new Russia.

In Chapter 6, Paul Kalinichenko takes a legal perspective. After emphasizing that Russia and the EU have common interests and constitutional values, he refers to Russian case law and shows that the Partnership and Cooperation Agreement (PCA) has been a useful instrument of economic cooperation for the two contracting parties. However, the two international actors have gradually become 'distant neighbours' due to the unwelcome competition entered into by the EU with the Eurasian projects. The Ukrainian crisis has affected the trade relations of the two parties within the context of the WTO and has led to the adoption of restrictive EU measures and Russian countermeasures. The author of the chapter believes that in order to revitalize their relations, the PCA, which is outdated, should be replaced by a new agreement. Indeed, global threats and economic interdependence demand a closer cooperation and partnership between the two partners rather than a confrontation.

Chapter 7 explains from the perspective of a historian the new values promoted by the Russian political leadership (as of 2000) to create a new image of a 'Great Russia' both inside and outside its borders. First of all, Elena Dundovich shows how the Eurasist vision was central to Putin's strategy, based on the idea of a Great Russian Empire, promoting the incorporation of the Russian-speaking populations that had remained outside the borders of Federal Russia. Second, she explains how the West and the idea of a nation state ceased to be a model for Russia after the West supported the so-called coloured revolutions. This was the time that Putin promoted patriotism (rather than nationalism) as the foundation of its policy and conceived Russia as a multinational empire where various nationalities could live together under the common roof of Russian culture. Third, the author argues that the role of the Orthodox Church has been crucial in forging Russian identity. Its support was guaranteed by the conservative policies of the governmental leadership (i.e. the laws against blasphemy and the homosexual and libertarian propaganda of the Western press) and its defence of Christian roots, 'traditional European values' (including the 'traditional family') as opposed to the new 'European values' based on 'boundless tolerance'. Fourth, the chapter explains how Putin has revisited the historical memory and has used it as an ideological weapon. The last pillar of Putin's strategy to build the idea of new Russia is based on the use of rituals, symbols and ceremonies to celebrate the grandeur of the president. Coming to Russia's foreign policy, the contribution emphasizes that the popularity of the president is not only the result of Putin's tight control on the media but also of Western attitudes and of the sanctions regime. Finally, the contribution highlights how Russia has become increasingly 'distant' from Europe and the West and looks with interest to its Asian allies of the Collective Security Treaty Organization (CSTO) and the partners of the Shanghai Cooperation Organization (SCO).

Part IV is dedicated to the principle of coherence in the ENP. In order to be credible *vis-à-vis* its ENP partners, the EU should be consistent. The EU's coherence can be explored from different angles. Chapters 8 and 9 focus on the internal coherence of the ENP with respect to the principles underlying this external policy and more broadly the whole spectrum of EU external relations. In this part the following questions are raised. Is the EU coherent in applying the principle of conditionality and in differentiating its relations with ENP countries accordingly? In addition, should the EU continue to use the principle of conditionality in the ENP? What are the alternative approaches? Chapter 8 explores all of these issues. A further problem pertaining to the internal coherence of the ENP is whether the EU is consistent in the way it promotes specific values in its relations with ENP countries. Chapter 9 focuses on this issue by examining the EU's consistency in exporting the rule of law, which is a relatively unexplored value in comparison with other EU values (e.g. democracy and human rights).

In Chapter 8 Elena Basheska and Dimitry Kochenov criticize the use of the principle of conditionality in the context of the ENP. First, the authors of the chapter contend that the values of Art. 2 TEU are not genuinely shared by the EU and many ENP partners. Second, the EU does not provide sufficient incentives ('a stake in the internal market') or sufficient financial resources through the ENI to ensure compliance with the values. Thus, the effectiveness of the principle of conditionality is questionable. Often, partner countries have not adhered to EU values; at the same time, in several cases the EU has set a very low threshold of adherence (e.g. Azerbaijan, Egypt). This flexible approach towards certain partners has served the EU's interests rather than the promotion of its values. This contribution criticizes the key EU instruments, principles, assumptions and approaches, aimed at creating a 'ring of friends' in the Union's neighbourhood. The EU's diplomatic conduct in its relations with Russia is also considered questionable: the EU believed that it could promote its values in a vacuum, with no opposition to its external policies. Finally, the authors argue that the new ENP should not be based on uniform approaches to all neighbours but on tailor-made engagement with them. The EU should give up the propaganda language of values and 'joint ownership' of the process. Depending on the needs of the partner in question, a clear choice has to be made whether to apply conditionality or not. It is suggested that the EU should export concrete rules – the *acquis* to 'willing countries', whereas it would be wrong for the EU to continue applying the conditionality principle in its relations with 'reluctant partners'.

In Chapter 9 Peter Van Elsuwege and Olga Burlyuk examine the way the EU reconciles its obligation to be coherent with the principle of differentiation of the ENP, in exporting 'the rule of law'. This contribution does not compare the EU's approach with eastern and southern neighbours. Indeed, this issue is touched upon in Chapter 1. Instead this last chapter focuses on the coherence-differentiation dynamic, taking into consideration the group of eastern neighbours. At the outset, the contribution highlights the problematic nature of the concept of the 'rule of law' and also the lack of particular indicators to assess whether a given country adheres to it. The rule of law is a fluid concept 'including certain core principles of which the precise interpretation largely depends upon the particular context.' The authors of the chapter note that considering the EU's lack of competence in enforcing the rule of law with respect to EU Member States – this is at least the Council's position – 'it appears impossible – and perhaps even undesirable – to apply a strict EU definition of the rule of law in relation to third countries.' This is rather a task for the Council of Europe. Attention is then shifted to the content of the 'rule of law clauses' of the Agreements with Ukraine, Moldova and Georgia. Is the rule of law included in the 'essential elements' clauses of these agreements, which are primarily used by the EU to export its values? This is the case for Ukraine alone. However, even in the other two cases, the 'rule of law clause' gives the Union a mandate to be involved in the domestic reforms in these countries. By contrast, the 'EU's rule of law export is much more difficult and, as a result, less developed with regard to non-associated eastern neighbours.' The legal relations with the latter countries are, for the time being, still based on largely outdated PCAs. This difference is not an element of incoherence. The final part of the chapter considers the EU's approach to migration as a case study to examine the interplay between differentiation and coherence. It is shown with which eastern neighbours countries the EU has concluded Mobility Partnerships, bilateral agreements on visa facilitation and readmission and Visa Liberalisation Action Plans (VLAPs). The latter instruments can be singled out since they include rule of law requirements, thus showing that there is a coherent framework for the export of the rule of law to those countries. The authors of the chapter conclude that there is a high degree of differentiation in EU-eastern neighbours cooperation in the field of migration. Whereas readmission and visa facilitation agreements have been concluded with Georgia, Moldova, Ukraine, Armenia and Azerbaijan, the process of visa liberalization was only started with the first three countries. Hence, 'the EU's leverage in terms of rule of law export is most developed with regard to the associated countries. For Armenia and Azerbaijan, their lower ambition of integration with the EU implies that the Union cannot apply the same pressure but, concomitantly, less far-reaching incentives are offered.' The conclusion is that the field of migration is thus an area in which a certain level of policy coherence can be reconciled with differentiated bilateral relations and mechanisms for exporting the rule of law abroad. On the other hand, there is a discrepancy between the policy on visa liberalization with Russia and the policies with Georgia, Moldova and Ukraine. The Common Steps document with Russia is less demanding and only requires discussion and cooperation regarding the relevant recommendations of international human rights organizations. This confirms that the export of EU values to Russia is based on a totally different approach from that with ENP countries.

Many of the ideas, insights and arguments presented in this book were discussed at an international workshop, 'The EU and Its Values: Contestation and Consistency', which was organized by the Jean Monnet Chair of the University of Pisa, on 3 October 2014. This conference was generously funded by the Lifelong Learning Programme Jean Monnet Action. The financial support of this Action is gratefully acknowledged and was essential both in exchanging ideas and stimulating a cross-disciplinary discussion in the context of this conference and in conceiving this book.

Part I
EU values and their contestation

1 The fluid concept of 'EU values' in the neighbourhood

A change of paradigm from East to South?

Nariné Ghazaryan

Introduction: setting the scene

Exporting European Union (EU) values has been a staple of the rhetoric of the European Neighbourhood Policy (ENP) since its early days in 2003. Values were to be promoted to and shared with all addressees of the policy, the list of which grew to cover a vast geographic area in the vicinity of the European Union, including both bordering and other countries.[1] The ENP applies to the EU's eastern and southern neighbours with varying intensities as some countries have seemingly advanced legally and politically in their cooperation with the EU, while others have not agreed on a basic framework of cooperation.[2] In 2008 and 2009, a few years following the ENP's inception, EU neighbourhood policies were divided into regional flanks, with the Eastern Partnership (EaP) and the Union for the Mediterranean (UfM).[3]

Exporting EU values is a means to an end, i.e. the achievement of the EU's wider policy objectives of securing a stable and safe zone around its post-2004 and 2007 enlargement borders.[4] The underlying idea is that the more the EU's neighbours replicate EU values, the safer and securer the EU will be. Ambitious in its scope, the policy aimed to integrate the neighbouring states into the EU in an

---

[1] The following countries are addressees of the policy (some do not have immediate borders with the EU at present): Ukraine, Moldova, Belarus, Georgia, Armenia, Azerbaijan, Egypt, Algeria, Tunisia, Morocco, Israel, the Occupied Palestinian Territories, Syria, Jordan, Lebanon and Libya.

[2] For instance, no ENP Action Plans have been established with Belarus, Algeria, Libya or Syria as of June 2015.

[3] Brussels European Council Conclusions, 19–20 June 2008, 19; Brussels European Council Conclusions, 13–14 March 2008, 19.

[4] For the centrality of security considerations within the ENP, see M. Smith and K. Webber, 'Political Dialogue and Security in the European Neighbourhood Policy: The Virtues and Limits of "New Partnership Perspective"' (2008) 13 *EFAR* 81; W. Wallace, 'Looking after the Neighbourhood: Responsibilities for the EU-25' (2003) 4 *Notre Europe Policy Papers* 27; R. Zaiotti, 'Of Friends and Fences: Europe's Neighbourhood Policy and the "Gated Community Syndrome"' (2007) 29 *European Integration* 143, 149; M. Cremona and C. Hillion, 'L'Union Fait La Force? Potential and Limitations of the ENP as an Integrated EU Foreign and Security Policy' in N. Copsey and A. Mayhew (eds), *European Neighbourhood Policy: The Case of Europe*, Sussex European Institute, (2006) 1 *SEI Seminar Papers Series* 24.

extensive range of areas.[5] In the absence of a membership agenda, the incentive of a deep and comprehensive free trade area has gradually emerged to motivate willing neighbours in their efforts to emulate the EU's values as well as its institutions and practices.

The application of ENP conditionality both in the east and in the south has faced much criticism.[6] Rather than considering EU values in the light of the policy of conditionality,[7] this chapter explores the normative agenda of this conditionality. Currently, Art. 2 TEU offers a list of EU values such as freedom, democracy, equality, the rule of law and respect for human dignity and human rights, including minority rights. While this list serves broadly as a signpost for the values to be promoted, it is worth analyzing what is meant by them. The chapter also considers how the EU has shaped these values in its relations with its eastern and southern neighbours.

The EU might be expected to require a more stringent standard from the Eastern Neighbourhood, for two reasons. First, the ENP was originally aimed at the EU's eastern neighbours, some of which, including Russia, were to be affected to a certain extent by the 2004 enlargement, and some of which were rather vocal about their aspirations for EU membership. Second, although the EU intended the ENP to be a replacement for EU membership for the countries concerned, it nevertheless did not entirely rule out such membership. Since there has been no membership rejection as in the case of Morocco in 1987, Art. 49 TEU allows any 'European' state to apply for membership upon fulfilling certain conditions. It was therefore legitimate to expect the EU to be stricter with European countries. However, this does not necessarily mean that the EU is imposing a strict standard

---

[5] Commission (EC) 'Wider Europe – Neighbourhood: A New Framework for Relations with Our Eastern and Southern Neighbours', COM (2003) 104 final, 11 April 2003, 5. On the legal aspects of ENP see M. Cremona, 'The European Neighbourhood Policy: More Than a Partnership?' in M. Cremona (ed.), *Developments in EU External Relations Law* (Oxford, Oxford University Press 2008); B. Van Vooren, *EU External Relations Law and the European Neighbourhood Policy: A Paradigm for Coherence* (London, Routledge 2014); N. Ghazaryan, *The European Neighbourhood Policy and the Democratic Values of the EU* (Oxford, Hart Publishing 2014).

[6] D. Kochenov, 'The ENP Conditionality: Pre-Accession Mistakes Repeated' in L. Delcour and E. Tulmets (eds), *Pioneer Europe? Testing EU Foreign Policy in the Neighbourhood* (Baden-Baden, Nomos 2008), 116; A. Magen, 'The Shadow of Enlargement: Can the European Neighbourhood Policy Achieve Compliance?' Centre on Democracy, Development and the Rule of Law, Stanford Institute for International Studies (2006) 68 *Working Paper* 415; K.E. Smith, 'The Outsiders: The European Neighbourhood Policy' (2005) 81 *International Affairs* 757, 765; N. Tocci, 'Can the EU Promote Democracy and Human Rights Through the ENP? The Case for Refocusing on the Rule of Law' in M. Cremona and G. Meloni (eds), *The European Neighbourhood Policy: A New Framework for Modernisation?*, (2007) 21 *EUI Working Papers*, LAW 23–35, 31; M. Emerson, 'Is There to Be a Real European Neighbourhood Policy?' in R. Youngs (ed.), *Global Europe: New Terms of Engagement* (Foreign Policy Centre, London 2005) 15–22, 20; P. Seeberg, 'The European Neighbourhood Policy, Post-Normativity and Pragmatism' (2010) 15 *EFAR* 676; Ghazaryan (n 5) 125–149; R.A. Del Sarto and T. Schumacher, 'From Brussels with Love: Leverage, Benchmarking, and the Action Plans with Jordan and Tunisia in the EU's Democratisation Policy' in S. Lavenex and F. Schimmelfennig (eds), *Democracy Promotion in the EU's Neighbourhood: From Leverage to Governance* (London, Routledge 2013) 49.

[7] See Kochenov and Basheska's chapter in this volume.

on all its eastern neighbours.[8] This chapter explores the extent to which the values of the EU differ depending on the specific grouping of neighbours. In the first section, 'values' as established in the ENP foundational policy documents, as well as the Action Plans (APs) – the initial bilateral policy documents – are examined. The second section traces the projection of EU values in the multilateral frameworks of cooperation created following the geographic division in the policy and considers the effects that the Arab Spring revolutions have had on both policy flanks. The third section presents a comparison between the essential elements clauses in the latest and most important instruments of cooperation in the East – the newly established Association Agreements (AAs) with Ukraine, Georgia and Moldova[9] – and the Euro-Mediterranean AAs in the South, some of which were concluded after the ENP was inaugurated.[10]

EU values as set out in ENP documents and Action Plans

The first ENP document, the 2003 Wider Europe Communication, contains an indication of the values dimension of the ENP initiative: it starts off by including democracy and respect for human rights and the rule of law within 'shared values' and, in a footnote, links these concepts to the Charter of Fundamental Rights.[11] Not only did the Charter have no binding legal force at that time, but also its content, although relevant for democracy and the rule of law, could be characterized as a bill of rights (including non-justiciable principles).[12] This was rather unusual since the EU refers to international standards in its contractual relations with third

---

[8] See, for instance, the comparison between the South Caucasian countries, Ghazaryan (n 5).
[9] Association Agreement between the European Union and the European Atomic Energy Community and their Member States, of the one part, and Georgia, of the other part [2014] OJ L261/4; Association Agreement between the European Union and the European Atomic Energy Community and their Member States, of the one part, and the Republic of Moldova, of the other part [2014] OJ L260/4; Association Agreement between the European Union and its Member States, of the one part, and Ukraine, of the other part [2014] OJ L161/5.
[10] Euro-Mediterranean Agreement establishing an Association between the European Community and its Member States, of the one part, and the People's Democratic Republic of Algeria, of the other part [2005] OJ L265/2; Euro-Mediterranean Agreement establishing an Association between the European Communities and their Member States, of the one part, and the Arab Republic of Egypt, of the other part [2004] OJ L304/39; Euro-Mediterranean Agreement establishing an Association between the European Communities and their Member States, of the one part, and the Hashemite Kingdom of Jordan, of the other part [2002] OJ L129/3; Euro-Mediterranean Agreement establishing an association between the European Communities and their Member States, of the one part, and the State of Israel, of the other part [2000] OJ L147/3; Euro-Mediterranean Agreement establishing an association between the European Communities and their Member States, of the one part, and the Kingdom of Morocco, of the other part [2000] OJ L070/2; Euro-Mediterranean Agreement establishing an association between the European Communities and their Member States, of the one part, and the Republic of Tunisia, of the other part [1998] OJ L97/2; Euro-Mediterranean Agreement establishing an association between the European Community and its Member States, of the one part, and the People's Democratic Republic of Lebanon, of the other part [2006] OJ L143/2.
[11] COM (2003) 104 final (n 5), 4.
[12] Charter of Fundamental Rights of the European Union [2010] OJ C83/389.

countries (see, for instance, human rights clauses of EU agreements). The Wider Europe Communication continues by including pluralism, civil liberties and core labour standards, which are viewed as 'essential prerequisites for political stability, as well as for peaceful and sustained social and economic development.'[13] In addition, the Communication stresses the institutional aspect of democracy and human rights by emphasizing the importance of 'strong democratic institutions' and 'the need to institutionalise respect for human rights.'[14] After defining these core 'values', the Communication makes a judgement about progress in political reform in the neighbourhood: 'Generally, the countries of the WNIS [Western Newly Independent States] and Russia have taken steps towards establishing democracy and market institutions over the past 12 years. Yet political reform in the majority of the countries of the Mediterranean has not progressed as quickly as desired.'[15] This judgement would have suggested at the time that the EU would be stricter in its approach towards values in its relations with its southern neighbours than with Moldova and Ukraine (part of the WNIS).

The concept of 'shared values' is further emphasized in a 2004 ENP Strategy Paper: 'The privileged relationship with neighbours will build on mutual commitment to common values principally within the fields of the rule of law, good governance, the respect for human rights, including minority rights, the promotion of good neighbourly relations'.[16] While it would seem that democracy is replaced here with good governance, the Strategy Paper also gives the Commission monitoring powers with respect to 'the strengthening of democracy, the rule of law and respect for human rights.'[17] Most importantly, the Strategy Paper specifies the 'values' that the APs will contain:

> strengthening democracy and the rule of law, the reform of the judiciary and the fight against corruption and organised crime; respect of human rights and fundamental freedoms, including freedom of media and expression, rights of minorities and children, gender equality, trade union rights and other core labour standards, and the fight against the practice of torture and prevention of ill-treatment; support for the development of civil society; and co-operation with the International Criminal Court.[18]

This appears to be an indicative list of priority actions, which includes general actions that can be implemented without any prioritization. The ENP Strategy Paper also makes it clear that international standards will form the basis for the promotion of these values. These international standards include UN human rights conventions, the European Convention on Human Rights (ECHR) (for

---

[13] COM (2003) 104 final (n 5) 7.
[14] Ibid. 12.
[15] Ibid. 7.
[16] Commission (EC) 'Communication from the Commission European Neighbourhood Policy' (Strategy Paper), COM (2004) 373, 12 May 2004, 3.
[17] Ibid. 10.
[18] Ibid. 13.

those neighbours who are members of the Council of Europe), the UN Charter, the Universal Declaration of Human Rights (UDHR) and, in relation to South Caucasian countries, the Organization for Security and Co-operation in Europe (OSCE).[19] The 2006 Commission Communication on strengthening the ENP did not add much to the understanding of the values and merely referred to their interlinked nature with the other areas of cooperation.[20] The Communication's muted stance might have been because most of the bilateral APs were already in place by then.

In terms of the priority actions that reflect the EU values with each ENP country, the APs can be divided into two main groups: Egypt, Jordan, Lebanon, Morocco, Tunisia, Ukraine and Moldova in one group and Georgia, Armenia and Azerbaijan in the other.[21] The APs for the first group can be grouped under a wider list of priority actions related to democracy and human rights. Despite the regional distinction and the presumption in the Wider Europe Communication that non-EU Mediterranean countries are lagging behind in their progress on political reform, a similar range of issues can be identified with a comparable intensity.[22]

Thus the priority areas relevant to our discussion are usually divided under two headings: (1) democracy and the rule of law, and (2) human rights and fundamental freedoms.[23] The first heading mainly focuses on strengthening democratic institutions, often with an emphasis on free and fair elections, decentralization, the independence and efficiency of the judiciary, the functioning of civil society and the fight against corruption. The second heading refers to specific rights and freedoms, with a major emphasis on political rights, including freedom of association, media pluralism, the prevention of torture, freedom of religion, women's and children's rights, social rights and labour standards.

Not all issues are equally reflected in all APs; for instance, the APs for Egypt, Jordan, Lebanon, Morocco and Tunisia (southern neighbours) have a stronger emphasis on women's rights, as well as on fighting discrimination, racism and xenophobia. The Ukrainian and Moldovan APs have additional actions, such as ensuring international justice related to the International Criminal Court.

The APs in the first group were much criticized for being overly general in nature, with a lack of precision and poor benchmarking.[24] The second group of

---

[19] Ibid. 10–13.
[20] Commission (EC) Communication from the Commission to the Council and the European Parliament on 'Strengthening the European Neighbourhood Policy', COM (2006) 726 final, 4 December 2006, 3.
[21] No APs have been established with other neighbours (n 2).
[22] Available online at http://eeas.europa.eu/enp/documents/action-plans/index_en.htm (accessed 3 June 2015).
[23] Only the EU–Ukraine AP does not divide the actions under two headings.
[24] On the EU–Tunisia and EU–Jordan APs, see R. Del Sarto and T. Schumacher (n 6) 51, 56–62; on EU–Israel, see W.T. Douma, 'Israel and the Palestinian Authority' in S. Blockmans and A. Lazowski (eds), *The European Union and Its Neighbours: A Legal Appraisal of the EU's Policies of Stabilisation, Partnership and Integration* (The Hague, TMC Asser Press 2006) 433–461, 457; R.A. Del Sarto, 'Wording and Meaning(s): EU-Israeli Political Cooperation according to the ENP Action Plan' (2007) 12 *Mediterranean Politics* 61–62; on the EU–Morocco AP, see K. Kausch, 'The European

APs (i.e. for the South Caucasian countries) is even more limited in its approach. Their priorities for political reform are structured around the issues of the separation of powers of the executive and judiciary, electoral reform, and guaranteeing basic rights. There are some significant omissions even from this shortened list. For instance, the Georgian AP largely omits the issue of human rights and fundamental freedoms: the prohibition of torture is the only issue that features on the human rights agenda of the Georgian AP. In the Azerbaijani AP, corruption features in a separate area related to the improvement of the business climate, suggesting that this issue was being depoliticized. In the case of Armenia, the functioning of the national parliament and the political parties was omitted. Overall, these APs take a much more restrictive interpretation of EU values than the APs of the first group.[25]

There are two APs that stand out from the rest. The EU–Palestine AP should be distinguished from other APs because of the manner in which the issue of values is presented: prioritizing the foundations of future state building in 'the rule of law and respect for human rights within a functioning deep democracy and with accountable institutions.'[26] Given the absence of statehood, it is understandable why no list of actions would be expected here, although there is a call for action in terms of political rights, women and girls' rights.

Israel's AP should also be viewed separately, although for a different reason. In this case, as distinct from the APs considered previously, there are no actions regarding state institutions and their practices, but rather both Israel and the EU are to strive to fight racism, xenophobia, Islamophobia (Israel) and anti-Semitism (EU).[27] It is the only AP where priorities are set for the EU as well. The impression that one draws from the content of the plan is that the values at the basis of the cooperation are perceived to be shared.

It can therefore be concluded that the normative content set out in the ENP Strategy Paper has been most closely replicated in the APs for Ukraine, Moldova, Egypt, Jordan, Lebanon, Morocco and Tunisia, although not in a fashion which can be seen as real benchmarking. This suggests that there was a divide at this stage in the way the EU defined its values within its eastern neighbours, rather than a split between the East and the South.

The geographic split of neighbourhood policies and the projection of EU values after the Arab Spring

A few years after the establishment of the ENP, with the enterprise of certain proactive Member States, a regional split occurred in EU policies towards the

---

Union and Political Reform in Morocco' (2009) 14 *Mediterranean Politics* 165, 171; M. Emerson and G. Noutcheva, 'From Barcelona Process to Neighbourhood Policy: Assessments and Open Issues' (2005) 220 *CEPS Working Document*.

[25] For a more detailed analysis of the APs with South Caucasian countries, see Ghazaryan (n 5) 130–149.
[26] Priority Objective 3 in the EU–Palestine AP.
[27] For a more detailed analysis of the EU–Israel Action Plan, see Del Sarto (n 24).

neighbourhood with the initiation of the EaP in the East and a somewhat revamped Barcelona Process, the UfM, in the South.[28] To an extent, the geographic split marked a return to the original rationale of the ENP, that is to offer preferential relations to its eastern neighbours.[29] In its proposal for the EaP, the Commission envisaged that the new initiative would 'make a step change in relations with these partners' in comparison with the ENP, which promised, inter alia, a free trade area.[30]

The EaP preserved the values rhetoric of the ENP and promised intensified bilateral cooperation through association agreements. According to the EaP Communication:

> a sufficient level of progress in terms of democracy, the rule of law and human rights, and in particular evidence that the electoral legislative framework and practice are in compliance with international standards, and full cooperation with the Council of Europe, OSCE/ODIHR and UN human rights bodies will be a precondition for starting negotiations and for deepening relations thereafter.[31]

This suggested that both international and regional standards would be applied to the EU's eastern neighbours. The OSCE instruments had previously formed the basis of cooperation with the EU via the essential elements clauses in the Partnership and Cooperation Agreements (PCAs).[32] Without dwelling on the problematic aspects of the application of ENP conditionality, the fact that negotiations were entered into with most EaP countries demonstrates that the Communication's preconditions were mostly rhetorical. Despite significant shortcomings in political reforms, testified to in the Commission's annual Progress Reports for each of the partners, negotiations had started with all EaP countries with the exception of Belarus.

---

[28] Brussels European Council Conclusions, 19–20 June 2008, 19. For the discussion of the Member States' position at this stage see B. Van Vooren, 'The European Union as an International Actor and Progressive Experimentation in Its Neighbourhood' in P. Koutrakos (ed.), *European Foreign Policy: Legal and Political Perspectives* (Edward Elgar Publishing 2011) 147–171, 152–153.

[29] E. Lannon and P. Van Elsuwege, 'The Eastern Partnership: Prospects of a New Regional Dimension within the ENP' in E. Lannon (ed.), *The European Neighbourhood Policy's Challenges* (P.I.E. Peter Lang 2012) 285–322, 286.

[30] Commission (EC), Communication from the Commission to the European Parliament and the Council 'Eastern Partnership', COM (2008) 823 final, 3 December 2008, 2.

[31] Ibid. 4.

[32] PCA between the European Communities and their Member States, of the one part, and Russia, of the other [1997] OJ L327/3; PCA between the European Communities and their Member States, of the one part, and the Republic of Armenia, of the other [1999] OJ L239/3; PCA between the European Communities and their Member States, of the one part, and the Republic of Azerbaijan, of the other [1999] OJ L246/3; PCA between the European Communities and their Member States, of the one part, and the Republic of Georgia, of the other [1999] OJ L205/3; PCA between the European Communities and their Member States, of the one part, and the Republic of Moldova, of the other [1998] OJ L181/3; PCA between the European Communities and their Member States, of the one part, and Ukraine, of the other [1998] OJ L049/3.

The EaP also introduced a multilateral framework of cooperation for eastern neighbours which was expected to provide 'added value' to the new project.[33] In this context, the novelty of the EaP was seen not in terms of the incentives or instruments on offer, but rather as the intention to enhance the relations between the eastern partners themselves.[34] The EaP was nonetheless aimed not only at introducing qualitative changes to the ENP, but also at counterbalancing, to a certain extent, the Russian presence, since its launch was linked to the August 2008 war in Georgia.[35]

On a structural level, the EaP introduced new forums for multilateral high-level meetings, which supports the suggestion that the EaP takes the political association between the EU and its partners further than a 'classical association.'[36] The conclusions of the first 2009 biannual Prague summit did not add much to the understanding of the values, simply aligning the relationship 'to the principles of international law and to fundamental values, including democracy, the rule of law and the respect for human rights and fundamental freedoms, as well as to market economy, sustainable development and good governance.'[37] The new agreements promised by the EaP were expected to clarify further the meaning of values.

The EaP established four thematic platforms for multilateral cooperation (the cooperation takes the form of an exchange of practices through meetings held twice a year for senior officials): (1) democracy, good governance and stability; (2) economic integration and convergence with EU policies; (3) energy security; and (4) contacts between people. The thematic platform on democracy and good governance follows the Action Plan requirements, mainly referring to the obligations the neighbouring states undertake in the Council of Europe or the OSCE.[38]

It can be argued that the real added value of the EaP for the purposes of EU democratic values is linked to the enhanced role of national parliaments and civil society. Parliamentary exchange is made possible through the Euronest parliamentary cooperation framework which, according to the ENP Commissioner, represents more than just another EaP structure: it is a tool to 'advance democratisation' via shared experiences between parliamentarians.[39] The establishment of a civil society forum in 2009, which convenes annually, is another important

---

[33] For the Polish policy makers the EaP was to transform the eastern neighbourhood based on the Visegrad accession experience; AK Cianciara, '"Eastern Partnership"– Opening a New Chapter of Polish Eastern Policy and the European Neighbourhood Policy?' (2008) 4 *The Institute of Public Affairs*, Warsaw, 3, 6.

[34] B. Van Vooren, 'The European Union as an International Actor and Progressive Experimentation in Its Neighbourhood' in P. Koutrakos (ed.), *European Foreign Policy: Legal and Political Perspectives* (Cheltenham, Edward Elgar 2011) 156.

[35] N. Popescu, 'ENP and EaP: Relevant for the South Caucasus?' in *South Caucasus: 20 Years of Independence* (Friedrich Ebert Stiftung 2011) available at: http://library.fes.de/pdf-files/bueros/georgien/08706.pdf (accessed 10 February 2016) 316–334, 327.

[36] C. Hillion and A. Mayhew, 'The Eastern Partnership – Something New or Window-Dressing' (2009) 109 *SEI Working Paper* 8–9.

[37] Eastern Partnership Prague Summit Declaration, 7 May 2009, 5.

[38] See Ghazaryan (n 5).

[39] S. Füle, European Commissioner for Enlargement and European Neighbourhood, Speech at the Euronest Parliamentary Assembly Baku, Speech/12/256, 3 April 2012.

development within the EaP and compensates to some extent for the sidelined role of civil society within the ENP. The forum has established its own working groups, including groups devoted to democracy, good governance and stability.

The UfM was a qualitatively different initiative from the ENP, as a mostly intergovernmental multilateral platform and with a wider membership than the EU Member States and the southern neighbours.[40] Driven by France, the aim of the UfM was to build on the Barcelona Process, which had already promised a trade area for partner states. The Barcelona Process chapters, including those on political dialogue, were to continue to be the focus of relations.[41] The values rhetoric was preserved in the 2008 Paris Summit Declaration, which stressed the parties' commitment to strengthening democracy and political pluralism:

> by the expansion of participation in political life and the embracing of all human rights and fundamental freedoms, ... full respect of democratic principles, human rights and fundamental freedoms, as enshrined in international human rights law, such as the promotion of economic, social, cultural, civil and political rights, strengthening the role of women in society, the respect of minorities, the fight against racism and xenophobia and the advancement of cultural dialogue and mutual understanding.[42]

However it became quite clear that political reform was not at the forefront of the new initiative, which was also characterized as being 'apolitical'[43] and lacking 'reform objectives'.[44] Moreover, the UfM was criticized for foregoing political conditionality altogether.[45] It also failed to establish parliamentary or civil society cooperation,[46] in the same way as the EaP.

The EU's approach came under its own scrutiny shortly after the Arab Spring. The first reaction came in the form of the Partnership for Democracy and Shared Prosperity with the Southern Mediterranean (PDSP) in 2011. The new partnership emphasized the need for joint efforts in political reform, linking political reform to economic growth and development.[47] The partnership for democracy

---

[40] It includes also current and potential candidate states (Montenegro, Albania, Bosnia and Herzegovina, Turkey) and other countries (Mauritania and Monaco); Commission (EC) Communication from the Commission to the European Parliament and the Council 'Barcelona Process: Union for the Mediterranean' COM (2008) 319 final, 20 May 2008.

[41] Economic Cooperation and Free Trade, and Human, Social and Cultural Dialogue, Migration, Social Integration, Justice and Security are the other chapters; ibid. 4.

[42] Joint Declaration of the Paris Summit for the Mediterranean, Paris, 13 July 2008, 10.

[43] Del Sarto and Schumacher (n 6) 50.

[44] R. Balfour, 'The Transformation of the Union for the Mediterranean' (2009) 14 *Mediterranean Politics* 99, 104.

[45] J.C. Völkel, 'More for More, Less for Less – More or Less: A Critique of the EU's Arab Spring Response à la Cinderella' (2014) 19 *EFAR* 263.

[46] R. Gillespie, 'A "Union for the Mediterranean" ... or for the EU?' (2008) 13 *Mediterranean Politics* 277, 284.

[47] European Commission/High Representative, 'A Partnership for Democracy and Shared Prosperity with the Southern Mediterranean', COM (2011) 200 final, 8 March 2011.

was to focus on 'democratic transformation and institution-building, with a particular stress on fundamental freedoms, constitutional reforms, reform of the judiciary and the fight against corruption' and 'a stronger partnership with the people, with specific emphasis on support to civil society.'[48] Although it can be suggested that 'constitutional reform' as such had not been mentioned hitherto in either ENP or UfM documents, all other components of political reform had already featured in ENP policy documents, as well as in the APs with the southern neighbours. An entry qualification was established in 'a commitment to adequately monitored, free and fair elections',[49] although without specifying what the 'entry' is for. Some have viewed the new partnership as having a sharper focus on the balance between the state and civil society,[50] whereby 'expanding support to civil society' has been placed at the heart of democracy and institution building.[51] Such reorientation was particularly seen as 'a clear mea culpa on behalf of the EU.'[52] A few years later, the Southern Neighbourhood Civil Society Forum was established, holding its first session in 2014.[53]

This revisionist approach is also seen in the Joint Communication of the Commission and the High Representative for Foreign Affairs, which reviewed the ENP in 2011. The review was initiated in 2010, prior to the turbulent events in the Southern Neighbourhood, and it is not clear whether the revolutions in the region left their mark on it or whether its contents had already been established and translated into the PDSP. According to Gillespie, 'the existing policy review was extended so that adjustments could be made to the outcome. Essentially, the review brought proposals to make democratising reforms more central to the policy content of future ENP Action Plans.'[54]

The revised ENP seemingly offers a closer partnership to build democracy, pursue economic development and manage migration.[55] This outlook is based on further differentiation – the so-called more for more approach, where it appears almost in an incentive-like role.[56] However, differentiation is not necessarily or exclusively linked to political reforms, but also to other internal and external

---

[48] Ibid. 3.
[49] Ibid. 5.
[50] A. Teti, 'The EU's First Response to the "Arab Spring": A Critical Discourse Analysis of the Partnership for Democracy and Shared Prosperity' (2013) 17 *Mediterranean Politics* 272–273, 276.
[51] COM (2011) 200 final (n 47).
[52] 'EU Action to Strengthen Respect for Human Rights and Democracy in the Process of Political Changes in the Middle East and North Africa', Directorate General for External Policies, European Parliament, 4 December 2012, 12. Available online at www.europarl.europa.eu/RegData/etudes/etudes/join/2012/457141/EXPO-DROI_ET(2012)457141_EN.pdf (accessed 3 June 2015).
[53] 'First EU–Southern Neighbourhood Civil Society Forum takes place in Brussels', Press Release, 28 April 2014, Brussels.
[54] R. Gillespie, 'The UfM Found Wanting: European Responses to the Challenge of Regime Change in the Mediterranean' in F. Bicchi and R. Gillespie (eds), *The Union for the Mediterranean* (London, Routledge 2012) 213.
[55] European Commission/High Representative 'A New Response to a Changing Neighbourhood', COM (2011) 303, 25 May 2011, 1.
[56] Ibid. 2, 8–9, 20–21; European Commission/High Representative, 'Delivering on a New European Neighbourhood Policy', JOIN (2012) 14, 15 May 2012, 2–4.

political developments.[57] The 'more for more approach' goes hand in hand with 'a new approach' in promoting democracy, which is meant to signal a reinforced commitment to political reforms.[58] On the one hand, it can be suggested that this was prompted by Art. 8 TEU, inserted by the Lisbon Treaty. The 'new approach' is included in the first post-Lisbon revision of the ENP, which should reflect the EU's commitments under Art. 8 TEU.[59] According to the latter provision, the 'Union *shall* develop a special relationship with neighbouring countries ... founded on the values of the Union.' This suggests that the 'new approach' is mostly about underlining the importance of a commitment to these values, particularly when the substance of the commitments has not changed in practice.[60] The 'new approach' therefore concerns the external rehabilitation of the EU's normative image in an attempt to distance itself from its past practice of cooperating with or even strengthening authoritarian regimes.

This 'new approach' is linked to the so-called deep democracy, or deep and sustainable democracy.[61] This understanding of democracy follows the trend of merging the concepts of democracy, human rights and the rule of law. It avoids commitments to core democratic values and instead focuses on the following formal criteria:

- free and fair elections;
- freedom of association, expression and assembly, and a free press and media;
- the rule of law administered by an independent judiciary and the right to a fair trial;
- the fight against corruption;
- security and law enforcement sector reform (including reform of the police) and the establishment of democratic control over armed and security forces.[62]

Most of these elements of deep democracy are part of the ENP's earlier approach, and do not add much specification to the content of the values, clarified at the previous stage of relations. However, such additions as the establishment of democratic control over armed and security forces and the right to a fair trial seem to be at odds with the rest of the elements, which are rather general in character. These additions can be clearly explained within the revolutionary context of the southern neighbours. The reference to sustainable democracy suggests a shift towards a more inclusive understudying of human rights, inclusive of social

---

[57] P. Van Elsuwege, 'Variable Geometry in the European Neighbourhood Policy: The Principle of Differentiation and Its Consequences' in E. Lannon (ed.), *The European Neighbourhood Policy's Challenges* (College of Europe Studies, Bruxelles, P.I.E. Peter Lang 2012) 66–67.
[58] COM (2011), 303 (n 55) 2–3.
[59] For the analysis of article 8 TEU, see P. Van Elsuwege and R. Petrov, 'Article 8 TEU: Towards a New Generation of Agreements with the Neighbouring Countries of the European Union?' (2011) 36 *ELR* 688.
[60] Council Conclusions on the European Neighbourhood Policy, Foreign Affairs, 20 June 2011.
[61] COM (2011), 303 (n 55) 3.
[62] Ibid.

and economic rights, as opposed to the previous practice of mainly focusing on political rights. However, in view of the following paragraph, this does not seem to be the case:

> Reform based on [the above] elements will not only strengthen democracy but help to create the conditions for sustainable and inclusive economic growth, stimulating trade and investment. They are the main benchmarks against which the EU will assess progress and adapt levels of support.[63]

It suggests that progress in institution-building and securing political freedoms is a prerequisite for economic development. However, securing social and economic rights for the peoples of the neighbouring countries is not a priority per se. As part of a more general approach, the Council endorsed the Commission's report for democratic governance in December 2013, indicating that the EU would support 'a rights based approach encompassing all human rights.'[64] It should be noted that in line with the PDSP, the 2011 Communication revising the ENP also emphasized the importance of 'a partnership with society', with a major emphasis on civil society and its funding.[65]

The idea of deep democracy has also been translated into the EaP framework with the 2011 and 2013 Summit Declarations, which both refer to the commitment to deep and sustainable democracy, but without much elaboration.[66] Deep and sustainable democracy has also become part of the ENP Progress Reports since the post-Arab Spring ENP review. It is under this heading that the Commission evaluates each country's progress in the area of political reform; however, the ever-changing and patchy monitoring makes the idea of deep and sustainable democracy seem somewhat fuzzy.[67]

Despite the coining of the new terms 'deep democracy' and 'deep and sustainable democracy', no new mechanisms have been established to achieve deep democracy,[68] and the 'new approach' has not made a difference to the application of ENP conditionality. Subsequent events have demonstrated that the 'new approach' did not last long and that strict compliance with the values could be overlooked. For instance, no serious consequences followed the overthrow of President Morsi in Egypt, with the exception of the suspension of export licences to Egypt for any equipment that could be used for internal repression.[69] Similarly

---

[63] Ibid. 4.
[64] Foreign Affairs (Development) Council Conclusions, 12 December 2013, para 2.
[65] COM (2011), 303 (n 55) 3–4.
[66] Joint Declaration of the Eastern Partnership Summit, Warsaw, 29–30 September 2011, 1; Joint Declaration of the Eastern Partnership Summit, Vilnius, 28–29 November 2013, Eastern Partnership Vilnius Summit Declaration, 2.
[67] For criticism of the Commission's monitoring, see Ghazaryan (n 5) 154–159.
[68] M. Emerson, 'Review of the Review – of the European Neighbourhood Policy' CEPS Commentary, 8 June 2011, 4. Available online at www.ceps.eu/publications/review-review---european-neighbourhood-policy (accessed 3 June 2015).
[69] Foreign Affairs Council Conclusions, 21 August 2013, para 8.

in the East, AAs were signed with Ukraine while it was in political turmoil, as well as with Georgia and Moldova earlier than expected despite the weaknesses in their political reform profiles.[70]

It can be concluded that there is no major difference in the understanding of values between the Southern Neighbourhood and the Eastern Neighbourhood. In fact, the concept of EU values is general enough to be used in relations with eastern and southern neighbours in equal measure. Predominantly, the values focus on institutional practices and political rights. There is, however, a stronger emphasis in the Eastern Neighbourhood on political reform, accompanied by a more meaningful mechanism (such as parliamentary and civil society cooperation), in comparison with the UfM following the initiation of the EaP. The events in the Southern Neighbourhood required the EU to declare its reinforced commitment to its own values, while the 'new approach' of deep and sustainable democracy remained shallow in both flanks of the policy. This seeming parity, however, does not hold true when comparing the essential elements clauses of the Euro-Mediterranean Association Agreements and the Eastern Association Agreements (Eastern AAs).

Human rights clauses as statements of EU values: Eastern AAs v. Euro-Mediterranean AAs[71]

The human rights clauses in the Eastern AAs and the Euro-Mediterranean AAs have been analyzed extensively elsewhere.[72] The purpose of this section is a much narrower comparison between the essential elements clauses of these two groups of agreements. The Eastern AAs are not the first post-ENP agreements in the neighbourhood, as several Euro-Mediterranean AAs were signed after the initiation of the ENP as noted above. However, the Eastern AAs are the first post-Lisbon agreements in the neighbourhood, which might suggest a more stringent standard in terms of political commitments.

The essential elements clauses constitute part of the so-called 'standard' human rights clauses, in addition to a reference in the preamble and a provision on the suspension of the agreement.[73] In certain cases, a Joint Declaration accompanies

---

[70] Joint Staff Working Document 'Implementation of the European Neighbourhood Policy in Georgia Progress in 2012 and Recommendations for Action' SWD (2013) 90 final, 20 March 2013, 4–8; Joint Staff Working Document 'Implementation of the European Neighbourhood Policy in Republic of Moldova Progress in 2012 and Recommendations for Action' SWD (2013) 80 final, 20 March 2013, 5–8.

[71] This section is based on N. Ghazaryan, 'A New Generation of Human Rights Clauses? The Case of Association Agreements in the Eastern Neighbourhood' (2015) 40 *ELR* 391.

[72] L. Bartels, 'A Legal Analysis of Human Rights Clauses in the European Union's Euro-Mediterranean Association Agreements' (2004) 9 *Mediterranean Politics* 368; Ghazaryan (n 71).

[73] E. Riedel and M. Will, 'Human Rights Clauses in External Agreements of the EC' in P. Alston, *The EU and Human Rights* (Oxford, Oxford University Press 1999) 731–732; A. Rosas, 'The European Union and Fundamental Rights/Human Rights' in C. Krause and M. Scheinin (eds), *International Protection of Human Rights: A Textbook* (University Institute for Human Rights 2009) 443–474, 467; M. Bulterman, *Human Rights in the Treaty Relations of the European Community: Real Virtues or Virtual*

the agreements, linking the essential elements clause to the suspension mechanism.[74] It is primarily the essential elements provision that creates the normative framework of the values that are promoted in both regions. Thus a comparison between the respective provisions of the Euro-Mediterranean AAs and the Eastern AAs may reveal whether there is a distinct normative pattern as far as different geographic neighbourhoods are concerned.

Before turning to the essential elements clauses, the preambular references should be noted because often they also contain indications as to the values dimension of the cooperation. The preambles of the Eastern AAs are much more vocal on value issues than their southern counterparts. Despite certain differences between the Eastern AAs, the rhetoric on common values in all three of them is more prevalent than in the Euro-Mediterranean AAs. In the case of Georgia and Moldova, the values – that is, democracy, human rights and fundamental freedoms, and the rule of law – are 'at the heart of political association and economic integration.'[75] In the case of Ukraine, they constitute the 'basis of the cooperation', whereas the values are spelled out in a rather detailed manner for a preamble in order to include democratic principles, the rule of law, good governance, human rights and fundamental freedoms, including the rights of persons belonging to national minorities, non-discrimination of persons belonging to minorities, and respect for diversity and human dignity.[76] They are found in previous policies and in past commitments made by the parties.

More toned down and narrower references are found in the Euro-Mediterranean AAs. Here values including human rights, political and economic freedoms and, in some cases, also democratic principles form the 'basis of cooperation'.[77] Furthermore, already the recitals of the Eastern AAs indicate a more extensive scope of obligations. In fact, they refer to the UN Charter, OSCE documents, the UDHR and the ECHR, as opposed to only the UN Charter in the case of the Euro-Mediterranean AAs.

As regards the essential elements themselves, the Eastern AAs are more onerous both in terms of the elements considered as essential, as well as in terms of the international standards that form their basis. The essential elements usually include respect for human rights and democracy. The scope of the essential elements can also be expanded to include references to the rule of law, as in the case of the EU's contractual relations with certain countries in the Balkans.[78] At times the rule of law is not part of the essential elements clause, but is included among

---

Reality (Mortsel, Intersentia 2001) 157; L. Bartels, *Human Rights Conditionality in the EU's International Agreements* (Oxford, Oxford University Press 2005) 23.

[74] For instance, the Euro-Med Agreement with Algeria.
[75] Preambles of the EU–Moldova and EU–Georgia Association Agreements.
[76] Preamble of the EU–Ukraine Association Agreement.
[77] Euro-Med Agreement with Egypt; Euro-Med with Israel (human rights and democracy, no reference to political and economic freedoms here); Euro-Med Agreement with Jordan.
[78] See, for instance, Art. 2, Stabilisation and Association Agreement between the European Communities and their Member States, of the one part, and the Republic of Albania, of the other part [2009] OJ L107/166.

the areas of cooperation.[79] The PCAs with Georgia, Armenia and Azerbaijan also include respect for the principles of international law, explained with reference to the outstanding conflicts in the region.[80] In addition, the essential elements provision of the PCAs and the Stabilisation and Association Agreement (SAA) with the Western Balkan states includes the principles of market economy, for which a rationale has been found in the communist past of the countries concerned.[81]

The widening of the scope of these provisions has been criticized as discrediting the 'essential' nature of these elements, since the longer the list, the less essential its elements.[82] However, this does not diminish the essential status of these provisions in terms of their function.[83] On the other hand, it can be argued that the scope of the essential elements clauses is the widest in the neighbourhood. The Euro-Mediterranean AAs that were signed both before and after the ENP make no reference to the rule of law, the principles of international law or the market economy, and instead are limited to human rights – at times 'fundamental human rights' – and democratic principles.[84]

In contrast, the Eastern AAs include 'democratic principles, human rights and fundamental freedoms', offering a more nuanced approach by including 'human rights and fundamental freedoms'.[85] In addition, a new element on countering the proliferation of weapons of mass destruction, related materials and their means of delivery is also included as an essential element in line with the 2003 Council Common Position on non-proliferation.[86] By contrast, none of the Euro-Mediterranean AAs concluded after the ENP initiation and the adoption of the relevant Council Position have a similar provision. In other agreements, the issue of non-proliferation surfaced only as part of the political dialogue.[87]

An interesting variation lies with the rule of law and certain other new elements, which are exclusive to the Eastern AAs among the ENP agreements. Ordinarily

---

[79] M. Cremona, 'The European Neighbourhood Policy: Legal and Institutional Issues', Centre on Democracy, Development and the Rule of Law (2004) 25 *Working Papers* 20; see also P. Van Elsuwege and O. Burlyuk's chapter in this volume.

[80] See, for instance, common Art. 2 PCAs with Armenia, Georgia and Azerbaijan, Riedel and Will (n 73) 743.

[81] E. Fierro, *The EU's Approach to Human Rights Conditionality in Practice* (Hague: Martinus Nijhoff 2003), 235.

[82] Bulterman (n 73) 161.

[83] Ghazaryan, 'A New Generation of Human Rights Clauses' (n 71) 399–400.

[84] Art. 2 of Euro-Med Agreements with Algeria, Egypt, Jordan, Israel, Lebanon, Morocco and Tunisia.

[85] Art. 2 of EU–Ukraine AA, EU–Moldova AA and EU–Georgia AA.

[86] Council Common Position 2003/805/CFSP of 17 November 2003 on the universalisation and reinforcement of multilateral agreements in the field of non-proliferation of weapons of mass destruction and means of delivery [2003] OJ L302/34; M. Cremona, 'Values in EU Foreign Policy' in M. Evans and P. Koutrakos (eds), *Beyond the Established Legal Orders: Policy Interconnections between the EU and the Rest of the World* (Oxford, Hart Publishing 2011) 305.

[87] See Arts. 4–5 of Euro-Med Agreement with Syria, not signed, Council of the European Union. Available online at http://register.consilium.europa.eu/doc/srv?l=EN&f=ST%209921%202009%20 INIT (accessed 3 June 2015).

no further explanations are provided as to the meaning of the rule of law,[88] which appears to be the case with the Ukrainian clause. This provision is further stretched to include the principles of sovereignty and territorial integrity, inviolability of borders and independence as essential elements. This can be explained with reference to the political situation in Ukraine, in view of the Russian annexation of Crimea, and can therefore be seen as an expression by the EU of its support for Ukraine.[89] The EU has been unequivocal in its condemnation of the illegal referendum on independence and the subsequent annexation of the peninsula.[90]

However, in the Georgian and the Moldovan AAs, the rule of law as such does not constitute part of the essential elements clause and is stipulated in a different paragraph of the same article, framed in a language of 'reaffirming respect' for the rule of law and good governance.[91] Unlike the Ukrainian AA, the Georgian and Moldovan AAs further clarify the principle of the rule of law, referring to partners' international obligations in the UN, the Council of Europe and the OSCE. Although this is not specified within any particular context in the case of Moldova, the Georgian AA ties the rule of law to a wider international and national context. In Art. 2(2) the rule of law is linked to the principles of sovereignty and territorial integrity, inviolability of borders and independence, which therefore do not feature as essential elements – as in the case of Ukraine – but merely indicate the meaning of the rule of law. While including the principles of sovereignty and territorial integrity, inviolability of borders and independence within the general principles of cooperation can similarly be explained by the existence of frozen conflicts; their exclusion from the essential elements clause might be related to a less pressing political situation around the Abkhazian and South Ossetian conflicts. In addition, the commitment to the rule of law is further specified with reference to good governance, the fight against corruption, organized crime, terrorism etc.[92]

The Moldovan and Georgian agreements, unlike their Ukrainian counterpart, provide for a commitment to the principles of a free market economy, sustainable development and effective multilateralism within the same article as the essential elements provision, albeit in a different paragraph. Although the principle of a free market economy has previously been referred to in the PCA and SAA essential elements clauses,[93] the reference to sustainable development and effective multilateralism is new. Both the PCAs and the SAAs establish the principles

---

[88] Pech finds exceptions in the Cotonou agreement: L Pech, 'Promoting the Rule of Law Abroad: On the EU's Limited Contribution to the Shaping of an International Understanding of the Rule of Law' in D. Kochenov and F. Amtenbrink (eds), *The European Union's Shaping of the International Legal Order* (Cambridge, Cambridge University Press 2013) 114.

[89] Following a referendum in Crimea on 16 March 2014 on the issue of acceding to Russia, an accession treaty was signed on 18 March 2014 to include the Republic of Crimea and Sevastopol as part of the Russian Federation.

[90] Foreign Affairs Council Conclusions, 17 March 2014, para. 1; European Council Conclusions, 20–21 March, para. 29.

[91] Art. 2(3) of the EU–Moldova AA.

[92] Arts. 2(3) and (4) of the EU–Georgia AA.

[93] The Euro-Med agreements do not make reference to the principle of market economy.

The fluid concept of 'EU values' 27

of a market economy as part of the essential elements clause, as reflected in the Commission on Security and Cooperation in Europe's (CSCE) Bonn document.[94] This document mentions the objectives and endeavours of the participants to achieve 'sustainable economic growth', which can be compared to the principle of sustainable development. The reference to effective multilateralism suggests that it potentially refers to the WTO membership of the parties concerned. Ultimately, these principles are not part of the essential elements clause as such and, similar to the rule of law, only constitute part of the general provisions, which reiterate the commitments of the parties but do not have the same status as essential elements.

In comparison, the Ukrainian AA provides for a separate article within the general provisions, emphasizing the importance of the principle of a free market economy, the rule of law, good governance, the fight against corruption, transnational organized crime and terrorism, the promotion of sustainable development and effective multilateralism.[95] Thus in all three cases, the general principles have been expanded beyond the essential elements clause, hence making a distinction between the 'hard core common values' and 'other general principles' that are important to the parties.[96] However, the variation between the Ukrainian AA and the Georgian and Moldovan AAs demonstrates the flexible and rather arbitrary nature of this distinction.

In terms of the normative framework, human rights clauses often contain references to certain international instruments. The insertion of such references opposes the so-called *tout court* approach, which does not provide for additional information.[97] The *tout court* approach is therefore characterized by a higher level of abstraction, which leaves the party with more flexibility to determine the meaning of the provision.[98] The most prevalent practice in standard human rights clauses is to refer to the UDHR, which is viewed as testimony to the universality of the principles to which the parties have to adhere.[99] The presumption of the universality of the norms here, to a certain extent, reflects the EU's constitutional framework, starting from Art. 11(1) TEU and continuing in Arts. 21(1) and 21(2) (c) TEU.

---

[94] See, for instance, Art. 2 in the Ukraine and Moldova PCAs; Art. 2 in the Stabilisation and Association Agreement with Albania; Stabilisation and Association Agreement between the European Communities and their Member States of the one part, and the Republic of Serbia, of the other part [2013] OJ L278/16.
[95] Art. 3 of the EU–Ukraine AA.
[96] G. Van der Loo, P. Van Elsuwege and R. Petrov, 'The EU-Ukraine Association Agreement: Assessment of an Innovative Legal Instrument' (2014) 9 *EUI Working Papers* 13.
[97] Fierro (n 81) 234, 231.
[98] P. Leino, 'The Journey towards All That Is Good and Beautiful: Human Rights and "Common Values" as Guiding Principles of EU Foreign Relations Law' in M. Cremona and B. de Witte (eds), *EU Foreign Relations Law: Constitutional Fundamentals* (Oxford, Hart Publishing 2008), 279.
[99] A. Rosas, 'The European Union and International Human Rights Instruments' in V. Kronenberger (ed.), *The European Union and the International Legal Order: Discord or Harmony?* (The Hague, TMC, Asser Press 2011) 61; B. de Witte, 'The EU and the International Legal Order: The Case of Human Rights' in M. Evans and P. Koutrakos (eds), *Beyond the Established Legal Orders: Policy Interconnections between the EU and the Rest of the World* (Oxford, Hart 2011) 141–142.

While the *tout court* approach can be found in some Euro-Mediterranean AAs,[100] in others the only international instrument referred to is the UDHR,[101] which is viewed as a compromise, opting for the middle ground between the *tout court* approach and a very loaded content.[102] This aspect of the Euro-Mediterranean AAs is in stark contrast with the practice found in the Eastern AAs, where the UDHR is supplemented by the ECHR, the Helsinki Final Act and the Paris Charter. Here, the regional instruments are used to define the normative framework of the essential elements, which would not have been applicable to the southern neighbours. What is surprising, however, is that by containing a reference to the ECHR, the Eastern AAs appear to be more onerous than certain SAA candidate countries.[103]

Although, as part of customary international law, the UDHR would be binding for members of the international community,[104] no other document cited in the essential elements clause is directly binding on the parties. It has been suggested that the reliance on non-binding instruments is 'an indirect strengthening of international human rights standards, as they add another enforcement mechanism to otherwise "toothless" international supervisory bodies.'[105] This dynamic is different as far as the ECHR is concerned: it is the only instrument to create directly binding legal obligations for the countries concerned, whereby they risk losing membership of the Council of Europe. In this respect, it is possible to conclude that the essential elements clause of the Eastern AAs is the strictest in the neighbourhood.

The essential elements clauses in the Eastern AAs have a more clearly defined normative scope. However, some view the enhancement of the list of international instruments negatively, claiming that the greater the number of instruments referred to in the provision, the more uncertain is the exact standard promoted.[106] Others argue for an open-ended list of human rights instruments, whereby including a phrase on 'other human rights instruments' could be considered as a positive evolution that would allow the normative basis of the human rights clauses to be updated in line with emerging practice.[107] Here a distinction should be made between the Ukrainian AA and the Georgian and Moldovan AAs. In the latter case, the list of acts appears to be exhaustive, while in the former, the

---

[100] Art. 2 of the Euro-Med Agreement with Israel, Euro-Med Agreement with Tunisia.
[101] References to UDHR, for instance, can be found in the Euro-Med Agreements with Algeria, Egypt, Jordan and Morocco.
[102] Fierro (n 81), 237.
[103] Ghazaryan, 'A New Generation of Human Rights Clauses' (n 71) 398.
[104] De Witte (n 99) 141–142.
[105] F. Hoffmeister, 'The Contribution of EU Practice to International Law' in M. Cremona (ed.), *Developments in EU External Relations Law* (Oxford, Oxford University Press 2008) 114.
[106] Nogueras and Martinez as cited in A. Williams, *EU Human Rights Policies: A Study in Irony* (Oxford, Oxford University Press 2004) 41.
[107] Art. 1, Framework Agreement between the European Union and its Member States, of the one part, and the Republic of Korea, on the other part [2013] OJ L20; L. Bartels, '*The European Parliament's Role in Relation to Human Rights in Trade and Investment Agreements*' (2014) 9, 14–15. Available online at http://papers.ssrn.com/abstract=2441926 (accessed 10 October 2015).

provision refers to 'other relevant human rights instruments', thus rendering the list open ended.

None of the agreements actually refer to the EU human/fundamental rights standards as general principles of law or as established in the Charter of Fundamental Rights. Presumably, this is to steer away from accusations of imposing EU standards on outsiders and thereby adhere to the universality of the values promoted.

Thus, judging from the essential elements provisions only, the human rights clauses in the Eastern AAs reveal a more enhanced approach in terms of the basis of cooperation that stretches beyond democratic principles and human rights as essential elements. They also show much wider international standards, defining those essential elements where the European regional instruments feature heavily. It clearly demonstrates the political and geographic proximity of the Eastern – European – neighbours of the EU.

Conclusions

The initial ENP policy documents suggest a common reference point for values. The detailing of what constitutes values in the first ENP bilateral documents, the APs, demonstrate that there is no East–South division, but rather one between the WNIS Moldova and Ukraine and southern neighbours on the one hand, and the South Caucasian countries on the other. In this respect, the Israeli and Palestinian counterparts stand on their own for specific reasons: Palestine, due to an absence of statehood; Israel, due to the perception of shared values, with a limited number of actions prescribed for both the EU and Israel. Nevertheless, all APs in combination confirm the fluid nature of the concept of values, which allows for much generalization.

As far as the regional policy division is concerned, the value rhetoric, although preserved on both sides, is nevertheless more in tune with the reality of the EaP than it is with the reality of the UfM. The ENP revisions, which to a certain extent coincided with the response to the Arab Spring, led the EU to acknowledge its failures. In response, the EU set up a 'new approach', focusing on 'more for more' and 'deep democracy', to help it rectify its record. However, the 'new approach' has proven to be more of a label rather than a qualitatively different framework or method of sharing EU values. The deep democracy rhetoric has also been translated to the Eastern flank of the policy, although in a similarly meaningless fashion. A noticeable addition to the revision of the policy was the acknowledgement of the importance of engagement with civil society in neighbouring countries.

The most prominent distinction between the two regions, however, concerns the essential elements clauses of the Eastern AAs and the Euro-Mediterranean AAs. The clauses of the Eastern AAs are wider in scope and therefore much more onerous, not only in terms of the essential elements themselves, but also in terms of the normative internal framework underpinning them. This can be explained by the geographic and political proximity of the eastern neighbours. The Eastern AAs acknowledge the European nature of the relevant countries.

Although EU membership is not currently on the cards for them, this will help to keep speculation alive.

Bibliography

Balfour, R. (2009) The Transformation of the Union for the Mediterranean. *Mediterranean Politics*. 14(1). pp. 99–105.

Bartels, L. (2004) A Legal Analysis of Human Rights Clauses in the European Union's Euro-Mediterranean Association Agreements. *Mediterranean Politics*. 9(3). pp. 368–395.

—(2005) *Human Rights Conditionality in the EU's International Agreements*. Oxford: Oxford University Press.

—(2014) The European Parliament's Role in Relation to Human Rights in Trade and Investment Agreements. Available online at http://papers.ssrn.com/abstract=2441926 (accessed 10 October 2015).

Bulterman, M.K. (2001) *Human Rights in the Treaty Relations of the European Community: Real Virtues or Virtual Reality?* School of Human Rights Research Series (7). Mortsel: Intersentia NV.

Cianciara A.K. (2008) 'Eastern Partnership' – Opening a New Chapter of Polish Eastern Policy and the European Neighbourhood Policy? no. 4. The Institute of Public Affairs. pp. 1–16.

Cremona, M. (2004) *The European Neighbourhood Policy: Legal and Institutional Issues*. Center on Democracy, Development, and the Rule of Law, Stanford Institute for International Studies. Paper 25.

—(2008) The European Neighbourhood Policy: More than a Partnership? In Cremona, M. *Developments in EU External Relations Law*. Oxford: Oxford University Press.

—(2011) Values in EU Foreign Policy. In Evans, M. and Koutrakos, P. *Beyond the Established Legal Orders: Policy Interconnections between the EU and the Rest of the World*. Oxford: Hart Publishing.

Cremona, M. and Hillion, C. (2006) L'Union Fait la Force? Potential and Limitations of the European Neighbourhood Policy as an Integrated EU Foreign and Security Policy. In Copsey, C. and Mayhew, A. *European Neighbourhood Policy: The Case of Europe*. Sussex European Institute, SEI Seminar Papers Series Number 1.

Del Sarto, R. (2007) Wording and Meaning(s): EU-Israeli Political Cooperation according to the ENP Action Plan. *Mediterranean Politics*. 12(1). pp. 59–75.

Del Sarto, R. and Schumacher, T. (2013) From Brussels with Love: Leverage, Benchmarking, and the Action Plans with Jordan and Tunisia in the EU's Democratization Policy. In Lavenex, S. and Schimmelfennig, F. *Democracy Promotion in the EU's Neighbourhood: From Leverage to Governance?* Abingdon: Routledge.

De Witte, B. (2011) The EU and the International Legal Order: the Case of Human Rights. In Evans, M. and Koutrakos, P. *Beyond the Established Legal Orders: Policy Interconnections between the EU and the Rest of the World*. Oxford: Hart Publishing.

Douma, W.T. (2006) Israel and the Palestinian Authority. In Blockmans, S. and Lazowski, A. *The European Union and Its Neighbours: A Legal Appraisal of the EU's Policies of Stabilisation, Partnership and Integration*. The Hague: T.M.C. Asser Press.

Emerson, M. (2005) Is there to Be a Real European Neighbourhood Policy? In Youngs, R. *Global Europe 2: New Terms of Engagement*. London: Foreign Policy Centre.

—(2011) Review of the Review – of the European Neighbourhood Policy. CEPS Commentary. 8 June 2011, 4. Available online at www.ceps.eu/publications/review-review---european-neighbourhood-policy (accessed 3 June 2015).

Emerson, M. and Noutcheva, G. (2005) From Barcelona Process to Neighbourhood Policy: Assessments and Open Issues. *CEPS Working Document.* 220.

Fierro, E. (2003) *The EU's Approach to Human Rights Conditionality in Practice.* Leiden: Martinus Nijhoff.

Ghazaryan, N. (2014) *The European Neighbourhood Policy and the Democratic Values of the EU: A Legal Analysis.* Oxford: Hart Publishing.

—(2015) A New Generation of Human Rights Clauses? The Case of Association Agreements in the Eastern Neighbourhood. *European Law Review.* 40 (3). pp. 391–410.

Gillespie, R. (2008) A 'Union for the Mediterranean' … or for the EU? Profile. *Mediterranean Politics.* 13(2). pp. 277–286.

—(2014) The UfM Found Wanting: European Responses to the Challenge of Regime Change in the Mediterranean. In Bicchi, F. and Gillespie, R. *The Union for the Mediterranean,* Abingdon: Routledge.

Hillion, C. and Mayhew, A. (2009) The Eastern Partnership: Something New Or Window-Dressing. SEI Working Paper No 109.

Hoffmeister, F. (2008) The Contribution of EU Practice to International Law. In Cremona, M. *Developments in EU External Relations Law.* Oxford: Oxford University Press.

Kausch, K. (2009) The European Union and Political Reform in Morocco. *Mediterranean Politics.* 14(2). pp. 165–179.

Kochenov, D. (2008) The ENP Conditionality: Pre-Accession Mistakes Repeated. In Tulmets, E. and Delcour, L. *Pioneer Europe? Testing EU Foreign Policy in the Neighbourhood.* Baden-Baden: Nomos.

Lannon, E. and Van Elsuwege, P. (2012) The Eastern Partnership: Prospects of a New Regional Dimension within the European Neighbourhood Policy. In Lannon, E. *The European Neighbourhood Policy's Challenges.* Bruxelles: P.I.E. – Peter Lang.

Leino, P. (2008) The Journey towards All That Is Good and Beautiful: Human Rights and 'Common Values' as Guiding Principles of EU Foreign Relations Law. In Cremona, M. and de Witte, B. *EU Foreign Relations Law: Constitutional Fundamentals.* Oxford: Hart Publishing.

Magen, A. (2006) The Shadow of Enlargement: Can the European Neighbourhood Policy Achieve Compliance? *Columbia Journal of European Law.* 12(2). pp. 383–428.

—(2006) The Shadow of Enlargement: Can the European Neighbourhood Policy Achieve Compliance? Centre on Democracy, Development and the Rule of Law, Stanford Institute for International Studies. Working Paper No 68.

Pech, L. (2012) Promoting the Rule of Law Abroad: On the EU's Limited Contribution to the Shaping of an International Understanding of the Rule of Law. In Kochenov, D. and Amtenbrink, F. *The European Union's Shaping of the International Legal Order.* Cambridge: Cambridge University Press.

Popescu, N. (2011) ENP and EaP: Relevant for the South Caucasus? In *South Caucasus: 20 Years of Independence.* Friedrich Ebert Stiftung. Available online at http://library.fes.de/pdf-files/bueros/georgien/08706.pdf (accessed 10 February 2016).

Riedel, E. and Will, M. (1999) Human Rights Clauses in External Agreements of the EC. In Alston, P. *The EU and Human Rights.* Oxford: Oxford University Press.

Rosas, A. (2001) The European Union and International Human Rights Instruments. In Kronenberger, V. *The European Union and the International Legal Order: Discord or Harmony.* The Hague: T.M.C. Asser Press.

—(2009) The European Union and Fundamental Rights/Human Rights. In Krause, C. and Scheinin, M. *International Protection of Human Rights: A Textbook.* Turku: Åbo Akademi University Institute for Human Rights. pp. 443–474.

Seeberg, P. (2010) European Neighbourhood Policy, Post-Normativity, and Pragmatism. *European Foreign Affairs Review*. 15(5). pp. 663–679.

Smith, K.E. (2005) The Outsiders: The European Neighbourhood Policy. *International Affairs*. 81(4). pp. 757–773.

Smith, K.E. and Webber, M. (2008) Political Dialogue and Security in the European Neighbourhood: The Virtues and Limits of 'New Partnership Perspectives'. *European Foreign Affairs Review*. 13(1). pp. 73–95.

Teti, A. (2012) The EU's First Response to the 'Arab Spring': A Critical Discourse Analysis of the Partnership for Democracy and Shared Prosperity. *Mediterranean Politics*. 17(3). pp. 266–284.

Tocci, N. (2007) Can the EU Promote Democracy and Human Rights Through the ENP? The Case for Refocusing on the Rule of Law. In Cremona, M. and Meloni, G. *The European Neighbourhood Policy: A New Framework for Modernisation?* EUI Working Papers. LAW 2007/21.

Van Elsuwege, P. (2012) Variable Geometry in the European Neighbourhood Policy: The Principle of Differentiation and Its Consequences. In Lannon, E. *The European Neighbourhood Policy's Challenges*. Bruxelles: P.I.E. – Peter Lang.

Van der Loo, G. Van Elsuwege, P. and Petrov, R. (2014) The EU-Ukraine Association Agreement: Assessment of an Innovative Legal Instrument. EUI Working Papers No 9.

Van Vooren, B. (2011) *EU External Relations Law and the European Neighbourhood Policy: A Paradigm for Coherence*. Abingdon: Routledge.

—(2011) The European Union as an International Actor and Progressive Experimentation in Its Neighbourhood. In Koutrakos P. (ed.) *European Foreign Policy: Legal and Political Perspectives*. Cheltenham: Edward Elgar.

Völkel, J.C. (2014) More for More, Less for Less – More or Less: A Critique of the EU's Arab Spring Response à la Cinderella. *European Foreign Affairs Review*. 19(2). pp. 263–281.

Wallace, W. (2003) Looking after the Neighbourhood: Responsibilities for the EU-25. Notre Europe Policy Papers No 4.

Williams, A.J. (2004) *EU Human Rights Policies: A Study in Irony*. Oxford: Oxford University Press.

Zaiotti, R. (2007) Of Friends and Fences: Europe's Neighbourhood Policy and the 'Gated Community Syndrome'. *European Integration*. 29(2). pp. 143–162.

2 Promoting EU values in the neighbourhood through EU financial instruments and restrictive measures

Sara Poli

Introduction

The European Neighbourhood Policy (ENP) is presented by EU institutions as a values-based policy which is implemented through the principle of conditionality. This is 'designed to ensure that a partner country's political, economic and regulatory development converges with EU values and norms.'[1] While the values-based approach is common to other aspects of EU external policy, it may be wondered whether there are distinctive features in the way the EU promotes its values in its relations with ENP countries.

This issue will be examined in relation to specific instruments that the EU employs to project its values in the context of the ENP. These are the European Neighbourhood Instrument (ENI), provided for by Regulation (EU) 232/2014[2] and other external financial instruments such as the Decisions on macro-financial assistance. We will also examine restrictive measures; these are used as tools to promote the objectives of the Union's external action, such as peace, democracy and the respect for the rule of law, human rights and international law.[3] This contribution is thus complementary to those of other authors in this collection.[4]

Before looking at the mentioned instruments, we define the common values that underpin EU–ENP relations, the rationale of the EU's values-based approach in this context and the criticism that has been leveled at the EU for the way in which it has implemented such an approach. In the next section, we turn our attention to the EU's external financial instruments. The ENI,[5] which was revised in the months preceding Crimea's proclamation of independence, is briefly explored. First, we examine to what extent the newly enacted financial regime encourages ENP countries

---

[1] On the principle of conditionality see M. Cremona, 'EU Enlargement: Solidarity and Conditionality' (2005) 30(1) *European Law Review* 15.
[2] Regulation (EU) 232/2014 of the European Parliament and of the Council of 11 March 2014 establishing a European Neighbourhood Instrument [2014] OJ L 77/27.
[3] Factsheet, *EU Restrictive Measures*, 29 April 2014, 1.
[4] See, in particular, chapter 1 of this volume, written by N. Ghazaryan, focusing on Action Plans and the content of Association Agreements with ENP countries. On the latter instruments, see also R. Petrov's chapter in this volume. On Action Plans and other soft law instruments, see B. Van Wooren, 'A Case-Study of "Soft Law" in EU External Relations: The European Neighbourhood Policy' (2009) 34(5) *European Law Review* 696–719.
[5] See (n 2).

to adhere to its values and how it differs from the preceding edition of 2006. Does the EU continue to attach importance to the respect for its values in the disbursement of funds, despite the criticism that its values-based approach to the ENP has attracted? Is the principle of conditionality, which in its modern form is the 'more for more' principle, safeguarded in the ENI Regulation? Are there differences between the neighbourhood and enlargement policies in the importance attached to EU values when comparing the ENI with the new Instrument of Pre-Accession Assistance (IPA II)?

Decisions on macro-financial assistance are the next type of financial instrument that is scrutinized. To what extent are they linked to respecting EU values? Were the ENP partners the only addressees of these measures, or has the EU extended its assistance to other third countries?

In the following section, we turn to restrictive measures. Our analysis is aimed at mapping out the various categories of sanctions adopted by the EU to enforce respect for EU values and international law in the ENP context, and to identify the distinctive elements of these measures compared to those enacted against other third countries and nationals thereof.

Finally, the last section puts forward a few concluding observations on the place that EU values should have in the EU's cooperation with ENP countries. This is one of the thorny issues that the EU will have to address when revising the ENP.

The EU values-based approach to the ENP: the rationale and the criticism

Universal values such as the inviolable and inalienable rights of the human person, freedom, democracy, equality and the rule of law are the basis of European integration.[6] Respect for human dignity and for the rights of persons belonging to minorities are additional values stipulated in Art. 2 TEU, which represent the foundations upon which the EU rests.[7]

Adherence of ENP partners to EU values is fundamental to the development of the EU's relations with these countries.[8] In principle, the EU negotiates the terms of cooperation with its neighbours on the basis of 'shared values', that is to say a

---

[6] This can be inferred from the Preamble of the EU Treaty (TEU).
[7] With the exception of minority rights, this provision reformulates the principles of Art. 6 TEU in the pre-Lisbon era. There is a certain ambiguity in the Treaty as to whether democracy, the rule of law, the universality and indivisibility of human rights and fundamental freedoms, and respect for human dignity are principles that inspire the EU's action on the international scene as indicated by Art. 21(1) TEU or rather "values" as provided for by Art. 2. Principles of EU law are justiciable before the Court whereas values are not. See M. Cremona, 'Values in EU Foreign Policy' in M. Evans and P. Koutrakos (eds), *Beyond the Established Orders: Policy Interconnections between the EU and the Rest of the World* (Hart Publishing, Oxford 2011) 280–281.
[8] 'In return of concrete progress demonstrating shared values and effective implementation of political economic and institutional reform, ... the EU neighbourhood should benefit from the prospect of closer economic relations with the EU', European Commission (EC), Communication from the Commission to the Council and the European Parliament, 'Wider Europe – Neighbourhood: A New Framework for Relations with our Eastern and Southern Neighbours' COM (2003) 104, 11 March 2003, 4.

mutual commitment to respect them. However, the EU refers to its own 'values'.[9] This is explicit in the text of Art. 8 TEU.[10]

In fact, the values mentioned by the Action Plans with ENP countries are broader than those identified in Art. 2 TEU. EU partners are offered cooperation in exchange for respect for economic and political standards that can be identified with 'Western values'. The principle of the market economy is considered as a value to be promoted through the ENP together with respect for human dignity, democracy (which is qualified as 'deep and sustainable' after the Arab Spring), the rule of law, liberty, human rights, including those of persons belonging to minorities, and tolerance (or respect for diversity). Respect for international law, including international humanitarian law, which appears amongst the objectives of the EU's external relations, is also expected from the EU's partners.

It is worth examining the reasons behind the EU's choice to support a values-based approach. First, the EU perceives itself as an international actor with responsibility to export its values abroad. Second, democratic institutions and a market-based economy are essential ingredients for the modernization of ENP partners and also to the stability of their institutions. In a Resolution preceding the Ukrainian crisis, the EU Parliament recalls that:

> democratic reforms promoted by the EU are in the interest of the partner countries themselves and can contribute to their economic and social development; points out that strong democratic institutions and closer ties with the EU through Association Agreements, DCFTAs [Deep and Comprehensive Free Trade Agreements] and visa facilitation measures will help to strengthen the sovereignty of these countries against the influence of powerful neighbours; is deeply concerned about the mounting pressure being exerted on some partner countries, such as Moldova, Ukraine and Armenia, which is ultimately aimed at slowing down their progress towards further engagement with the EU; calls for the EU to address these issues in a politically coherent manner; reaffirms the EU's readiness to be a reliable and strong partner for these countries on the basis of shared common values and solidarity, and to share with them all the advantages of the EU acquis, along the lines of an Economic Area Plus arrangement.[11]

The model of pre-accession conditionality, which characterizes EU relations with candidate countries, was reiterated in the ENP in the hope that democracy and the rule of law would take root in the neighbouring countries. As the High Representative of the Union for foreign affairs and security policy (High

---

[9] M. Cremona (n 7) 302.
[10] This provision bases the EU's special relationship with neighbouring countries on the values of the EU. P. Van Elsuwege and R. Petrov, 'Article 8 TEU: Towards a New Generation of Agreements with the Neighbouring Countries of the European Union?' (2011) 36(5) *European Law Review* 688–703.
[11] European Parliament Resolution of 24 October 2013 on the Annual Report from the Council to the European Parliament on the Common Foreign and Security Policy (2013/2081(INI)), point 53.

Representative) put it, 'There is no stability without democracy. There is no security, without human rights. Stability and security cannot exist without a fair trial system, a serious commitment towards good governance, the rule of law and the fight against corruption. Stability versus democracy or security versus human rights are false dilemmas. We should never fall into this trap.'[12]

Third, it has been suggested that the EU may also have an internal reason for sticking to its values: it sees them as a tool to facilitate consensus amongst Member States 'to evade or minimize the[ir] ever-present resistance ... in the Council to a common European neighborhood policy.'[13] It is clear that there is a divide amongst the EU's southern and northern Member States as far as the ENP is concerned. Mediterranean countries are more interested in the southern dimension of this policy; the rest of the Union, in the northern dimension. Giving a soul to the ENP and making it based on the projection of EU values is a way of keeping Member States committed to developing EU relations with its neighbours within a single framework.

Finally, a link can be established between respect for selected EU values and the security, in its broadest sense, of the ENP and the EU.[14]

Sometimes the EU is criticized for being a realist power, pursuing its own interests in the ENP,[15] rather than a promoter of values. Del Sarto has recently defined 'the EU's exporting of rules and practices to neighbouring states as the modus operandi of empires in pursuit of their own interests; this modus operandi also serves the construction of a "normative" identity.'[16]

The same Treaty framework leaves the EU free to balance the export of its values with its interests. Article 3(5) TEU states: 'In its relations with the wider world, the Union shall uphold and promote its values and interests and contribute to the protection of its citizens.' It is clear from this wording that the projection of EU values abroad is placed on an equal footing with respect to the advancement of its interests. A similar idea is conveyed by Art. 13 TEU, which states: 'The Union shall have an institutional framework which shall aim to *promote its values*, advance

---

[12] Speech by High Representative/Vice-President Federica Mogherini at the UN Security Council: Cooperation between the UN and Regional and Sub-Regional Organisations, 09 March 2015. Available online at http://eeas.europa.eu/statements-eeas/2015/150309_01_en.htm (accessed 31 August 2015).

[13] I. Tömmel, 'The EU's New Neighbourhood Policy: An Appropriate Response to the Arab Spring?', 29 May 2013. Available online at www.e-ir.info/2013/05/29/the-new-neighbourhood-policy-of-the-eu-an-appropriate-response-to-the-arab-spring (accessed 1 September 2015).

[14] 'The promotion of stability, security and sustainable development gave rise to the ENP and remains a major EU objective. Security, in the broadest possible sense, demands transparent and accountable governance, respect for fundamental rights and freedoms, and economic and employment prospects', Joint Communication to the European Parliament, the Council, the European Economic and Social Committee and the Committee of the Regions 'Neighbourhood at the Crossroads: Implementation of the European Neighbourhood Policy in 2013', JOIN/2014/012 final, 27 March 2014.

[15] A. Hyde-Price, ' "Normative" Power Europe: A Realist Critique' (2006) 13(2) *Journal of European Public Policy* 217 ff.

[16] R. Del Sarto, 'Normative Empire Europe: The European Union, Its Borderlands, and the "Arab Spring" ' (2015) 54(2) *Journal of Common Market Studies* 216.

its objectives, *serve its interests*, those of its citizens and those of the Member States' (emphasis added). Article 21(2)(a) also mandates the EU to safeguard its values, fundamental interests, security, independence and integrity. This legal framework enables the EU to privilege its interests and continue to engage with strategic partners even if their adherence to universal values, such as democracy and respect for human rights and freedom, is not satisfactory. However, when this happens, the EU's credibility as an exporter of universal values is undermined.

It is true that several ENP countries are not interested in accepting the whole range of Western values.[17] As Korosteleva puts it, 'many countries of the former Soviet Union demonstrate an enduring proclivity for strong leadership and adherence to other-than-liberal values – those of community, tolerance, cultural heritage, etc. as opposed to democracy, lawfulness and human rights – which invariably make them different and so less susceptible to values and ideals of the liberal democracy, as practised by the West.'[18] She further argues elsewhere: 'The EU … often takes its "soft power" appeal for granted, as reforms that the EU demands from its neighbours are hard, laborious and in the short term, socially alienating.'[19] This was acknowledged by the consultation paper of the High Representative/the Commission of March 2015: 'The approach of "more for more" underlines the EU's commitment to its core values, but … has not always been successful in providing incentives [to] further reforms in the partner countries.'[20] The incentives that the EU can offer to ENP countries are considered too small.[21] Should the EU continue to follow its values-based approach? We will get to this question in the final section of this chapter.

We now explore the way the EU reacts when the values and principles at the basis of cooperation with ENP countries are breached within the territory of partner countries. The practice is that the EU condemns these moves through the European External Action Service (EEAS), as it does with other third countries. This has happened, for example, when in a given ENP country human rights are violated,[22] or death sentences are carried out,[23] or minority rights[24] are repressed,

---

[17] See S. Gstöhl's chapter in this volume.
[18] E. Korosteleva, 'Questioning democracy promotion: Belarus' response to the "colour revolutions"' (2012) 19(1) *Democratization* 49.
[19] E. Korosteleva, 'Moldova's European Choice: "Between Two Stools"?' (2010) 62(8) *Europe-Asia Studies* 1280.
[20] Joint consultation paper from the Commission and the Vice-President/High Representative, 'Towards a new European Neighbourhood Policy', 4 March 2015.
[21] J.C. Völkel, 'More for More, Less for Less – More or Less: A Critique of the EU's Arab Spring Response à la Cinderella' (2014) 19(2) *European Foreign Affairs Review* 272–273.
[22] This is the case of the Egyptian anti-terrorism law. See European Parliament Resolution of 17 July 2014 on freedom of expression and assembly in Egypt, P8_TA-PROV(2014)0007.
[23] See, for example, 'The EU Missions in Jerusalem and Ramallah condemn the death sentence issued in Gaza'. Available online at http://eeas.europa.eu/delegations/westbank/documents/news/2014/20140520_eu_local_statement_gaza_executions_en.pdf (accessed 5 October 2015).
[24] 'The rights of persons belonging to minorities are challenged in most of the neighbourhood countries. The spectrum of exclusion extends from increasing violence and hate speech in political life against minorities in Armenia, Ukraine, Palestine and Israel to sectarian fighting during all of 2013 in Egypt', JOIN/2014/012 final (n 14), 8.

as most recently in the case of the shutdown of most of Crimean Tatar-language media outlets on 1 April 2014.[25] Violations of international law by neighbours and near neighbours such as Russia have also been stigmatized. This has happened in the case of the illegal referendum held in Crimea and in the case of the annexation of Crimea and Sevastopol by the Russian Federation[26] and, most recently, with the signature of the 'Treaty on Alliance and Integration' between the Russian Federation and Georgia's breakaway region of South Ossetia.[27] The European Parliament is traditionally vocal and goes as far as condemning the adoption of legislation that unduly restricts human rights.[28]

Yet, while the EU's official reaction to breaches of democratic standards and human rights is negative, the EU's policy is not substantially affected vis-à-vis the ENP country concerned, be it an eastern or southern neighbours. This is the main reason why the values-based approach of the ENP has been criticized.

Three specific examples can be made to illustrate this point. First, Egypt can be singled out as a country that does not respect human rights and can hardly be considered a democracy. Despite this, the EU has limited itself to condemning in mild terms the way the elections of May 2014 were administered.[29] In addition, although the EU recognizes that there are violations of human rights in Egypt,[30] and has also criticized the death sentences against former President Morsi,[31] this has

---

[25] See Statement by the Spokesperson on the shutdown of Crimean Tatar ATR TV, doc. n. 150401_02_en, 01 April 2015.

[26] Declaration by the High Representative on behalf of the EU on Crimea, press release n. 119/05, 16 March 2015.

[27] Statement by High Representative/Vice-President Federica Mogherini on the announced signature of a 'Treaty on Alliance and Integration' between the Russian Federation and Georgia's breakaway region of South Ossetia, doc. n. 150317_04_en, 17 March 2015.

[28] For example, the Parliament has called on Egypt to revoke the repressive and unconstitutional laws that severely restrict basic human rights and freedoms, in particular the presidential decree Law 136 of 2014, which places all 'public and vital facilities' under military jurisdiction for two years, and also Law 107 of 2013 on the Right to Public Meetings, Processions and Peaceful Demonstrations (Protest Law). See European Parliament Resolution of 15 January 2015 on the situation in Egypt, P8_TA-PROV(2015)0012, points 8 and 9.

[29] As noted in an EU document, 'Presidential elections were held in May 2014 and the EU stated that these were technically administered in line with the law. Although the overall electoral process was judged to be satisfactory on polling day itself, the Election Observation Mission was critical of partial media coverage, very limited space for dissent, and the political/legal context the elections were held in.' See Joint Staff Working Document 'Implementation of the European Neighbourhood Policy Partnership for Democracy and Shared Prosperity with the Southern Mediterranean Partners Report Accompanying the document Joint Communication to the European Parliament, the Council, the European Economic and Social Committee and the Committee of the Regions Implementation of the European Neighbourhood Policy' SWD/2015/75 final, 25 March 2015.

[30] For example, the EU called on the Egyptian authorities 'to allow journalists to operate freely; to ensure peaceful protest notably by amending the protest law, to launch independent and credible investigations into the violent events since 30 June 2013; to ensure the defendant's rights to a fair and timely trial based on clear charges; to ensure humane prison conditions in line with international law and standards; to review the numerous death sentences imposed on political opponents in mass trials and to respect due process', EU Council, Declaration on behalf of the European Union on the presidential elections in Egypt, 5 June 2014, doc. n. 10649/1/14 REV 1.

[31] See Statement by the High Representative/Vice-President Federica Mogherini on Court sentences in Egypt, doc. n. 150616_03_en, 6/06/2015.

not led the EU to substantially alter the terms of EU–Egypt relations,[32] as one might expect if the values-based approach of the ENP were properly implemented. So far, only the European Parliament has stated that 'the EU will deliver on its financial support only if the necessary political and democratic conditions are met, with the democratic transition being pursued, strengthened and fully inclusive, with full respect for human and women's rights.'[33] The Parliament has also proposed that the EU enact a ban on the export to Egypt of intrusion and surveillance technologies which could be used to spy on and repress citizens, and has called for a ban on the export of security equipment or military aid that could be used in the suppression of peaceful protest or against the EU's strategic and security interests.[34] The enactment of this ban would be a limited but symbolic reaction by the EU to serious violations of its values in this country.

The second example concerns EU–Israel relations. The EU has clearly condemned Israel's violations of international humanitarian law in response to the firing of rockets by Hamas in the summer of 2014.[35] Human rights violations (house demolitions, appropriation of lands) were also denounced. Yet, the EU has continued to upgrade its relations with Israel despite the lack of implementation of the two-State solution.[36]

Azerbaijan is the third problematic case. This country needs to make significant efforts to meet its commitments regarding democracy.[37] The EU recognizes that '[T]he democratic and human rights environment significantly deteriorated in 2014'[38] and human rights activists and journalists are often imprisoned. Generally speaking, Azerbaijan has not shown much interest in EU values.[39] Yet, this country is

---

[32] For an overview of these relations see P. Seeberg, 'The EU and Constitutionalism in Egypt: EU Foreign and Security Policy Challenges with a Special Focus on the Changing Political Setting in the MENA-region' (2013) 18(3) *European Foreign Affairs Review* 411–428.

[33] European Parliament Resolution of 15 January 2015 on the situation in Egypt (n 28), point X.

[34] Ibid. point 23.

[35] See Joint Staff Working Document 'Implementation of the European Neighbourhood Policy in Israel Progress in 2014 and Recommendations for Actions Accompanying the document Joint Communication to the European Parliament, the Council, the European Economic and Social Committee and the Committee of the Regions-Implementation of the European Neighbourhood Policy in 2014', SWD/2015/72 final, 25/03/2015, 7.

[36] See R.A. Del Sarto, 'Defining Borders and People in the Borderlands: EU Policies, Israeli Prerogatives and the Palestinians' (2014) 52(2) *Journal of Common Market Studies* 200 ff.

[37] European Commission (EC), 'Implementation of the European Neighbourhood Policy in Azerbaijan: Progress in 2011 and Recommendations for Action', SWD (2012) 111 final, 15 May 2012, 2, quoted by K. Nielsen and M. Vilson, 'The Eastern Partnership: Soft Power Strategy or Policy Failure?' (2014) 19(2) *European Foreign Affairs Review* 257.

[38] See EEAS statements, doc n. 140717/04, 17 July 2014; see also EEAS Statement Brussels, doc. n. 140802/01, 02 August 2014; the Statements of HR/Vice-President Mogherini and Commissioner Hahn on the sentencing of Khadija Ismayilova in Azerbaijan, doc. 150901_04_en, 01 September 2015.

[39] Joint Staff Working Document 'Implementation of the European Neighbourhood Policy in Azerbaijan Progress in 2014 and Recommendations for Actions Accompanying the document Joint Communication to the European Parliament, the Council, the European Economic and Social Committee and the Committee of the Regions -Implementation of the European Neighbourhood Policy in 2014', SWD/2015/0064 final, 25 March 2015, 4.

important for the EU's energy security and this has prevented the EU from freezing its relations with the Azerbaijani political leadership.

The preceding examples show that there is a certain degree of rhetoric in the EU's proclamation that the ENP is a principled policy. However, it should also be acknowledged that in 2014 the EU has taken a united front in enacting sanctions against Russia in the face of its blatant breaches of international law, even when this might endanger its energy security and commercial interests.[40]

The reinforcement of the importance of EU values and the principle of conditionality in the ENI Regulation

The most important financial instrument for ENP countries is the ENI Regulation.[41] It was approved on 11 March 2014, at the height of the Crimean crisis, in order to replace the previous legislative framework of 2006. The new rules detail the allocation of funds to be distributed to ENP countries and Russia[42] for the period 2014–2020.

As in the previous regime, the ENI is aimed at 'contributing to achieve an area of shared prosperity and good neighbourliness in the partner countries by developing a special relationship founded on cooperation, peace and security, mutual accountability and a *shared commitment* (emphasis added) to the universal values of democracy, the rule of law and respect for human rights.'[43] The language of the IPA II is more prescriptive with respect to adherence to EU values. Indeed, in this context the objective of financial assistance is to support reform in the acceding countries so that 'they *comply* (emphasis added) with EU values'[44] and align with the Union's rules and standards.

Analysis of the ENI Regulation reveals that the importance attached to political values has increased in EU–ENP relations, despite the criticism that the values-based approach has attracted. This is due to the prioritization of the actions to be financed. These include the promotion of human rights and fundamental freedoms, the rule of law, principles of equality and the fight against discrimination in all its forms, the establishment of deep and sustainable democracy, the promotion of good governance and the fight against corruption. The protection of human rights, good governance and the rule of law, including the reform of justice, the public administration and the security sector have particular priority for the EU.[45] Note that in the 2006

---

[40] See infra the section on restrictive measures but also P. Kalinichenko's chapter in this volume.
[41] Regulation (EU) 232/2014 (n 2).
[42] In one of the last statements of this kind, Russia is defined as 'both a Union neighbour and a strategic partner in the region.' See recital n. 7 of Regulation (EU) 232/2014 (n 2).
[43] See Art. 1 of Regulation (EU) 232/2014 (n 2).
[44] Art. 1 of Regulation (EU) 231/2014 of the European Parliament and of the Council of 11 March 2014 establishing an Instrument for Pre-Accession Assistance (IPA II) [2014] OJ L 77/11.
[45] Other priorities included: institutional cooperation and capacity development, including for the implementation of Union agreements; support to civil society actors and to their role in reform processes and democratic transitions; sustainable and inclusive economic development, including at regional and local level, and territorial cohesion; development of the social sectors, in particular for the youth, with a focus on social justice and cohesion and employment; trade and private-sector development, including support to small and medium-sized enterprises, employment

Regulation, the promotion of these values, especially respect for human rights, did not receive the same attention.[46] The IPA II remains slightly different from the ENI, as while it is intended to promote political reforms and strengthen democracy and respect for human rights,[47] good governance and good neighbourly relations in the future EU countries, priority is given to actions that enable state institutions to work properly and to the building of a functioning market economy.

A further novelty of the 2014 Regulation is that for the first time it also envisages 'the prevention and settlement of conflicts, including protracted conflicts',[48] amongst the actions to be funded through EU financial resources. In this provision, the EU institutions' intention to link the external financial instrument to the objectives of the Common Foreign and Security Policy (CFSP) is clear. Thus, in this respect, the goals of this Regulation are not that far from those of the IPA, which sets out to promote reconciliation and peace-building and confidence-building measures.[49]

Finally, whereas the development of a functioning market economy is one of the aims of the 2006 European Neighbourhood Policy Instrument (ENPI) Regulation, the ENI does not finance actions with such an objective.[50] This confirms that in the 2014 Regulation the EU places more emphasis on the convergence of ENP countries towards the EU's political values than on giving incentives to replicate its economic model.

An examination of the position of EU values within the EU financial instrument should also be accompanied by that of the principle of conditionality. Has the EU also become more selective in distributing its funds depending on the ENP partner's adherence to EU values? In other words, has this principle been

---

and implementation of deep and comprehensive free trade areas; agriculture and rural development, including food security; sustainable management of natural resources; the energy sector, with a focus on energy efficiency and renewable energy; transport and infrastructure; education and skills development, including vocational education and training; mobility and migration management, including the protection of migrants; confidence-building and other measures contributing to the prevention and settlement of conflicts, including support to affected populations and reconstruction.

[46] The promotion and protection of human rights and fundamental freedoms was not on the top of the list of actions to be financed but it came after other areas of cooperation (i.e. promoting sustainable development and the environment). The rights of persons belonging to minorities were not mentioned at all; by contrast, in the ENI Regulation they are cross-cutting objectives in all actions undertaken under the new rules. See Regulation (EC) 1638/2006 of the European Parliament and of the Council of 24 October 2006 laying down general provisions establishing a European Neighbourhood and Partnership Instrument [2006] OJ L 310/1.

[47] The IPA II Regulation is more detailed than the ENI instrument in explaining that acceding countries should defend all EU values, including rights such as those of lesbian, gay, bisexual, transgender and intersex persons, and promote gender equality, non-discrimination and tolerance. See Art. 2(1)(a)(ii) of Regulation (EU) 231/2014 (n 44).

[48] Art. 2(2)(e) of Regulation (EU) 232/2014 (n 2).

[49] Art. 2(1)(a)(iv) of Regulation (EU) 231/2014 (n 44).

[50] By contrast in the IPA II, the achievement of Union standards in the economy, including the functioning of a market economy, is a specific objective of the assistance to acceding countries. See Art. 2(1)(b)(i) of Regulation (EU) 231/2014 (n 44).

reinforced in the ENI Regulation? The answer is not straightforward. The EU is clearly more willing than in the past to differentiate its relations with partner countries that have undertaken the path toward democracy.[51] Indeed, the 2014 Regulation is based on the so-called incentive-based approach,[52] which is an example of positive conditionality. The EU's allocation of funds depends on a number of factors, indicated by Art. 4 of the mentioned act. Presumably, these factors are ranked in order of priority. The first factor listed is the size of the population of the ENP country and the level of development. The second is the commitment to and progress in implementing mutually agreed political, economic and social reforms. The third is commitment to and progress in building deep and sustainable democracy.[53] Indicators to measure the level of commitment to democracy and the achievement of the objectives of cooperation are specified in the text of the ENI Regulation.[54]

However, neither the ENI nor the two other external financial instruments[55] envisage the possibility of suspending financial assistance. The EU is reluctant to apply negative conditionality. Given the reinforced position of values and principles in the ENI Regulation compared to the previous regime, the absence of negative conditionality is conspicuous and surprising. This is in contrast to the 2006 Regulation, whose Art. 28 stated: '[W]here a partner country fails to observe the principles referred to in Article 1,[56] the Council, acting by a qualified majority on a proposal from the Commission, may take appropriate steps in respect of any Community assistance granted to the partner country under this Regulation.' The suspension of financial assistance was clearly one of the possible measures available to EU institutions as a reaction to the failure of the partner country to respect values such as liberty, democracy, human rights, fundamental freedoms and the rule of law. As noted in a statement of the European Parliament included at the end of the 2014 Regulation, none of the three EU external financial instruments contain any explicit reference to the possibility of suspending assistance in cases where a beneficiary country fails to observe

---

[51] I. Tömmel (n 13).
[52] Art. 4(1).
[53] Other criteria are the following: (a) 'partnership with the Union, including the level of ambition for that partnership' (meaning that the higher the ambition of the partnership, the greater the financial effort of the Union); and (b) 'absorption capacity and the potential impact of Union support under this Regulation' Art. 4(1)(d) and (e).
[54] Indicators are included in Art. 2(3) second paragraph of the 2014 Regulation. These are, for example, adequately monitored democratic elections; respect for human rights and fundamental freedoms; an independent judiciary; cooperation on issues of justice, freedom and security, the level of corruption, trade flows, gender equality. The aforementioned criteria and indicators were absent in the ENPI, as was the principle of differentiation, indicated by Art. 4.
[55] These are the IPA II (see n 44) and the Instrument for Development Cooperation (regulated by Regulation (EU) 233/2014 of the European Parliament and of the Council of 11 March 2014 establishing a financing instrument for development cooperation for the period 2014–2020 [2014] OJ L 77/44.
[56] It should be noted that Art. 1(3) refers to 'values' (such as values of liberty, democracy, respect for human rights and fundamental freedoms and the rule of law) and not to 'principles'.

the basic principles enunciated in the respective instrument and, notably, where it fails to observe the principles of democracy, the rule of law and respect for human rights.

However, this does not mean that the new Regulation is deprived of any elements of negative conditionality. Indeed, the EU has the right to reconsider its support 'in the event of serious or persistent regression'[57] in building deep and sustainable democracy and in implementing agreed reforms.[58] Suspension of assistance is one way of the EU reconsidering its decision to assist, should EU values be breached[59] and is therefore one of the measures that the EU may enact.

In its Declaration in the text of the Regulation, the European Parliament claims that any suspension of assistance under the ENI and the other external financial Regulations would need the Parliament's approval, given its status as co-legislator and co-branch of the budgetary authority. In the past, suspension decisions were in the hands of the Commission and were never taken. The reinforcement of the Parliament's external powers after the Lisbon Treaty and its vocation of human rights defender might make the prospect of a decision to suspend assistance more likely than in the past.

The overall conclusion is that in the ENI Regulation the principle of conditionality, both in its positive and negative dimensions, is not only safeguarded but also strengthened.

Finally, the 2014 Regulation places unprecedented emphasis on the fact that 'funding under this Regulation shall comply with ... the Union's commitments under international law, taking into account relevant Union policies and positions.'[60] It is not easy to grasp the meaning of this provision. Does it mean that the EU can suspend assistance to ENP partners if they fail to observe international rules which the EU is committed to respect (i.e. human rights)?[61] One possible interpretation is that this provision was inserted to make sure that the EU can suspend its assistance in a situation where the ENP countries are targeted by sanctions adopted in the UN context. The EU is not directly bound by United Nations Security Council (UNSC) Resolutions, but it is bound to respect international law and to enable EU Members States to respect the UN Treaty from which the UNSC's authority stems.

---

[57] Art. 3(2) third paragraph.
[58] The incentive-based approach shall not apply to support to civil society, people-to-people contacts, including cooperation between local authorities, support for the improvement of human rights, or crisis-related support measures. In the event of serious or persistent regression, such support may be increased (see Art. 4(3)).
[59] The suspension of the EU's assistance would also be imposed by the principle of consistency between the ENP and the objectives and principles of the Union's external policies and, in particular, the common foreign and security policy. Indeed, should the Council condemn the violation of EU values by the ENP partner in the context of the CFSP, all its decisions with an external dimension, including those granting financial assistance, would have to be coherent with this position.
[60] Art. 1(4).
[61] As protected under ECHR (after the EU's accession to this Convention) or as principles of EU law.

EU values and political conditionality in the EU's macro-financial assistance

The EU has been providing macro-financial assistance (MFA) since 1995 to third countries in the neighbourhood who have a deteriorated economic situation.[62] The MFA's Decisions are made on an *ad hoc* basis, upon request of the third country that urgently needs assistance. The EU's financial support may take the form of loans or, under specific circumstances, grants financed through the EU budget. It is complementary to financial support from the International Monetary Fund and conditional upon the existence of an adjustment and reform programme agreed with this organization.[63]

The Parliament is co-legislator with the Council in this area, and therefore the procedure to decide in favour of an MFA is lengthy. A relevant question is thus whether respect for EU values is amongst the substantive conditions that the recipient countries must fulfil. There is no legislation that details in a single and legally binding framework the principles and economic and political conditions that country beneficiaries of macro-financial assistance should comply with in order to obtain the EU's support. An attempt to define a legislative framework was made in 2011. The Commission submitted a proposal for a Regulation of the European Parliament and of the Council, founded on Arts. 209 and 212 TFEU, laying down general provisions for macro-financial assistance to third countries ('the proposal for a framework Regulation').[64] One of the questions that this measure was intended to address concerns the legislative process leading to the adoption of MFA Decisions. However, as a result of major disagreements between the Parliament and the Council on the one hand, and the Commission on the other, the proposal was withdrawn in 2013. The Court has confirmed the legality of the Commission's withdrawal of its proposal.[65]

It is necessary to examine how the EU has exercised its powers in the context of macro-financial assistance over the years and in particular what the criteria were that led to the intervention in favour of third countries. Did the EU grant financial assistance to countries that were transitioning towards democracy and were struggling to adhere to Western values? Did the EU privilege candidate and neighbour countries over other third countries?

In the mid-1990s, the first recipients of macro-financial assistance were candidate countries (such as Romania and Bulgaria), other countries with a European perspective (such as Albania, Bosnia-Herzegovina and the Former Yugoslav

---

[62] At that time, there was no specific legal basis for this kind of action in the Treaties; reliance on Art. 308 TEC was therefore necessary. It is only with the Lisbon Treaty that a specific competence was conferred on the EU on the basis of Art. 212 TFEU. This enables the EU to provide financial support specifically to non-developing countries.

[63] Report from the European Commission to the European Parliament and the Council on the implementation of macro-financial assistance to third countries in 2014, COM (2015) 290 final, 11 June 2015, 1.

[64] Proposal for a Regulation of the European Parliament and of the Council laying down general provisions for Macro-Financial Assistance to third countries, COM (2011) 396 final, 4 July 2011.

[65] Judgment of 14 April 2015 in Case C409/13 *Council* v. *Commission*, ECLI:EU:C:2015:217.

Republic of Macedonia)[66] and also neighbour countries (such as Ukraine[67] and Moldova[68]). It is interesting that the EU's decision to assist these countries was linked to their undertaking political and economic reform, including changes aimed at establishing an open market economy.[69] In the case of Ukraine and Moldova, the EU seems to have been more interested in supporting a transition to an open market economy than in supporting a transition to democracy. At the time these early decisions were taken, the so-called Genval Criteria applied. These criteria were agreed informally at an Ecofin Council on 9 October 1993 and later revised on 20 March 1995. An Ecofin Council of 8 October 2002 reviewed the principles and criteria behind the EU's financial assistance. These were the exceptional character of the financial support, the so-called political precondition, the complementary nature of the grant, (economic) conditionality, financial discipline and geographic delimitation.[70]

In this context, we will focus on the political and geographic criteria. Regarding the former, third countries are required to fully respect effective democratic mechanisms, including multiparty parliamentary systems, the rule of law and guarantee respect for human rights. As to the geographic criteria, the EU assists third countries with which the Union 'maintains close political and economic links, taking into account especially their geographical proximity and the Union's economic, commercial and political interests.'[71] Due to the withdrawal of the Commission's proposal for a framework regulation on macro-financial assistance in 2011,[72] the Genval Criteria remain informal conditions.

Did the EU actually respect the conditions it set out in 2002? The first beneficiaries of the EU's financial support after the launch of the ENP were Armenia and Georgia, in 2009. It should be noted that neither the MFA Decision on Armenia[73] nor that on Georgia,[74] both based on the current Art. 352 TFEU, refer

---

[66] Serbia received assistance only in 2009 after the EU had developed its relations with this country in the context of the Stabilisation and Association Process and the European Partnership. See Council Decision of 30 November 2009 providing macro-financial assistance to Serbia [2009] OJ L 320/9.
[67] Council Decision of 23 October 1995 providing further macro-financial assistance for Ukraine [1995] OJ L 258/63.
[68] Council Decision of 25 March 1996 providing further macro-financial assistance for Moldova [1996] OJ L 80/60.
[69] See, for example, Council Decision of 10 May 1999 providing macro-financial assistance to Bosnia and Herzegovina [1999] OJ L123/57, recital n. 2 and Council Decision of 25 March 1996 (n 68).
[70] Ecofin Council, doc. n. 12592/02, 8 October 2002, 11–12. Available online at www.consilium.europa.eu/uedocs/cms_data/docs/pressdata/en/ecofin/72608.pdf (accessed 30 September 2015).
[71] Ibid. 11.
[72] The proposed legislative act was adopted amongst other reasons to clarify and formalize the Genval Criteria 'in order to strengthen the legal force, transparency and predictability of the rules applicable to MFA.' See Art. 6 of the Commission proposal (n 64).
[73] Council Decision of 30 November 2009 providing macro-financial assistance to Armenia [2009] OJ L 320/3.
[74] Council Decision of 30 November 2009 providing macro-financial assistance to Georgia [2009] OJ L 320/1.

to the political conditions as defined in 2002. The constitutional contexts of the beneficiaries are not taken into consideration.

In the case of Georgia, the geopolitical context is merely hinted at.[75] The decision to provide financial support to this country is due to the political commitment made at the European Council level in September 2008 to strengthen EU–Georgia relations in the aftermath of Georgia's armed conflict with the Russian Federation. The decision to come to the aid of Georgia was taken without any elements of conditionality.

We have to wait until 2013 to have the first MFA Decision, based on Art. 212 TFEU, showing a link between the EU's decision to assist and the commitment of ENP countries to respect EU values.[76] In a Decision concerning Georgia, a Joint Declaration of the Parliament and the Council emphasizes their willingness to financially support third countries for their commitment 'to common values shared with the Union, including democracy, the rule of law, good governance, respect for human rights, sustainable development and poverty reduction, and to the principles of open, rules-based and fair trade.'[77] In addition, beneficiary countries have to respect effective democratic mechanisms, including a multi-party parliamentary system and the rule of law, and guarantee respect for human rights. It is further stressed that EU financial support should strengthen the efficiency, transparency and accountability of public finance management in beneficiary countries. Finally, the Commission is tasked with monitoring respect for these conditions.[78] According to this institution, Georgia benefited from the 'more for more principle' in recognition of its progress in the fields of democracy and respect for human rights, for which it received additional grants of €50 million in 2012–2013.[79]

In post-2013 practice, the EU has granted financial assistance to neighbouring countries on the basis of their commitment to EU values. Decisions on macro-financial assistance to Tunisia,[80] Jordan[81] and Ukraine[82] adopted between 2013 and 2015 are a case in point. In these three Decisions, it is clearly stated that

[75] 'The extraordinary European Council of 1 September 2008 confirmed the EU's willingness to strengthen EU–Georgia relations in the aftermath of the armed conflict in August 2008 between Georgia and Russia.' See Council Decision of 30 November 2009 providing macro-financial assistance to Georgia (n 74), recital n. 2.
[76] Decision 778/2013/EU of the European Parliament and of the Council of 12 August 2013 providing further macro-financial assistance to Georgia [2013] OJ L 218/15.
[77] Recital n. 8.
[78] Recitals n. 9–10. In post-Lisbon practice, the monitoring task is shared by the Commission and the European External Action Service.
[79] Report from the Commission to the European Parliament and the Council on the implementation of macro-financial assistance to third countries in 2014, SWD (2015) 115 final, 11 June 2015.
[80] Decision 534/2014/EU of the European Parliament and of the Council of 15 May 2014 providing macro-financial assistance to the Republic of Tunisia [2014] OJ L151/9.
[81] Decision 1351/2013/EU of the European Parliament and of the Council of 11 December 2013 on providing macro-financial assistance to the Hashemite Kingdom of Jordan [2013] OJ L 341/4.
[82] Decision 2015/601/EU of the European Parliament and of the Council of 15 April 2015 providing macro-financial assistance to Ukraine [2015] OJ L100/1.

the EU is willing to support these countries as a result of their transition to democracy. For example, the Decision on Jordan mentions democratic developments that took place there in 2011.[83] In the context of the macro-financial assistance to Tunisia, emphasis is placed on the first free and democratic elections that took place on 23 October 2011, on the concerted efforts by the main political actors to proceed with reforms towards a fully-fledged democratic system and on the Constitution adopted by the National Constituent Assembly of Tunisia, which includes some advances in individual rights and freedoms, and gender equality.[84]

In the latest Decision on Ukraine, it is also clear that the EU is seeking to support the country's difficult transition after democratic elections were held in the country. Recital n. 2 states: 'Following the reinstatement of the Ukrainian Constitution of 2004, presidential as well as parliamentary elections were successfully held on 25 May 2014 and 26 October 2014, respectively. After the formation of a new government on 2 December 2014 reflecting the outcome of the parliamentary elections, Ukraine has reconfirmed its commitment to political and economic reforms.'[85]

Ukraine has benefited on two occasions from the EU's financial support between 2014 and 2015. Indeed, 'the violation of Ukraine's sovereignty and territorial integrity and the resulting military conflict have had damaging effects on Ukraine's already precarious economic and financial stability.'[86] In the most recent macro-assistance decision, €1.8 billion were granted to support 'Ukraine's economic stabilisation and a substantive reform agenda.'[87] This sum is in addition to €11 billion granted to Ukraine by the EU for the period 2014–2020.[88]

However, the Union does not use financial assistance only for the benefit of ENP countries that are taking the path of democratization. This is illustrated by the MFA Decision on the Kyrgyz Republic in 2013, linked to this country's commitment to values shared with the Union, including democracy, the rule of law, good governance, respect for human rights, sustainable development and poverty reduction, as well as to its commitment to the principles of open, rules-based and fair trade.[89] The precondition for granting the Union's macro-financial assistance should be that the Kyrgyz Republic respects effective democratic mechanisms,

---

[83] It is stated: 'Jordan has embarked on a series of political reforms, most in particular leading to the adoption by the Jordanian Parliament in September 2011 of over 40 constitutional amendments, representing a significant step towards a fully-fledged democratic system. Political and economic support from the Union to Jordan's reform process is consistent with the Union's policy towards the Southern Mediterranean region, as set out in the context of the ENP.' Decision 1351/2013/EU of the European Parliament and of the Council of 11 December 2013 on providing macro-financial assistance to the Hashemite Kingdom of Jordan [2013] OJ L 341/4.
[84] Decision 534/2014/EU (n 80), recitals n. 3 and 4.
[85] Decision 2015/601/EU (n 82).
[86] Ibid. recital n. 3.
[87] Ibid. Art. 1.
[88] Council Decision of 14 April 2014 providing macro-financial assistance to Ukraine [2014] OJ L 111/85. This Decision is based for the first time ever on Art. 213 TFEU (and not on Art. 212) making possible to request urgent financial assistance.
[89] Decision 1025/2013/EU of the European Parliament and of the Council of 22 October 2013 providing macro-financial assistance to the Kyrgyz Republic [2013] OJ L 283/1, recital n. 17. This Decision is based on Art. 209 TFEU.

including a multiparty parliamentary system and the rule of law, and guarantees respect for human rights.[90]

The Kyrgyz Republic lies outside the normal geographic scope of the MFA instrument, but is justified by the strength of pro-democratic political and economic reform momentum in the country and the fact that it is part of a region of particular economic and political importance for the EU.[91] The fact that the EU decided to support this Asian country is interesting for two reasons: the first is that macro-financial assistance is a form of support that the EU does not reserve for its neighbours and candidate countries, but also for partners that are in the EU's geographic proximity and are strategically important for the EU. The practice of MFA shows that the EU does not have a privileged relationship with its ENP partners. Second, the threshold of commitment towards EU values expected from the requesting country is not very high, considering the rates of the Kyrgyz Republic reported by Freedom House.[92]

The distinguishing features of the restrictive measures in the context of the ENP

Attaching importance to respect for the principles of international law and EU values in EU primary and secondary law has little meaning if it is not accompanied by an attempt by the EU to sanction countries that disregard these principles. Currently, there are thirty-four countries subject to sanctions, of which seven are ENP countries and one is the Russian Federation. With the exception of measures taken vis-à-vis Lebanon[93] and (to some extent) Libya,[94] restrictions imposed on neighbours and near neighbours are taken outside the UN context.[95] In addition to classic arms and trade embargos, the EU subjects governmental leaderships and often leaders' relatives – but also people and companies who benefit from autocratic regimes – to targeted sanctions. These take the form of asset freezes and travel bans, as well as bans on the provision of services.

Travel bans against the separatists of Transnistria[96] in 2003 were the first restrictions to be enacted by the EU, a few months before the launch of the

---

[90] Ibid. recital n. 18.
[91] COM (2015) 290 final (n 63) 8.
[92] Kyrgyzstan is rated Partly Free in 'Freedom in the World 2014' and Not Free in 'Freedom of the Press 2014'. Kyrgyzstan receives a democracy score of 6.61 on a scale of 1 to 7, with 7 as the worst possible score, in 'Nations in Transit 2014'. See https://freedomhouse.org/article/freedom-h ouse-statement-criminal-investigation-kyrgyzstan (accessed 5 October 2015).
[93] Council Common Position 2005/888/CFSP of 12 December 2005 concerning specific restrictive measures against certain persons suspected of involvement in the assassination of former Lebanese Prime Minister Rafiq Hariri [2005] OJ L 327/26.
[94] See Council Decision 2011/137/CFSP of 28 February 2011 concerning restrictive measures in view of the situation in Libya [2011] OJ L 58/53. However, the EU has also adopted additional autonomous sanctions vis-à-vis Ghadaffi's family and the Libyan political leadership.
[95] Algeria, Armenia, Azerbaijan, Morocco, Israel and the Palestinian Authority are not subject to sanctions.
[96] Council Common Position 2003/139/CFSP of 27 February 2003 concerning restrictive measures against the leadership of the Transnistrian region of the Moldovan Republic [2003] OJ L 53/60.

ENP. Sanctions targeted against Lebanon and Belarus followed in 2005 and 2006. The events of the Arab Spring in 2011 were at the basis of sanctions against the governmental leadership or nationals of southern neighbours, such as Egypt,[97] Libya,[98] Syria[99] and Tunisia.[100] The Ukraine–Russia crisis in 2014 shifted restrictions towards the east, with the adoption of an unprecedented number and range of sanctions against Ukraine's secessionist republics and the Russian Federation. In several cases concerning nationals of Libya,[101] Syria,[102] Belarus,[103] Egypt,[104] Tunisia[105] and Russia,[106] the inclusion of some persons in the list of people subject to restrictions was challenged before the General Court and EU Court of Justice on the grounds of breach of due process rights or lack of a legal basis to be included in the list. There have been a number of successes before the General Court by Tunisian, Belarusian and Syrian nationals;[107] by contrast, where appealed by the addressees of the targeted sanctions, the judgments of the General Court, rejecting the annulment actions, were confirmed.[108]

Sanctions were adopted in various situations where EU values or principles of international law were breached. Whereas most EU targeted sanctions *vis-à-vis* third

---

[97] Council Decision 2011/172/CFSP freezing of funds and economic resources of persons identified as being responsible for the misappropriation of Egyptian State funds, and natural or legal persons, entities and bodies associated with them OJ [2011] L 76/63, as subsequently amended.

[98] See (n 95).

[99] Council Decision 2011/273/CFSP of 9 May 2011 concerning restrictive measures against Syria [2011] OJ L 121/11.

[100] Council Decision 2011/72/CFSP of 31 January 2011 concerning restrictive measures directed against certain persons and entities in view of the situation in Tunisia [2011] OJ L 28/62.

[101] Case T-348/13 *Ahmed Mohammed Qadhaf Al Dam* v. *Council*, ECLI:EU:T:2014:806.

[102] Case T-509/11 *Mohammad Makhlouf* v. *Council*, ECLI:EU:T:2015:33; Case T-203/12 *Mohamad Nedal Alchaar* v. *Council*, ECLI:EU:T:2014:602; T-293/12 *Syria International Islamic Bank* v. *Council*, ECLI:EU:T:2014:439; T-202/12 *Bouchra Al Assad* v. *Council*, ECLI:EU:T:2014:113; T-383/11 *Eyad Makhlouf* v. *Council*, ECLI:EU:T:2013:431; and Cases T-563/11 & T-592/11 *Issam Anbouba* v. *Council*, ECLI:EU:T:2013:429; T-329/12 and T-74/13 *Mazen Al-Tabbaa* v. *Council*, ECLI:EU:T:2014:622.

[103] C-535/14 P *Vadzim Ipatau* v. *Council*, ECLI:EU:C:2015:407; T-163/12 *Ternavsky* v. *Council*, ECLI:EU:T:2015:271; T-196/11 and T-542/12 *Aliaksei Mikhalchanka* v. *Council*, ECLI:EU:T:2014:801.

[104] C-220/14 P *Ezz & Others* v. *Council*, ECLI:EU:C:2015:147.

[105] T-133/12 *Ben Ali* v. *Council*, ECLI:EU:T:2014:176; Case T-200/11 *Al Matri* v. *Council*, ECLI:EU:T:2013:275; T-187/11 *Trabelsi and others* v. *Council*, ECLI:EU:T:2013:273; T-188/11 *Chiboub* v. *Council*, ECLI:EU:T:2013:274.

[106] Case T-715/14, *Rosneft a.o.* v. *Council*, pending; T-720/14 *Rotenberg* v. *Council*, pending; T-734/14, *VTB Bank* v. *Council*, pending.

[107] Actions were upheld in T-133/12 (n 105), T-163/12 (n 103), Case T-200/11 (n 105), T-187/11 (n 105), T-188/11 (n 105), T-542/12 (n 103), Case T-203/12 (n 102), T-293/12 (n 102), T-329/12 and T-74/13 (n 102).

[108] See the appeals rejected by the CJEU in Case C-220/14 P (n 104) and Case C-605/13 P *Issam Anbouba* v. *Council*, ECLI:EU:C:2015:248.

country regimes are adopted to react to human right abuses[109] and in relation to post-conflict institutional consolidation,[110] those addressing the situations of ENP countries were enacted for a wider variety of reasons. We can distinguish different categories of restrictions, depending on the violations at their basis. Apart from the unique case of Lebanon, where sanctions were applied in connection with the terrorist bombing that killed President Hariri,[111] a first category of targeted measures was enacted against the breaches of democratic rules and at a subsequent stage to sanction violations of human rights. Other restrictions were adopted to support the transition towards democracy (as in the cases of Tunisia and Egypt) and to react to violations of principles of international law such as the principle of territorial integrity, as in the case of the Separatist Republics of Ukraine.[112] The EU's targeted sanctions were also enacted against the governmental leaderships of Libya[113] and Syria.[114] The motivation was the breach of international law consisting in repressing in a violent manner the civilian population. There are also situations in which sanctions were adopted against people who obstructed the peaceful resolution of a conflict and unduly restricted human rights, as in the case of the political leadership of the Transnistria Region of the Republic of Moldova. Finally, targeted sanctions against Russia were enacted due to its destabilization of the situation in Ukraine.

Having mapped out these restrictive measures, we will examine the way they have evolved and seek to identify the specificities of these restrictions with respect to those targeting nationals of third countries in other geopolitical contexts.

The Belarus leadership was sanctioned in 2006, following the disappearance of well-known people, the fraudulent elections and referendum, and the severe human rights violations in the repression of peaceful demonstrators in the aftermath of the elections and referendum.[115] New measures were enacted in 2011 after the presidential elections of 19 December 2010 and the violent crackdown on political opposition, civil society and representatives of the independent mass media.[116] In 2013, another wave of restrictions was imposed after the elections of 23 September 2012 were considered inconsistent with OSCE

---

[109] Human rights abuses have given rise to restrictive measures in several cases (i.e. Central African Republic, Côte d'Ivoire, the Democratic Republic of Congo, Democratic People's Republic of Korea, Iran, Libya, Somalia, South Sudan, Syria, Sudan, Ukraine, Yemen and Zimbabwe).

[110] F. Giumelli, 'How EU Sanctions Work', EUISS Chaillot paper n. 129, May 2013. Available online at www.iss.europa.eu/uploads/media/Chaillot_129.pdf (accessed 5 October 2015). See generally on restrictive measures C. Eckes, 'EU Restrictive Measures against Natural and Legal Persons: From Counterterrorist to Third Country Sanctions' (2014) 51(3) *Common Market Law Review* 869–906.

[111] Sanctions were adopted against persons suspected of involvement in the planning, sponsoring, organizing or perpetrating of the terrorist bombing. See Council Common Position 2005/888/CFSP (n 94).

[112] Sometimes the justification for sanctions is the breach of international law and human rights, as in the case of Ukraine.

[113] See (n 95).

[114] See (n 99).

[115] Common Position 2006/276/CFSP of 10 April 2006 concerning restrictive measures against certain officials of Belarus and repealing Common Position 2004/661/CFSP [2006] OJ L 101/5.

[116] Council Decision 2011/69/CFSP of 31 January 2011 amending Council Decision 2010/639/CFSP concerning restrictive measures against certain officials of Belarus [2011] OJ L 28/40.

standards.[117] Amongst those targeted were judges and prosecutors said to be involved in human rights violations (including the right to a fair trial of political prisoners) and military commanders said to be involved in internal repression, and also the rectors of a Belarusian university, military personnel and the persons responsible for the administration of the penal colony and detention centres. Interestingly, Ukraine and a few candidate countries aligned with the EU's restrictive measures against Belarus.[118] Here, the breaches of democratic rules and human rights were the justifications for the EU's restrictive measures. The latter are not unique in the EU's external relations: sanctions of this kind have been adopted against leaders of governmental regimes of third countries and other non-state entities (Myanmar in 1996 and Zimbabwe in 2002).[119]

A second category, this time specific to the ENP context, is the restrictive measures taken against the governmental leaderships of Tunisia and Egypt.[120] The justification is that the targeted people undermined the development of democracy and deprived the Egyptian and Tunisian people of the benefits of the sustainable development of their economy and society.[121]

Inaugurated after the Arab Spring, the sanctions consist in the freezing of funds and economic resources against natural or legal persons identified as responsible[122] for the misappropriation of state funds. The restrictions concern 48 individuals in Tunisia and 19 in Egypt. Several of those targeted are now dead. However, the investigation of the misappropriation of funds continued within the domestic jurisdiction and EU's assistance was requested so that the funds could then be returned to the new government. In 2012 '[T]he Council took steps to facilitate the return of misappropriated funds to the Egyptian and Tunisian authorities. The new legislative framework authorises EU member states to release frozen assets on the basis of judicial decisions recognized in EU member states.'[123]

The aim of the EU's action is to assist countries that are in transition towards democracy through judicial cooperation. Restrictions are instigated by the authorities in the third countries and rely on a high level of judicial cooperation with

---

[117] Council Decision 2012/642/CFSP of 15 October 2012 concerning restrictive measures against Belarus [2012] OJ L 285/1.

[118] Declaration by the High Representative on behalf of the EU on the alignment of certain countries concerning restrictive measures against Belarus, 11 August 2015. Available online at www.consilium.europa.eu/en/press/press-releases/2015/08/11-eeas-alignment-belarus (accessed 5 October 2015).

[119] K. Gerbert, 'Shooting in the Dark? EU Sanctions Policies', January 2013. Available online at www.ecfr.eu/page/-/ECFR71_SANCTIONS_BRIEF_AW.pdf (accessed 30 September 2015).

[120] Sometimes they include members of the governments and also relatives thereof and people associated with them. For example, as well as former President Ben Ali, his wife Leila Trabelsi and other members and close associates of the Trabelsi families are included in the list.

[121] On Decisions related to misappropriation of funds in the annulment actions introduced by a few of the addressees, see M. Cremona's chapter in this volume.

[122] This means that in the case of Tunisia, the EU enables the freezing of funds against people who are subject to judicial investigations for complicity in the misappropriation of public monies by a public office holder.

[123] Press release n. 16078/12, 26 November 2012.

EU Member States to release frozen assets. Thus, they are very different in nature from the more classic restrictions adopted against Belarusians and citizens of other countries. It is not coincidental that they were used by the EU mostly in the context of the ENP.[124] The implication is that the EU is ready to closely cooperate with its neighbouring countries in their transition to democracy.

The misappropriation of Ukrainian state funds was also invoked as a reason to impose asset freezes and travel bans against Janukovich, his sons and members of the government and administration (18 people in total), who breached human rights and were identified as responsible for the misappropriation of Ukrainian state funds.[125] These measures, adopted in March 2014 and later extended to other persons, show that the EU cooperates with the judicial authorities of Ukraine just as it did in the cases of Tunisia and Egypt.[126] However, this time the reason for assisting Ukraine was to support the establishment not only of democracy but of other EU values as well, such as the consolidation of the rule of law and respect for human rights.[127]

As the Ukrainian crisis unfolded with the proclamation of the Autonomous Republic of Crimea, the EU imposed travel restrictions and the freezing of funds and economic resources of a third type in March 2014. These were directed against the political leadership of the new unrecognized entity within Ukraine and Russian nationals (i.e. members of the Federal Council of the Russian Federation), for their actions undermining or threatening the territorial integrity, sovereignty and independence of Ukraine.[128] Thus, here the EU was acting to contribute to the strict observance of international law as provided for in EU primary law (Art. 3(5)TEU) by targeting non-state actors. These sanctions were extended in July to Ukrainian enterprises nationalized on the basis of the Republic of Crimea's laws, but also to self-proclaimed leaders of the People's Republic of Luhansk[129]

---

[124] An exception is represented by the restrictive measures against Côte d'Ivoire adopted in 2010 to implement a UNSC Resolution. In one of the latest changes to the sanctions against this country, the target of these measures is a person (Mr. Gossio) who is the subject of an international arrest warrant and is involved in the misappropriation of public funds and in the funding and arming of a militia. His activity is also central in the illegal trafficking of arms. See Council implementing Decision 2014/271/CFSP of 12 May 2014 implementing Decision 2010/656/CFSP renewing the restrictive measures against Côte d'Ivoire [2014] OJ L 138/108.

[125] The EU will later clarify that the freezing of funds is addressed to people (those in the close circle of Janukovich) who may be subject to investigation for misappropriation of funds and to persons responsible for human rights violations. See Council Decision 2015/143/CFSP of 29 January 2015 amending Decision 2014/119/CFSP concerning restrictive measures directed against certain persons, entities and bodies in view of the situation in Ukraine [2015] OJ L 24/16.

[126] It is not clear whether the EU's cooperation was requested by the ENP country concerned.

[127] Council Decision 2014/119/CFSP of 5 March 2014 concerning restrictive measures directed against certain persons, entities and bodies in view of the situation in Ukraine [2014] OJ L 66/30.

[128] Council Decision 2014/145/CFSP of 17 March 2014 concerning restrictive measures in respect of actions undermining or threatening the territorial integrity, sovereignty and independence of Ukraine [2014] OJ L 078/16; Council Regulation (EU) No 269/2014 of 17 March 2014 concerning restrictive measures in respect of actions undermining or threatening the territorial integrity, sovereignty and independence of Ukraine [2014] OJ L 078/6.

[129] Council Decision 2014/455/CFSP of 11 July 2014 amending Decision 2014/145/CFSP concerning restrictive measures in respect of actions undermining or threatening the territorial integrity,

Values, financial instruments and sanctions 53

(which declared its independence in May 2014), key figures in the Security Council of the Russian Federation, leaders of the People's Republic of Donetsk, leaders of other republics who had supported these secessions and 'acquaintances of President Putin', such as shareholders of Russian banks, who often also controlled television stations and state-owned companies, and military commanders.[130] Between September and November 2014, this line of sanctions was expanded as a result of the intensification of the fighting in Eastern Ukraine to include, amongst others, people (including members of the Russian Duma) who had favoured the formation of new entities within the Russian Federation[131] and leaders of the Luhansk People's Republic.[132] Trade bans[133] against the new entity followed the illegal annexation of Crimea and Sevastopol in June of the same year. The imposition of a commercial embargo was a measure giving effect to the United Nation General Assembly's resolution inviting all UN members not to recognize the change of status of Crimea.[134]

The adoption of restrictions against non-state entities for their breach of the principle of territorial integrity is not common in the European context.[135] These restrictions are a specificity of the ENP. This shows how an unlawful unilateral secession in a third country of the neighbourhood can trigger the EU's toughest

sovereignty and independence of Ukraine [2014] OJ L 205/22; Council implementing Regulation (EU) No 753/2014 of 11 July 2014 implementing Regulation (EU) No 269/2014 concerning restrictive measures in respect of actions undermining or threatening the territorial integrity, sovereignty and independence of Ukraine [2014] OJ L 205/7; Council Decision 2014/508/CFSP of 30 July 2014 amending Decision 2014/145/CFSP concerning restrictive measures in respect of actions undermining or threatening the territorial integrity, sovereignty and independence of Ukraine [2014] OJ L 226/23.

[130] Council Decision 2014/499/CFSP of 25 July 2014 amending Decision 2014/145/CFSP concerning restrictive measures in respect of actions undermining or threatening the territorial integrity, sovereignty and independence of Ukraine [2014] OL L 221/15.

[131] Council Decision 2014/658/CFSP of 8 September 2014 amending Decision 2014/145/CFSP concerning restrictive measures in respect of actions undermining or threatening the territorial integrity, sovereignty and independence of Ukraine [2014] OJ L 271/47.

[132] Council Decision 2014/855/CFSP of 28 November 2014 amending Decision 2014/145/CFSP concerning restrictive measures in respect of actions undermining or threatening the territorial integrity, sovereignty and independence of Ukraine [2014] OJ 344/22.

[133] These were later expanded to other sectors and foreign investments. See Council Decision 2014/933/CFSP of 18 December 2014 amending Decision 2014/386/CFSP concerning restrictive measures in response to the illegal annexation of Crimea and Sevastopol [2014] OJ L 365/152.

[134] Council Decision 2014/386/CFSP of 23 June 2014 concerning restrictions on goods originating in Crimea or Sevastopol, in response to the illegal annexation of Crimea and Sevastopol [2014] OJ L 183/70 and Council Regulation (EU) No 692/2014 of 23 June 2014 concerning restrictions on the import into the Union of goods originating in Crimea or Sevastopol, in response to the illegal annexation of Crimea and Sevastopol [2014] OJ L 183/9.

[135] Similar decisions were taken with respect to a candidate country. See Council Decision 2011/173/CFSP of 21 March 2011 concerning restrictive measures in view of the situation in Bosnia and Herzegovina [2011] OJ L 76/68. Recital n. 2 states: 'Restrictive measures should be imposed against certain natural and legal persons whose activities undermine the sovereignty, territorial integrity, constitutional order and international personality of Bosnia and Herzegovina, seriously threaten the security situation in Bosnia and Herzegovina or undermine the Dayton/Paris General Framework Agreement for Peace.'

non-military reaction against non-state entities. By contrast, no sanctions were adopted against South Ossetia and Abkhazia,[136] given that they have not formally seceded from Georgia.

The examination of the EU's position vis-à-vis breakaway regions, which violate the principle of territorial integrity, should not be concluded without reference to Transnistria. Although the EU is not playing an active role in the settlement of Transnistria's dispute with Moldova, it has adopted a number of interesting restrictive measures against Transnistrian leaders for purposes that are unusual in the practice of the EU's autonomous[137] restrictive measures. The EU has sanctioned with travels bans the separatists' lack of cooperation in promoting a solution to the conflict with Moldova.[138] Travel bans are particularly suitable in the case of leaders, for whom international recognition is a necessary resource to obtain their main policy goal.[139] A second set of measures was adopted in 2004 against those responsible for the design and implementation of the intimidation and closure campaign against Latin-script Moldovan schools in the Transnistrian region. Officials responsible for education were targeted. Some of these measures were selectively lifted in order to encourage progress in reaching a political settlement of the Transnistrian conflict and in restoring the free movement of persons across the administrative boundary of the Transnistrian region. In 2013 Russia's support of the Transnistrian authorities, who had taken action forbidding the use of the Latin alphabet in schools, was also found to breach the European Convention of Human Rights and Fundamental Freedoms.[140] In 2014–15, the restrictions were extended against both the political leadership of Moldova and the people responsible for the campaign against Latin-script schools in the Transnistrian region. Indeed, despite the EU sanctions, measures that hinder the right to education (for example, through non-justified increases in rent, measures concerning school staff, double taxation) were still in force in 2014.[141]

---

[136] However, the EU has condemned the 'Treaty on Alliance and Integration' concluded between Russia and these regions. See (n 27).

[137] However, there are examples of restrictive measures adopted against people who 'obstruct the political process' in an unstable country in order to implement a UNSC Resolution. See, amongst others, Council Regulation (EU) 2015/735 of 7 May 2015 concerning restrictive measures in respect of the situation in South Sudan, and repealing Regulation (EU) n. 748/2014 [2015] OJ L 117/13.

[138] Council Common Position 2003/139/CFSP of 27 February 2003 concerning restrictive measures against the leadership of the Transnistrian region of the Moldovan Republic [2003] OJ L 53/60. See also Council Common Position 2008/160/CFSP of 25 February 2008 concerning restrictive measures against the leadership of the Transnistrian region of the Republic of Moldova [2008] OJ L 51/23; Council 2010/573/CFSP of 27 September 2010 concerning restrictive measures against the leadership of the Transnistrian region of the Republic of Moldova [2010] OJ L 253/54.

[139] F. Giumelli (n 110) 22.

[140] *Catan v. Moldova and Russia* (App no 43370/04, 8252/05 and 18454/06) ECHR 19 October 2012.

[141] See 'EU statement regarding the situation of the Latin-script schools in the Transnistrian region of the Republic of Moldova', 19 March 2014. Available online at http://eeas.europa.eu/delegations/council_europe/press_corner/all_news/news/2014/2014031902_en.htm (accessed 30 August 2015).

Finally, restrictive measures were taken against Russia due to its destabilization of the situation in Ukraine.[142] The motivation behind these measures, which are specific to the ENP, is not common. Russia was hit for the first time at the end of July 2014.[143] Later reinforced,[144] these measures provoked the immediate retaliation of Russia, which enacted trade restrictions in August 2014, extending them in August 2015. Although there are UN-based measures that target people of a country because they threaten peace and stability in their countries or obstruct or undermine the successful completion of its political transition,[145] the sanctions against Russia are directed against the interferences with the stability of a country by a third country and are therefore special.

EU values in the reform of the ENP

In the Action Plan on human rights and democracy, High Representative Mogherini makes it clear that '[T]he implementation of reforms that foster inclusive dialogue, promote good governance, strengthen the independence of the judiciary and ensure protection of fundamental rights' continue to be at the heart of the ENP,[146] thus showing that the EU continues to see itself as a promoter of values in the neighbourhood. In the author's opinion, the new ENP should differentiate its relations depending on whether or not a particular ENP country is willing to follow the EU on the path of modernization, democracy and respect for the rule of law. The 'more for more' principle should be a non-negotiable component of the new ENP policy to build better relations with willing countries. As to unwilling countries, the EU should make more efforts to support their civil society.

The EU should design a neighbourhood policy in which privileged relations are reserved for those countries that subscribe to the EU's democratic standards and genuinely implement democracy, regardless of whether they are southern or eastern European neighbours. The EU should be as open as possible to these countries.

However, what are the implications of this strategy? Does it imply that the EU should conceive EU values as a 'shield' to protect and strengthen the sovereignty

---

[142] On the content of these trade restrictions, see P. Kalinichenko's chapter in this volume.

[143] Council Decision 2014/512/CFSP of 31 July 2014 concerning restrictive measures in view of Russia's actions destabilising the situation in Ukraine [2014] OJ L 229/13.

[144] Council Decision 2014/659/CFSP of 8 September 2014 amending Decision 2014/512/CFSP concerning restrictive measures in view of Russia's actions destabilising the situation in Ukraine [2014] OJ L 271/54; Council Regulation (EU) No 960/2014 of 8 September 2014 amending Regulation (EU) No 833/2014 concerning restrictive measures in view of Russia's actions destabilising the situation in Ukraine [2014] OJ L 271/3; Council Decision 2014/872/CFSP of 4 December 2014 amending Decision 2014/512/CFSP concerning restrictive measures in view of Russia's actions destabilising the situation in Ukraine; and Decision 2014/659/CFSP amending Decision 2014/512/CFSP [2014] OJ L 349/58.

[145] There are many examples. See, amongst others, Council Decision 2010/127/CFSP of 1 March 2010 concerning restrictive measures against Eritrea [2010] OJ L 51/19.

[146] See JOIN (2015) 16 final, Joint Communication to the European Parliament and the Council Action Plan on Human Rights and Democracy (2015–2019) 'Keeping human rights at the heart of the EU agenda action plan', 28 April 2015.

56 *Sara Poli*

of ENP countries against the influence of powerful neighbours? In this case, adherence by the EU's partners to EU values would serve to delimit the 'sphere of influence' between the EU and Russia. The answer is no, particularly given that such an approach would lead to a conflictual relationship with this country. And this would go against the fundamental principles of the EU integration process, including the promotion of peace and security both within its borders and amongst its neighbours.

Conclusions

This chapter has highlighted that the EU values-based approach, despite its contestation, is still reflected in the ENI Regulation. EU assistance is geared to the promotion of EU political values, while the development of a functioning market economy is no longer mentioned. There continue to be forms of positive and negative conditionality in this instrument. Overall, the ENI is similar in content to IPA II, although candidate countries are expected to fully comply with EU values.

Examination of the practice of Decisions regarding macro-financial assistance to ENP countries shows that they incrementally de facto (if not *de jure*) reflect the EU's values-based approach. However, it was also highlighted how this kind of exceptional economic assistance is reserved not only for ENP partners, but also for other countries of the wider neighbourhood. Thus, EU relations with its close neighbours is not special, as Art. 8 TEU envisages.

The overview of the restrictive measures taken against legal and natural persons and the governmental leadership of ENP countries shows that some of them present special features. The EU's judicial assistance to democracies in transition, such as Tunisia and Egypt, in fighting the misappropriation of funds is specific to the ENP. It underlines that the EU is more committed to supporting the establishment of its values in its relations with its neighbours than with more distant third countries. Restrictive measures adopted against the secessionist Ukrainian Republic (in reaction to their breach of the principle of territorial integrity and sovereignty) and those enacted against Russia are worth highlighting because they are uncommon. Despite some rhetoric in the EU's narrative of exporting its values to the ENP, it can be concluded that the EU is more committed to doing so in the neighbourhood than in other contexts and it is to be hoped that the EU's values-based approach will continue to be a non-negotiable component of this policy.

Bibliography

Cremona, M. (2005) EU Enlargement: Solidarity and Conditionality. *European Law Review*. 30(1). pp. 3–22.

—(2011) Values in EU Foreign Policy. In Evans, M. and Koutrakos, P. *Beyond the Established Orders: Policy Interconnections between the EU and the Rest of the World*. Hart Publishing: Oxford.

Del Sarto, R. (2014) Defining Borders and People in the Borderlands: EU Policies, Israeli Prerogatives and the Palestinians. *Journal of Common Market Studies*. 52(2). pp. 200–216.

—(2015) Normative Empire Europe: The European Union, Its Borderlands, and the 'Arab Spring'. *Journal of Common Market Studies*. 54(2). pp. 215–232.
Eckes, C. (2014) EU Restrictive Measures against Natural and Legal Persons: From Counterterrorist to Third-Country Sanctions. *Common Market Law Review*. 51(3). pp. 869–906.
Gerbert, K. 'Shooting in the Dark? EU Sanctions Policies', January 2013. Available online at www.ecfr.eu/page/-/ECFR71_SANCTIONS_BRIEF_AW.pdf (accessed 30 September 2015).
Giumelli, F. How EU Sanctions Work. *EUISS Chaillot Paper* n. 129. May 2013. Available online at www.iss.europa.eu/uploads/media/Chaillot_129.pdf (accessed 5 October 2015).
Hyde-Price, A. (2006) 'Normative' Power Europe: A Realist Critique. *Journal of European Public Policy*. 13(2). pp. 217–234.
Korosteleva, E. (2010) Moldova's European Choice: 'Between Two Stools'? *Europe-Asia Studies*. [Online] 62(8). pp. 1267–1289.
—(2012) Questioning Democracy Promotion: Belarus' Response to the 'Colour Revolutions'. *Democratization*. 19(1). pp. 37–59.
Nielsen, K.L. and Vilson, M. (2014) The Eastern Partnership: Soft Power Strategy or Policy Failure? *European Foreign Affairs Review*. 19 (2). pp. 243–262.
Seeberg, P. (2013) The EU and Constitutionalism in Egypt: EU Foreign and Security Policy Challenges with a Special Focus on the Changing Political Setting in the MENA-region. *European Foreign Affairs Review*. 18(3). pp. 411–428.
Tömmel, I. (2013) The New Neighborhood Policy of the EU: An Appropriate Response to the Arab Spring? Available online at www.e-ir.info/2013/05/29/the-new-neighbourhood-policy-of-the-eu-an-appropriate-response-to-the-arab-spring (accessed 1 September 2015).
Van Elsuwege, P. and Petrov, R. (2011) Article 8 TEU: Towards a New Generation of Agreements with the Neighbouring Countries of the European Union? *European Law Review*. 36(5). pp. 688–703.
Van Wooren, B. (2009) A Case-Study of 'Soft Law' in EU External Relations: The European Neighbourhood Policy. *European Law Review*. 34(5). pp. 696–719.
Völkel, J.C. (2014) More for More, Less for Less – More or Less: A Critique of the EU's Arab Spring Response à la Cinderella. *European Foreign Affairs Review*. 19(2). pp. 263–281.

3 The contestation of values in the European Neighbourhood Policy
Challenges of capacity, consistency and competition

Sieglinde Gstöhl

Introduction: an expanding community of values?

When launching the European Neighbourhood Policy (ENP), the European Union (EU) expected that through a steady process of rapprochement, the neighbouring countries would progressively become part of the EU's community of values. The European Commission declared that: 'The European Neighbourhood Policy's vision involves a ring of countries, sharing the EU's fundamental values and objectives, drawn into an increasingly close relationship, going beyond co-operation to involve a significant measure of economic and political integration.'[1] This declaration raised high expectations for a comprehensive regulatory and legislative alignment of the neighbours with significant socio-economic and political reforms according to the priorities set out in jointly agreed Action Plans and with benchmarks that could be monitored and assessed. The Action Plans would cover 'first, commitments to specific actions which confirm or reinforce adherence to shared values and ... secondly, commitments to actions which will bring partner countries closer to the EU in a number of priority fields.'[2]

Ten years later, it has become clear that the ambitious goal of expanding the 'zone of prosperity, stability and security' beyond the EU's borders is far – perhaps even further away – from being achieved. The EU's neighbourhood has become politically more fragmented and unstable, the pace of economic and democratic transition has slowed down, and the EU reluctantly finds itself in competition with Russia over the common Eastern Neighbourhood while its engagement in the south has been questioned by the Arab uprisings and their unintended consequences. In other words, 'there is hardly any other external policy of the EU with a larger gap between its stated objectives and the actual outcome.'[3] This chapter addresses this puzzle by looking into the promotion of values, since values were given a prominent role in the ENP. Although the inclusion of values is not unique to the ENP, the rhetoric and the process of monitoring compliance – inspired by

---

[1] Commission (EC), 'European Neighbourhood Policy (Strategy Paper)', COM (2004) 373, 12 May 2004, 5.
[2] Ibid. 9.
[3] S. Lehne, 'Time to Reset the European Neighbourhood Policy', *Carnegie Europe* (February 2014). Available online at http://carnegieeurope.eu/publications/?fa=54420 (accessed 5 October 2015).

the enlargement methodology – are much more elaborate compared to the EU's other external policies.

The EU has since the early 1990s – since the end of the Cold War and since the completion of its internal market – increasingly pursued normative foreign policy objectives and explicitly committed itself to the externalization of both political and economic norms. The political momentum after the fall of Communism had brought about the perspective of democratization and market liberalization worldwide. The EU's aspiration to project these values beyond its borders has further been reinforced by the Treaty of Lisbon. According to Art. 2 TEU, '[t]he Union is founded on the values of respect for human dignity, freedom, democracy, equality, the rule of law and respect for human rights, including the rights of persons belonging to minorities.' Any European state which respects these values and is committed to promoting them may apply to become a member of the Union (Art. 49 TEU); and the EU shall uphold and promote these values in its relations with the wider world (Art. 3(5) TEU). In addition to human rights and democratic standards, the European Union frequently cites the principles of market economy and sustainable development among the values that it intends to share with its neighbours. These political and economic values are thus constitutive of the EU's self-perception and self-projection abroad.

Manners' seminal concept of 'normative power Europe' conceives of the EU as a values-driven foreign policy actor based on the core norms that form its own identity (peace, liberty, democracy, the rule of law and respect for human rights and fundamental freedoms).[4] Among the 'minor' norms are social solidarity, anti-discrimination, sustainable development and good governance. Manners defines normative power as 'the ability to define what passes for "normal" in world politics', and the most important factor shaping the EU's international role 'is not what it does or what it says, but what it is.'[5]

In response to the 'normative power Europe' debate, which has mostly focused on political values, Damro argues that because the European Union is, at its core, a market, it may also be conceptualized as a 'market power Europe' which 'exercises its power through the externalization of economic and social market-related policies and regulatory measures.'[6] He sees the internal market as an alternative basis of the EU's identity, and thus its power, with three interrelated characteristics predisposing the Union to act as a market power: the large size of its market, its institutional features as a regulatory entity and the interest group contestation that this generates.[7] Indeed, the European Commission also perceives the internal market as 'a powerful engine to promote EU high quality rules and values around the world' because '[t]hrough the enlargement process and the European Neighbourhood Policy, the Community rulebook is gradually being

---

[4] I. Manners, 'Normative Power Europe: A Contradiction in Terms?' (2002) 40(2) *Journal of Common Market Studies* 242.
[5] Ibid. 236, 252.
[6] C. Damro, 'Market Power Europe' (2012) 19(5) *Journal of European Public Policy* 682.
[7] Ibid. 686.

adopted across large parts of the European continent', and the internal market is 'increasingly serving as a reference point in third countries as well as in global and regional fora.'[8]

Values underpin more concrete norms and guide action in a given situation. Cremona argues that 'in order to lead to concrete outcomes, the "values" which have a symbolic significance for the EU must find practical expression in legal norms', whether these norms are derived from the Treaties or imported into the EU's legal order.[9] However, norms may not only be of a legal nature but may also comprise social norms about appropriate behaviour, and may have both regulative and constitutive functions. Norms can be more broadly defined as 'intersubjective understandings that constitute actors' interests and identities, and create expectations as well as prescribe what appropriate behaviour ought to be.'[10]

In the framework of the European Neighbourhood Policy, the common values are located 'principally within the fields of the rule of law, good governance, the respect for human rights, including minority rights, the promotion of good neighbourly relations, and the principles of market economy and sustainable development.'[11] The Lisbon Treaty took this policy up and asked the EU to 'develop a special relationship with neighbouring countries, aiming to establish an area of prosperity and good neighbourliness, founded on the values of the Union and characterised by close and peaceful relations based on cooperation' (Art. 8(1) TEU).

At the outset of the European Neighbourhood Policy, the EU has to a large extent taken these values and their export for granted. This chapter asks why the promotion of values in the ENP has become a matter of contestation. It argues that, first, the values themselves have been challenged because of their ambiguous nature, because the potential conflicts between them can result in policy incoherence, and because of the (re-)emergence of competing values in the Arab world and in the post-Soviet space. Second, the mechanisms of value export have been challenged because some neighbours have been incapable or unwilling to absorb the values; the EU and its Member States have failed to conduct a consistent, credible policy; and the EU is facing normative rivalry from other actors, such as Russia. In other words, the European Neighbourhood Policy faces challenges of capacity, consistency and competition.

Following this line of reasoning, the chapter is structured in two main parts, the first focusing on issues linked to the values themselves and the second dealing with the mechanisms of exporting the values, followed by some conclusions.

---

[8] Commission Staff Working Document, 'The External Dimension of the Single Market Review', SEC (2007) 1519, 20 November 2007, 5.

[9] M. Cremona, 'Values in EU Foreign Policy' in M. Evans and P. Koutrakos (eds), *Beyond the Established Orders: Policy Interconnections between the EU and the Rest of the World* (Oxford, Hart Publishing 2011), 275.

[10] A. Björkdahl, 'Norms in International Relations: Some Theoretical and Methodological Reflections' (2002) 15(1) *Cambridge Review of International Affairs* 21.

[11] COM (2004) 373 (n 1) 3.

Contestation of values

The values in the ENP have been queried for three main reasons: (1) the manifold ambiguities of the nature and substance of the values; (2) the shift of focus from political to economic values in the ENP, especially with the advent of Deep and Comprehensive Free Trade Areas (DCFTAs); and (3) the (re-)emergence of competing values in the neighbourhood.

The ambiguity of values

At least three ambiguities can be discerned besides the fact that the Treaties tend to conflate different concepts into an overlapping terminology of values, principles and objectives.[12]

First, the EU on the one hand actively promotes its values in the neighbourhood through various instruments, including conditionality, while on the other hand it appears to assume that these values are already shared and form the basis for developing relations. Art. 21(1) TEU requires the Union to seek to build partnerships with third countries 'which share the principles on which it is founded.' In particular the neighbouring countries are thereby associated with shared values, as many EU statements on the Stabilization and Association Process with the Western Balkans and on the ENP show.[13]

A second ambiguity is pointed out by Leino and Petrov, who argue that EU institutions use the notion of 'common values' as both a universal concept and as an EU concept: on the one hand, the values constitute the EU's foundation, while on the other hand, they are universal.[14] When promoting the values abroad, the Union can thus claim not to be imposing its own values on others but rather to be using its influence to bring the practice of foreign governments into line with their own professed values. The EU also explicitly encourages ENP countries to embrace international norms, for instance by signing up to international agreements. The abstraction of values results in a European Neighbourhood Policy which 'formally promotes jointly shared values but which, in practice, amounts to the EU's own reading of them.'[15] Hence, views may differ with regard not only to the identification of the relevant values as such but also to their definition, for instance what kind of democracy, market economy or conception of human rights should be promoted. Even within the European Union the Member States do not always interpret the 'shared values' in the same way. Interestingly, the very first Wider Europe Communication of the European Commission referred to shared values with a footnote to the

---

[12] Cremona (n 9) 278.
[13] Ibid. 301–303.
[14] P. Leino and R. Petrov, 'Between "Common Values" and Competing Universals – The Promotion of the EU's Common Values through the European Neighbourhood Policy' (2009) 15(5) *European Law Journal* 654–671.
[15] Ibid. 656.

Charter of Fundamental Rights of the EU,[16] whereas the ENP Strategy Paper one year later focused on international standards, including the human rights conventions of the United Nations, the Council of Europe and the Organization for Cooperation and Security in Europe.[17]

Third, the question arises how the rather abstract values should be implemented. They need to be transposed into concrete reform steps in the Action Plans that can be monitored and, if necessary, enforced. Ghazaryan, for example, finds with regard to democracy promotion in the Southern Caucasus that the ENP Action Plans fall short of translating the political rhetoric on democratic reforms into operational and measurable plans of action and that democratic values are in fact only partially and to varying degrees included.[18] Moreover, the monitoring process and the assistance provided for the implementation of the Action Plans 'renders the democratic reform subsidiary, or in some cases irrelevant, within the ENP.'[19] More generally, Bosse argues that there is no coherent discourse on values nor an agreement among EU actors or among and within ENP partners on the contents and significance of these values.[20] Furthermore, there is a gap between the political rhetoric on shared values and the capability to enforce these values. In a similar vein, Kochenov contends that more attention needs to be paid to the export of values because 'the *acquis* is not necessarily about the values on which the Union is founded', nor can the *acquis* 'be taken as guarantor of such values' enforcement and promotion.'[21] In the EU's perspective, the acceptance of values includes the legislative approximation to the often technical, legal *acquis*. While conditionality may promote the export of *acquis*, it may be less suitable for the export of values, which actors need to internalize for an effective implementation. The internalization of values is more likely when the target countries view them as appropriate and legitimate and not just as a means to obtain the rewards that come with the policy import.[22] In this regard, processes of persuasion, socialization and learning resulting from social interaction and joint ownership appear to be more effective compared to incentives or the risk of sanctions in case of non-compliance.

In addition to the ambiguous nature of values, their substance and coherence has also been questioned.

---

[16] Commission (EC), 'Wider Europe – Neighbourhood: A New Framework for Relations with our Eastern and Southern Neighbours', COM (2003) 104 final, 11 March 2003, 3–4.
[17] COM (2004) 373 (n 1) 12–13.
[18] N. Ghazaryan, *The European Neighbourhood Policy and the Democratic Values of the EU: A Legal Analysis* (Oxford, Hart Publishing 2014) 136, 148.
[19] Ibid. 175.
[20] G. Bosse, 'Values in the EU's Neighbourhood Policy: Political Rhetoric or Reflection of a Coherent Policy?' (2007) 7 *European Political Economy Review* 38–62.
[21] D. Kochenov, 'The Issue of Values' in P. Van Elsuwege and R. Petrov (eds), *Legislative Approximation and Application of EU Law in the Eastern Neighbourhood of the European Union: Towards a Common Regulatory Space?* (London, Routledge 2014) 53.
[22] S. Gstöhl, 'Blurring Economic Boundaries? Trade and Aid in the EU's Near Abroad' in D. Mahncke and S. Gstöhl (eds), *Europe's Near Abroad: Promises and Prospects of the EU's Neighbourhood Policy* (Bruxelles, Peter Lang 2008) 135–161.

Conflict potential of values

In the literature and policy debate the focus has largely been on political values rather than on economic values. Yet, the EU Charter of Fundamental Rights covers both civil and political rights as well as social and economic rights, and the Union's aim to promote 'the well-being of its peoples' (Art. 3(1) TEU) includes the establishment of an internal market, sustainable development and 'a highly competitive social market economy' (Art. 3(3) TEU). Moreover, solidarity is an express goal of EU external action (Art. 21(1) TEU).

On the eve of Eastern enlargement, the European Council stated that the dynamics of the accession process presented 'an important opportunity to take forward relations with neighbouring countries based on shared political and economic values.'[23] The economic reform agenda normally includes accession to the World Trade Organization (WTO) as a prerequisite for concluding a free trade agreement with the EU. The development of the ENP soon embraced deep integration as well as deep democracy. Deep economic integration – as exemplified by the DCFTAs – refers to 'behind-the-border integration', such as common standards or competition rules, in contrast to shallow integration, which focuses on the removal of barriers at the border like tariffs and quotas.[24] In the context of EU external relations, deep economic integration implies legal approximation to or adoption of parts of the EU's *acquis*. The 2011 review of the ENP introduced the notion of deep democracy which, inter alia, includes free and fair elections, freedom of association and expression, the rule of law, the fight against corruption, security and law enforcement sector reform and the establishment of democratic control over armed and security forces.[25] The new Association Agreements with DCFTAs contain a 'common values conditionality' that goes beyond human rights and democratic principles and embraces, for instance, respect for sovereignty and territorial integrity and the fight against corruption, organized crime, terrorism and proliferation of weapons, as well as respect for the principles of the free market economy and the promotion of sustainable development and effective multilateralism.[26] However, the economic norms are not part of the 'essential elements clause' and cannot trigger a suspension of the agreement in case of a breach.[27]

Nevertheless, economic and political values can be at odds – and the economic concerns often prevail. For example, the pursuit of trade interests may conflict with the promotion of democratization or human rights. As pointed out by Panebianco, 'economic liberalization and the establishment of free

---

[23] European Council, Presidency Conclusions, Copenhagen, 12–13 December 2002, para 22.
[24] R.Z. Lawrence, *Regionalism, Multilateralism, and Deeper Integration* (Washington, The Brookings Institutions 1996). Available online at www.brookings.edu/research/books/1996/regional (accessed 5 October 2015).
[25] European Commission/High Representative, 'A New Response to a Changing Neighbourhood' COM (2011) 303, 25 May 2011, 3.
[26] G. Van der Loo, P. Van Elsuwege and R. Petrov, 'The EU-Ukraine Association Agreement: Assessment of an Innovative Legal Instrument' (2014) *EUI Working Paper* n. 9, 12.
[27] Ibid. 12–13.

markets – which are also crucial EU values – seem to come before human rights and democratic principles.'[28] The Union faces the general problem of how to prioritize among competing ENP goals such as security, good governance and economic aspirations. Art. 21 TEU does not provide a ranking of objectives, but simply calls for consistency between the different areas of EU external action and between these and its other policies. Consistency implies, for example, that the EU treats countries in a comparable human rights situation in a similar way in terms of sanctions. Consistency is crucial for the EU's credibility, as is the example set by Europe itself. Taking a principled stance on human rights and democracy but then backtracking on this stance in function of the economic or political importance of the third country concerned, risks damaging the EU's credibility. Overall in its external relations, the EU has tended to prioritize the first generation of human, civil and political rights over the second generation of economic, social and cultural rights.[29] Moreover, the EU is said to have a longstanding, marked preference for positive over negative measures in its external relations, with suspension being only a measure of last resort.

Conflicts may also arise within the same group of values, for instance between sustainable development and poverty reduction on the one hand and trade liberalization on the other, or between political stability and democratization.[30] Eurosceptic Islamist parties winning free elections in Southern ENP countries are a case in point. Although the EU viewed the Arab Spring as a 'window of opportunity' for democracy, as events unfolded it still prioritized security concerns as a response to the threat of instability in North Africa.[31]

Promoting regional economic integration in the neighbourhood could also be seen as a value, as stated by the European Commission: 'The European Neighbourhood Policy will reinforce existing forms of regional and subregional cooperation and provide a framework for their further development.'[32] However, economic relations between the EU and its partners, reinforced by the principles of differentiation and conditionality, have so far resulted rather in a bilateral

---

[28] S. Panebianco, 'The Constraints on EU Action as a "Norm Exporter" in the Mediterranean' in O. Elgström and M. Smith (eds), *The European Union's Roles in International Politics: Concepts and Analysis* (London, Routledge 2006) 141.

[29] See, for instance, B. Kerremans and J. Orbie, 'The Social Dimension of European Trade Policies' (2009) 14(5) *European Foreign Affairs Review* 638; J. Orbie and O. Babarinde, 'The Social Dimension of Globalization and EU Development Policy: Promoting Labour Standards and Corporate Social Responsibility' (2008) 30(3) *Journal of European Integration* 467; L. Bartels, 'Legal Analysis of Human Rights Clauses in the European Union's Euro-Mediterranean Association Agreements' (2004) 9(3) *Mediterranean Politics* 386; I. Byrne, 'The Importance of Economic, Social and Cultural Rights in Guaranteeing Civil and Political Rights with the Euro-Mediterranean Partnership' (2004) 9(3) *Mediterranean Politics* 344–367.

[30] T.A. Börzel and V. van Hüllen, 'One Voice, One Message, but Conflicting Goals: Cohesiveness and Consistency in the European Neighbourhood Policy' (2014) 21(7) *Journal of European Public Policy* 1033–1049.

[31] A. Dandashly, 'The EU Response to Regime Change in the Wake of the Arab Revolt: Differential Implementation' (2015) 37(1) *Journal of European Integration* 37–56.

[32] COM (2004) 373 (n 1) 4.

'hub-and-spoke' pattern which militates against regional cooperation.[33] This is also pointed out by Pace:

> The ideal of 'shared' and 'common' values is ... reflected in the kind of Europe that is projected to the south: a model of cooperation and peace that should be emulated in the Mediterranean. Yet, the ENP is highly focused on bilateral (rather than multilateral, cooperative and intra-regional) relations.[34]

Finally, although the EU likes to refer to universal values, its policy has been criticized as being Eurocentric or confined to 'Western values'.

The (re-)emergence of competing values

In the post-Western world the EU is but one among several regional actors promoting its norms. Yet in order to be a normative power, the outside world has to attribute such a distinct role to an actor. The outside perception of the EU as an international economic power is predominant, while it is seen as a weaker political and diplomatic actor.[35] More specifically, studies have found that 'the EU is not viewed as a normative power in Brazil, China, India, Russia and South Africa', nor in the United States, but in its Eastern and Southern Neighbourhoods the EU is to some extent perceived as a normative power and values such as human rights and democracy are associated with Brussels.[36] Nevertheless, the rise of BRICS and other emerging economies has turned the international system into a multipolar order in which the EU is but one major actor among others. Instead of the 'end of history' – a universalization of Western liberal democracy – alternative models and values have persisted or (re-)surfaced.

Since the end of the Cold War triggered a wave of democratization and the triumph of the market economy, the European Union has worked on the assumption that its neighbourhood is likely to subscribe to common values. However, while the post-modern European states have been further pooling their sovereignty, many of the 16 ENP partners have been struggling with authoritarian regimes or 'managed democracies'. Whereas Europe has become more secular, political Islam has been on the rise in Turkey and the Arab world. To varying degrees, and with the exception of Azerbaijan and Lebanon, predominantly Muslim societies in ENP countries appear to favour the application of Islamic law (sharia), or at least parts thereof, and a role for religious leaders in politics.[37]

In the post-Soviet space, many policymakers have remained attached to traditional concepts such as national sovereignty and non-interference or zero-sum

---

[33] Gstöhl 2012: 100.
[34] M. Pace, 'Norm Shifting from EMP to ENP: The EU as a Norm Entrepreneur in the South?' (2007) 20(4) *Cambridge Review of International Affairs* 662.
[35] H. Larsen, 'The EU as a Normative Power and the Research on External Perceptions: The Missing Link' (2014) 52(4) *Journal of Common Market Studies* 902.
[36] Ibid. 903–904.
[37] Pew Research Center, *The World's Muslims: Religion, Politics and Society*, 30 April 2013. Available online at www.pewforum.org/2013/04/30/the-worlds-muslims-religion-politics-society-overview (accessed 5 October 2015).

game spheres of influence. As argued by Korosteleva, the normative disjunction between the West and the former Soviet Union is 'deeply rooted in public perceptions whereby people clearly and uncompromisingly differentiate between Western values – of market economy, human rights, democracy and lawfulness – and their own values – of peace, tolerance, respect for cultural heritage and religion.'[38] Many post-Soviet countries also demonstrate an enduring proclivity for strong leadership and a strong corporate state. In particular the Russian elite considers the Western understanding of human rights 'as a dubious concept, insofar as it extends beyond the protection of personal freedom to impose and promote other values that contradict the traditional Russian religious and national values.'[39] Orthodoxy and Russian culture and language are emphasized as key elements of a Russian civilization.[40] Kratochvíl finds that the Russian foreign policy elite believes in state-centrism and in Russia's great power status, and believes that Russia has frequently been treated unfairly.[41] 'The deeply ingrained normative underpinnings of Russian foreign policy remain largely incompatible with those of the EU.'[42]

Contestation of the promotion of values

For Manners, EU norm diffusion takes place through unintentional diffusion (contagion), informational diffusion (strategic and declaratory communications), procedural diffusion (in an institutionalized relationship), transference (for instance, through trade and aid) and overt diffusion (through physical EU presence).[43] If the export of values is understood – as is the case in the ENP – as a deliberate and active attempt by the Union to externalize norms rather than as just an essentially passive influence, the main mechanisms of EU norm diffusion are linked to procedural and transference diffusion. In a similar vein, Damro argues that the EU exercises its market power through tools 'such as the use of positive and negative conditionality, international legal instruments and internal regulatory measures' in its relations to both state and non-state actors.[44] The 'market access conditionality' in the DCFTAs, for instance, is based on a strict monitoring process, inspired by the pre-accession methodology, and the process of legislative approximation and the effective enforcement and implementation of the agreement are subject to permanent scrutiny.[45]

---

[38] E. Korosteleva, 'Questioning Democracy Promotion: Belarus' Response to the "Colour Revolutions"' (2012) 19(1) *Democratization* 49.
[39] Leino and Petrov (n 14) 668.
[40] D. Shlapentokh, 'The Death of the Byzantine Empire and Construction of Historical/Political Identities in Late Putin Russia' (2013) 15(1) *Journal of Balkan and Near Eastern Studies* 69–96.
[41] P. Kratochvíl, 'The Discursive Resistance to EU-Enticement: The Russian Elite and (the Lack of) Europeanisation' (2008) 60(3) *Europe-Asia Studies* 417.
[42] Ibid. 398.
[43] Manners (n 4) 244–245.
[44] Damro (n 6) 692.
[45] Van der Loo, Van Elsuwege and Petrov (n 26) 28.

The EU engages in promoting its values and norms through unilateral instruments, bilateral agreements and non-binding instruments such as human rights or policy dialogues, Council conclusions, people-to-people exchanges, Action Plans and Progress Reports.[46] *Ex ante* conditionality may require that certain conditions be fulfilled by neighbouring countries before the EU enters into or upgrades a relationship, or lifts sanctions under the Common Foreign and Security Policy. *Ex post* conditionality – which foresees a reaction of the EU in an already established relationship with a neighbouring country in case the latter fails to comply with its commitments – is present in various EU instruments. The most common are human rights and democracy clauses in bi- or multilateral agreements and in regulations of financial aid (except for humanitarian assistance) or in autonomous trade preferences. Positive conditionality promises benefits to a country for desired action, while negative conditionality threatens punitive sanctions for not respecting crucial norms and values. These incentives and disincentives may also be combined in a 'carrot and stick' policy, as in the ENP.

These mechanisms of value export have been challenged. Some neighbours have been unable or unwilling to accept and absorb the values, or the EU and its Member States have failed to conduct a consistent and credible policy, especially with regard to conditionality, and they have had to face the normative rivalry of other external actors.

Lack of capacity and/or willingness in ENP countries

The European Union enjoys weaker political leverage, the lower the willingness and the capacity of governments and other domestic actors in ENP countries to deal with reforms.[47]

First, a crucial precondition for a successful norm export is the political will in ENP countries to tackle the domestic reforms required. In authoritarian regimes veto players are most likely placed at the governmental level, and an EU norm export will in particular depend on its anticipated effects on the executive's power; that is, the political costs of adopting reforms.[48] In other words, the EU's challenge 'remains how to put pressure on … governments to aim for "common values" (in particular democratic reforms) when these governments view such norms as threatening their own hold on power.'[49] Moreover, the resonance of EU values is not the same in all societies. Socialization research suggests that persuasion is more likely if the target is in a novel and uncertain environment, has few ingrained beliefs inconsistent with the socializing institution and wants to belong

---

[46] Cremona (n 9) 292–307.
[47] T.A. Börzel, 'When Europe Hits … beyond Its Borders: Europeanization and the Near Abroad' (2011) 9(4–5) *Comparative European Politics* 400; S. Gstöhl, 'The EU as a Norm Exporter?' in D. Mahncke and S. Gstöhl (eds) (n 22) 285–288.
[48] F. Schimmelfennig and U. Sedelmeier, 'Governance by Conditionality: EU Rule Transfer to the Candidate Countries of Central and Eastern Europe' (2004) 11(4) *Journal of European Public Policy* 670.
[49] Pace (n 33), 663.

to the latter.[50] Transition countries tend to be more receptive to EU norms than authoritarian regimes because they are likely to be more open to new ideas after their old governance systems are discredited.

Second, a lack of absorption capacity may hamper political and economic reforms. For economies without strong institutions or administrative capacities, regulatory approximation to EU standards can involve onerous costs, possibly resulting in higher domestic prices and trade diversion.[51] It can, for instance, be questioned whether the DCFTAs requiring alignment to and selective adoption of EU *acquis* are the most suitable instruments for countries facing serious development challenges. The DCFTAs cover substantially all trade in goods and services as well as 'behind-the-border' issues, such as technical and other standards, competition policy, industrial policy, intellectual property rights, company law, public procurement and financial services. By replicating the enlargement process, the ENP causes the EU's neighbours 'to lose a level of independence at a crucial time in their democratic reform and economic restructuring programmes', while they are receiving fewer benefits in return than applicant countries did.[52]

The Association Agreements with Ukraine, Moldova and Georgia, signed in June 2014, contain several legislative approximation mechanisms with varying degrees of obligation and various procedures to amend the incorporated rules. Also the dispute settlement varies across sectors from consultation, arbitration or mediation to rulings by the Court of Justice of the EU.[53] In particular, the countries commit to incorporate the relevant *acquis* regarding technical barriers to trade and certain services. The Association Council monitors the application of the agreement and serves as a forum to discuss new, relevant legislation. As already mentioned, the DCFTAs are based on far-reaching 'market access conditionality' which links additional access to the internal market to the country's progress in implementation. They entail 'a move from the soft law approach based on persuasion and assistance to a comprehensive, binding and detailed legal framework structuring relations between the EU and its Eastern neighbours.'[54] Nevertheless, a country's commitment to adopt and implement EU norms does not necessarily mean that this is actually followed up by their transposition into domestic law, nor by their application.[55] The will and the

---

[50] J.T. Checkel, 'International Institutions and Socialization in Europe: Introduction and Framework' (2005) 59(4) *International Organization* 813.

[51] P. Messerlin et al., *An Appraisal of the EU's Trade Policy towards Its Eastern Neighbours: The Case of Georgia* (CEPS and Sciences Po 2011) i-ii. Available online at www.ceps.eu/publications/appraisal-eu%E2%80%99s-trade-policy-towards-its-eastern-neighbours-case-georgia (accessed 5 October 2015).

[52] Leino and Petrov (n 14) 665.

[53] Van der Loo, Van Elsuwege and Petrov (n 26) 14–22.

[54] L. Delcour and K. Wolczuk, 'Eurasian Economic Integration and Implications for the EU's Policy in the Eastern Neigbhourhood' in R. Dragneva and K. Wolczuk (eds), *Eurasian Economic Integration: Law, Policy, and Politics* (London, Edward Elgar 2013) 190.

[55] J. Langbein and K. Wolczuk, 'Convergence without Membership? The Impact of the European Union in the Neighbourhood: Evidence from Ukraine' (2012) 19(6) *Journal of European Public Policy* 863–881.

capacity to adapt, as necessary, the political systems, economies and societies to the imported norms remain crucial.

Lack of capacity and/or willingness in the EU

The value export may be hampered not only by shortcomings in the ENP countries but also by inadequacies on the side of the European Union: the lack of political will, capacity or, as a result, inconsistency.

First, the (un)willingness of EU actors and Member States to deliver certain incentives can be seen in light of the transposition of the enlargement methodology to the ENP despite the lack of an EU membership perspective. The European Union was not ready to make any accession promises to the Eastern partners and left the ENP's ultimate objective open. In 2006 the European Commission introduced the concept of 'a longer-term vision of an economic community emerging between the EU and its ENP partners', which 'would include such points as the application of shared regulatory frameworks and improved market access for goods and services among ENP partners, and some appropriate institutional arrangement such as dispute settlement mechanisms.'[56] Such a Neighbourhood Economic Community would offer the neighbours 'a stake' in the internal market.[57] This future perspective may not be sufficiently attractive or concrete for some neighbours. The existence of a membership option may encourage not only the partner countries to make a bigger effort, but also the EU. Without such a perspective, the EU's ability to deliver real incentives, such as the liberalization of agricultural exports, labour migration or EU involvement in the resolution of regional conflicts, remains constrained because it includes areas in which the Union faces strong vested interests in some EU Member States. Some progress has been made over time with regard to trade in agricultural products and visa liberalization. Although the ENP was intended to 'reinforce stability and security and contribute to efforts at conflict resolution' and to promote good neighbourliness,[58] in practice the EU has been rather reluctant to get involved in the conflicts in Moldova (Transnistria), Georgia (Abkhazia and South Ossetia), Azerbaijan–Armenia (Nagorno–Karabakh), the Western Sahara and Israel–Palestine, not to mention the wars in Libya and Syria. Nevertheless, the EU established several civilian missions under the Common Security and Defence Policy, such as, in 2005, the European Union Border Assistance Mission (EUBAM) for the Rafah Crossing Point in Gaza, as well as the EUBAM to Moldova and Ukraine; in 2008, the European Union Monitoring Mission (EUMM) in Georgia; and, in 2013, the EUBAM in Libya. In 2011

---

[56] Commission (EC) 'Strengthening the European Neighbourhood Policy,' COM (2006) 726 final, 4 December 2006, 5.
[57] See S. Gstöhl, 'What Is at Stake in the Internal Market? Towards a Neighbourhood Economic Community' in E. Lannon (ed.), *The European Neighbourhood Policy's Challenges / Les Défis de la Politique Européenne de Voisinage* (Bruxelles, Peter Lang 2012) 85–108.
[58] COM (2004) 373 (n 1) 4.

the EU decided on a military operation in support of humanitarian assistance operations in response to the crisis in Libya (EUFOR Libya). However, EUFOR Libya was never deployed because the required call from the UN Office for the Coordination of Humanitarian Affairs was not issued.

Second, the EU may lack not only the necessary Member State support but also the legal competences, or face other constraints to acting on certain issues. A case in point is the non-participation of neighbours in the decision-making process about the actual meaning of common values and their further development.[59] This lack of 'input legitimacy' – or real joint ownership – hampers the internalization of norms in ENP countries. As non-EU members, neighbours risk facing a fundamental dilemma the more closely they become involved with the EU. Other neighbourhood models of deep economic integration, such as the EU–Turkey customs union, the EU–Switzerland bilateralism or the European Economic Area, have in recent years reached their limits because they cover more and more sectors but lack efficient institutional arrangements for ensuring the necessary market homogeneity.[60] The Council of the EU underlined that any close relationships with neighbouring countries must be guided by the principles of homogeneity and legal certainty because these principles 'guarantee the efficiency, sustainability and ultimately the credibility of the single market.'[61] This increasingly implies the conclusion of agreements which foresee a dynamic adaptation to the *acquis*, its uniform interpretation and independent surveillance and judicial enforcement. Such a measure of supranationality without full participation in the relevant EU decision-making processes encroaches upon national autonomy. The DCFTAs provide only for a limited form of 'decision-shaping' in specific areas where full internal market treatment is foreseen.[62]

Third, the lack of capacity or willingness to offer ENP countries certain benefits or to endorse the values by reacting to non-compliance may generate inconsistent EU policies. This may concern either vertical consistency between EU policies and national policies of the Member States or horizontal consistency between different EU policies. For example, the EU's promotion of human rights and democracy in the ENP has frequently been trumped by economic or security interests.[63] The Arab Spring caught Europe off guard and revealed how the EU and its Member States had, for the sake of political stability (including containing the flows of migration, terrorism and organized crime), connived with authoritarian regimes. The EU's engagement with autocratic regimes in ENP countries has become more pragmatic over time, shifting towards functional cooperation.

---

[59] Leino and Petrov (n 14) 666–667.
[60] S. Gstöhl, 'Models of External Differentiation in the EU's Neighbourhood: An Expanding Economic Community?' (2015) 22(6) *Journal of European Public Policy* 854–870.
[61] Council of the EU, 'Council Conclusions on EU relations with EFTA countries,' 3213th Transport, Telecommunications and Energy Council meeting, 20 December 2012, 5–6.
[62] Van der Loo, Van Elsuwege and Petrov (n 26) 19.
[63] See R. Balfour, 'Principles of Democracy and Human Rights: A Review of the European Union's Strategies towards its Neighbours' in S. Lucarelli and I. Manners (eds), *Values and Principles in European Union Foreign Policy* (London, Routledge 2006) 114–129; Ghazaryan (n 18), 172–176.

For Bosse, '[t]his development is potentially serious, as it appears to mark the beginning of the end of the EU's ambition to act as a successful democratizer in its immediate neighbourhood.'[64] Kurki argues that the technocratic approach glosses over the unclear normative meaning of democracy in EU discourse and pulls EU democracy promotion 'towards depoliticisation, assumptions of harmony, rationalistic and economistic methods, objectivist measurements and management, and technocratic rather than democratic ways of legitimising policies.'[65] On the other hand, a low-profile approach to democracy promotion may help promote the socialization and internalization of norms in societies and officials. While EU institutions are entangled in bureaucratic technicalities, EU Member States often ignore conditionality in their bilateral dealings with ENP countries. In order to be effective, however, Member States must be willing to support EU conditionality policy instead of disengaging or even pursuing detrimental policies.

Finally, in addition to domestic factors in either the ENP countries or the EU, the role of external competitors may play a role because of competing mechanisms of value export. The Russia–Georgia war in 2008, the consequences of the Arab Spring since 2010, and in particular Russia's annexation of Crimea in 2014 and the war in eastern Ukraine have served as wake-up calls for the EU to think more strategically, in particular in its own neighbourhood. Russia's policy in Ukraine and its creation of the Eurasian Economic Union in 2015, confronting the EU's DCFTAs with Eastern Partnership countries, clearly demonstrate that the Russian leadership thinks in terms of geopolitical spheres of influence.

In 2015 both the ENP and the European Security Strategy, born in 2003, are undergoing a review to assess how the changing global environment impacts the Union. With regard to the revision of the ENP, the Council of the EU has called to make the ENP 'more political and responsive to the diverse challenges in the neighbourhood' and to take into consideration the ENP countries' broader geographic context and their relations with their neighbours.[66] The joint consultation paper of the European Commission and High Representative acknowledges that some of the assumptions on which the ENP was constructed have been called into question and that the 'more for more' principle, underlining the commitment to values, has not contributed to a sense of shared ownership.[67] Moreover, it admits that many challenges need to take into account 'the neighbours of the neighbours' as well.[68]

[64] G. Bosse, 'A Partnership with Dictatorship: Explaining the Paradigm Shift in European Union Policy towards Belarus' (2012) 50(3) *Journal of Common Market Studies* 367.
[65] M. Kurki, 'Democracy through Technocracy? Reflections on Technocratic Assumptions in EU Democracy Promotion Discourse' (2011) 5(2) *Journal of Intervention and Statebuilding* 230–231.
[66] Council of the EU, 'Council Conclusions on the Review of the European Neighbourhood Policy', Press release 188/15, 20 April 2015.
[67] European Commission/High Representative, 'Towards a New European Neighbourhood Policy', JOIN (2015) 6 final, 4 March 2015, 4.
[68] Ibid.; see also S. Gstöhl, 'Conclusion: Models of Cooperation with the Neighbours of the EU's Neighbours' in S. Gstöhl and E. Lannon (eds), *The Neighbours of the EU's Neighbours: Diplomatic and Geopolitical Dimensions beyond the European Neighbourhood Policy* (Farnham, Ashgate 2014) 269–289.

Normative (market) power rivalry

The EU's efforts at value promotion are based on the assumption that the European models of democracy and market economy can and should be exported. However, this assumption may be questioned not only by the ENP countries themselves but also by external actors. While the east struggles with the 'Russia factor', in the south a number of players, ranging from the US to Turkey, Russia, China, Saudi Arabia and Qatar, pursue their own agenda.[69]

In the Southern Mediterranean several countries, especially Tunisia, Egypt, Libya and Syria, have rebelled against Western-backed authoritarian rulers. In some countries powerful counter-revolutions have taken place. The richer Gulf monarchies have tried to 'buy off' their citizens and have supported regressive forces in the region, including in the Maghreb, while the poorer monarchies of Morocco and Jordan have implemented rather cosmetic domestic reforms.[70] Democracy promotion implies that the EU must engage in dialogue with all political groups, not just with those that mirror Western values. Political Islam is not a unitary force but is characterized by important splits between different interpretations of Islam, such as between the Shiites and Sunnis, and between the Muslim Brotherhood and the Salafists. As argued by Leonard, the political awakening in the Arab Spring 'is about people claiming democratic rights to emancipate themselves from the traditional influence of the West, rather than trying to join it.'[71]

In the east, the European Union shares an overlapping neighbourhood with an increasingly assertive Russia that has reverted to great power aspirations. Russia from the very beginning opted out of the ENP and insisted on a strategic partnership 'between equals' with the EU. In addition, the Russian government began to increasingly put forward its own normative agenda in the region. As argued by Haukkala, energy-rich Russia can use mechanisms that are not at the EU's disposal to foster bilateral relations, plays a role in many 'frozen conflicts' in the region, and has sought to develop 'an alternative model of economic modernisation and societal development to that promoted by the EU.'[72] By offering a different set of national, cultural and religious values for the post-Soviet space, 'the language of values also provides Russia with a possibility to challenge the conditionality policy attached to the EU's reading of the values it declares.'[73]

Moreover, the Russian market is broadly accessible to countries that share the legacy of Soviet standards. The GOST technical standards are less competitive than the EU standards, and the implementation of the DCFTAs would imply a

---

[69] Lehne (n 3) 9.
[70] M. Leonard, 'Seven Reasons Why the Arab Uprisings Are Eclipsing Western Values', European Council on Foreign Relations, 23 January 2014. Available online at www.ecfr.eu/article/seven_reasons_why_the_arab_uprisings_are_eclipsing_western_values (accessed October 2015).
[71] Ibid.
[72] H. Haukkala, 'The Russian Challenge to EU Normative Power: The Case of European Neighbourhood Policy' (2008) 43(2) *International Spectator* 41.
[73] Leino and Petrov (n 14) 669.

gradual phasing out of GOST standards.[74] When Russia in 2011 proposed to develop its customs union with Belarus and Kazakhstan into a Eurasian Economic Union that could then extend to the post-Soviet space, it de facto compelled countries in the common neighbourhood to choose between this project and a DCFTA with the EU, unless the EU concluded an FTA with the entire Eurasian customs union.[75] Russia presented Eurasian integration as a project of economic modernization based on international law but did not shy away from threatening sanctions vis-à-vis its neighbours.[76] The announcement by the Armenian government, in the run-up to the Eastern Partnership Summit in Vilnius in November 2013, that it intended to join the Eurasian customs union, and the decision of the Ukrainian government to suspend the signature of its Association Agreement and DCFTA with the EU, clearly demonstrates that these countries are facing two 'centres of gravity'. The Eurasian integration project 'means that the EU is no longer the only actor promoting deep economic integration premised on regulatory convergence in the post-Soviet space.'[77] However, the economic benefits of the Eurasian Economic Union are questionable given the high tariff levels, which make imports from the EU and China more expensive and question the commitments of WTO members Armenia and Kyrgyzstan while complicating Kazakhstan's negotiations on WTO accession. Russia therefore offers a range of subsidies to its (potential) partners in the form of cheaper gas or loans and access to its labour market.[78]

In the end, the ENP's value export proved more attractive for Moldova, Georgia and finally – after the 'EuroMaidan revolution' – to Ukraine than to Armenia, Azerbaijan or Belarus, although the latter share some concerns about Russia's dominance in the Eurasian Economic Union.

Conclusions: conceptual flaws beyond implementation problems

In the post-Cold War era the EU has increasingly emphasized the role of values in its external actions and, in particular, in its neighbourhood. The Lisbon Treaty made it even clearer that any EU foreign policy strategy should be based upon both values and interests. As the European Neighbourhood Policy has unfolded, the resistance that the promotion of values encountered in some countries has

---

[74] I. Dreyer and N. Popescu, 'Trading with Moscow: The Law, the Politics and the Economics', (2014) 31 *EUISS Brief* 2. Available online at www.iss.europa.eu/uploads/media/Brief_31_Russia-Ukraine.pdf (accessed 5 October 2015).

[75] L. Delcour and H. Kostanyan, 'Towards a Fragmented Neighbourhood: Policies of the EU and Russia and their Consequences for the Area that Lies in Between', *CEPS Essay* 17, 17 October 2014, 5. Available online at www.ceps.eu/system/files/CEPS%20Essay%20No%2017%20Fragmented%20Neighbourhood%20-%20H%20Kostanyan%20L%20Delcour.pdf (accessed 5 October 2015).

[76] Delcour and Wolczuk (n 53) 192–197.

[77] Ibid. 180.

[78] N. Popescu, 'Eurasian Union: The Real, the Imaginary and the Likely', (2014) 132 *EUISS Chaillot Papers* 11–14. Available online at www.iss.europa.eu/publications/detail/article/eurasian-union-the-real-the-imaginary-and-the-likely (accessed 5 October 2015).

been growing instead of fading away. This chapter has examined the role of values in the ENP and the reasons for their unexpected contestation in recent years. It has been argued that the values themselves have been challenged because of their ambiguity, potential conflicts between them and the (re-)emergence of competing values abroad. In addition, the promotion of values has been questioned due to factors linked to the incapacity or unwillingness both of the neighbours and of the EU and its Member States, and because of the normative rivalry of other external actors. More precisely, the ENP has been plagued by an inconsistent and selective application of political conditionality, often disengaged EU Member States and a techno-bureaucratic approach that has turned out to be too demanding for many countries.

In a nutshell, the role of values in the ENP has been facing challenges of capacity, consistency and competition. In addition to such implementation problems, the ENP has suffered from certain conceptual flaws:[79] first of all, the policy embraces 16 countries that have little in common except for their geographic proximity to the EU. Originally designed for Wider Europe to the immediate east of the EU, the ENP was quickly extended to the Southern Mediterranean and the Southern Caucasus. The heterogeneity of the countries in these two geographic dimensions led, a few years later, to the creation of the Union for the Mediterranean and the Eastern Partnership.

Second, the ENP has produced a 'hub-and-spoke' system of bilateral relationships at the expense of a regional approach, as illustrated by the patterns of trade and investment flows.[80] The EU's initiatives to promote regional cooperation in its neighbourhood have also been hampered by the contested nature of the regions and confusion over the goals of regional cooperation, by the gap between the ends sought by the EU and the means available to it, and by the existence of enduring conflicts in these regions.[81]

Third, the ENP applies a methodology that has largely been derived from the enlargement process, such as targeted expert assistance, twinning arrangements with Member State administrations, participation in EU programmes and agencies, conditionality policy and monitoring and Progress Reports, as well as the bilateral rather than multilateral focus. Moreover, the EU's assumption that all partner countries were trying to emulate the European model was mistaken. The long-term perspective of a Neighbourhood Economic Community may, however, not make up for the lack of an accession perspective as a motivation for reforms and approximation. The ENP has largely been driven by the European Commission, later joined by the newly created European External Action Service, but Member States have often remained disengaged or have pursued their own bilateral foreign

---

[79] See also Lehne (n 3).
[80] D. Kallioras, 'Trade Activity between the EU and the ENP Countries: A "Reproduction" of the "Core-Periphery" Pattern?', SEARCH Working Paper 2/06. Available online at www.ub.edu /searchproject/wp-content/uploads/2013/09/SEARCH_Working-Paper_2.06.pdf (accessed 5 October 2015).
[81] A. Cottey, 'Regionalism and the EU's Neighbourhood Policy: The Limits of the Possible' (2012) 12(3) *Journal of Southeast European and Black Sea Studies* 375–391.

policy vis-à-vis ENP countries. In this context, the lack of participation of ENP countries in the decision-making – or at least the decision-shaping – process sits, in the long run, squarely with the principle of joint ownership and an expanding 'stake' in the internal market.

Fourth, the ENP's principle of joint ownership appears somewhat at odds with the principle of political conditionality, which states that 'the level of ambition of the EU's relationships with its neighbours will take into account the extent to which these values are effectively shared', resulting in a policy of differentiation among ENP partners.[82] The 2011 review of the ENP introduced an even more explicit 'more for more' approach: 'only those partners willing to embark on political reforms and to respect the shared universal values of human rights, democracy and the rule of law have been offered the most rewarding aspects of the EU policy, notably economic integration …, mobility of people …, as well as greater EU financial assistance.'[83] Finally, joint ownership allows ENP countries to downgrade the role in Action Plans of values to which they are opposed.

Fifth, a Eurocentric approach to the ENP tends to ignore the role of other influential actors in the neighbourhood. These other actors may pursue different and competing objectives. The EU was not prepared for the challenges that its supposedly universal values and their promotion have met. It did not sufficiently think strategically ahead. Adding a more geopolitical approach may help sharpen the EU's strategic focus and make it a more influential international partner. The Union and its Member States need to rely on clear values, interests and matching capabilities and avoid incoherent policies in order to credibly address growing expectations regarding the export of stability, peace and prosperity. The EU needs to strike a better balance between the promotion of values and geostrategic thinking – which does not imply a zero-sum game vision. The ENP review that the European Commission is carrying out in 2015 offers an opportunity to reconsider this approach.

Bibliography

Balfour, R. (2006) Principles of Democracy and Human Rights: A Review of the European Union's Strategies towards Its Neighbours. In Lucarelli, S. and Manners (eds), I. *Values and Principles in European Union Foreign Policy*. London: Routledge.

Bartels, L. (2004) Legal Analysis of Human Rights Clauses in the European Union's Euro-Mediterranean Association Agreements. *Mediterranean Politics*. 9(3). pp. 368–395.

Björkdahl, A. (2002) Norms in International Relations: Some Theoretical and Methodological Reflections. *Cambridge Review of International Affairs*. 15(1). pp. 9–23.

Börzel, T.A. (2011) When Europe Hits … beyond Its Borders: Europeanization and the Near Abroad. *Comparative European Politics*. 9(4–5). pp. 394–413.

Börzel, T.A. and van Hüllen, V. (2014) One Voice, One Message, but Conflicting Goals: Cohesiveness and Consistency in the European Neighbourhood Policy. *Journal of European Public Policy*. 21(7). pp. 1033–1049.

---

[82] COM (2004) 373 (n 1), 3.
[83] European Commission/High Representative, 'Delivering on a New European Neighbourhood Policy', JOIN (2012) 14–15 May 2012, 3–4.

Bosse, G.A. (2012) Partnership with Dictatorship: Explaining the Paradigm Shift in European Union Policy towards Belarus. *Journal of Common Market Studies*. 50(3). pp. 367–384.

Bosse, G. (2007) Values in the EU's Neighbourhood Policy: Political Rhetoric or Reflection of a Coherent Policy? *European Political Economy Review*. 7. pp. 38–62.

Byrne, I. (2004) The Importance of Economic, Social and Cultural Rights in Guaranteeing Civil and Political Rights with the Euro-Mediterranean Partnership. *Mediterranean Politics*. 9(3). pp. 344–367.

Checkel, J.T. (2005) International Institutions and Socialization in Europe: Introduction and Framework. *International Organization*. 59(4). pp. 801–826.

Cottey, A. (2012) Regionalism and the EU's Neighbourhood Policy: The Limits of the Possible. *Journal of Southeast European and Black Sea Studies*. 12(3). pp. 375–391.

Cremona, M. (2011) Values in EU Foreign Policy. In Evans M. and Koutrakos, P. (eds) *Beyond the Established Orders: Policy Interconnections between the EU and the Rest of the World*. Oxford: Hart Publishing.

Damro, C. (2012) Market Power Europe. *Journal of European Public Policy*. 19(5). pp. 682–699.

Dandashly, A. (2015) The EU Response to Regime Change in the Wake of the Arab Revolt: Differential Implementation. *Journal of European Integration*. 37(1). pp. 37–56.

Delcour, L. and Kostanyan, H. (2014) Towards a Fragmented Neighbourhood: Policies of the EU and Russia and Their Consequences for the Area That Lies in Between. *CEPS Essay*. 17. Available online at www.ceps.eu/system/files/CEPS%20Essay%20No%20 17%20Fragmented%20Neighbourhood%20-%20H%20Kostanyan%20L%20Delcour. pdf (accessed 5 October 2015).

Delcour, L. and Wolczuk, K. (2013) Eurasian Economic Integration and Implications for the EU's Policy in the Eastern Neigbhourhood. In Dragneva, R. and Wolczuk, K. (eds) *Eurasian Economic Integration: Law, Policy, and Politics*. London: Edward Elgar.

Dreyer, I. and Popescu, N. (2014) Trading with Moscow: The Law, the Politics and the Economics. *EUISS Brief*. n. 31. Available online at www.iss.europa.eu/uploads/media/ Brief_31_Russia-Ukraine.pdf (accessed 5 October 2015).

Ghazaryan, N. (2014) *The European Neighbourhood Policy and the Democratic Values of the EU: A Legal Analysis*. Oxford: Hart Publishing.

Gstöhl, S. (2008) Blurring Economic Boundaries? Trade and Aid in the EU's Near Abroad. In Mahncke, D. and Gstöhl, S. (eds) *Europe's Near Abroad: Promises and Prospects of the EU's Neighbourhood Policy*. Bruxelles: Peter Lang.

—(2008) The EU as a Norm Exporter? In Mahncke D. and Gstöhl, S. (eds) *Europe's Near Abroad: Promises and Prospects of the EU's Neighbourhood Policy*. Bruxelles: Peter Lang.

—(2012) What is at Stake in the Internal Market? Towards a Neighbourhood Economic Community. In Lannon, E. (ed.) *The European Neighbourhood Policy's Challenges / Les Défis de la Politique Européenne de Voisinage*. Bruxelles: Peter Lang.

—(2014) Conclusion: Models of Cooperation with the Neighbours of the EU's Neighbours. In Gstöhl S. and Lannon, E. (eds) *The Neighbours of the EU's Neighbours: Diplomatic and Geopolitical Dimensions beyond the European Neighbourhood Policy*. Farnham: Ashgate.

—(2015) Models of External Differentiation in the EU's Neighbourhood: An Expanding Economic Community? *Journal of European Public Policy*. 22(6). pp. 854–870.

Haukkala, H. (2008) The Russian Challenge to EU Normative Power: The Case of European Neighbourhood Policy. *International Spectator*. 43(2). pp. 35–47.

Kallioras, D. (2013) Trade Activity between the EU and the ENP Countries: A 'Reproduction' of the 'Core-Periphery' Pattern? *SEARCH Working Paper*. 2/06. Available online at www. ub.edu/searchproject/wp-content/uploads/2013/09/SEARCH_Working-Paper_2.06. pdf (accessed 5 October 2015).

Kerremans, B. and Orbie, J. (2009) The Social Dimension of European Trade Policies. *European Foreign Affairs Review.* 14(5). pp. 629–641.

Kochenov, D. (2014) The Issue of Values. In Van Elsuwege, P. and Petrov, P. (eds) *Legislative Approximation and Application of EU Law in the Eastern Neighbourhood of the European Union: Towards a Common Regulatory Space?* London: Routledge.

Korosteleva, E. (2012) Questioning Democracy Promotion: Belarus' Response to the 'Colour Revolutions'. *Democratization.* 19(1). pp. 37–59.

Kratochvíl, P. (2008) The Discursive Resistance to EU-Enticement: The Russian Elite and (the Lack of) Europeanisation. *Europe-Asia Studies.* 60(3). pp. 397–422.

Kurki, M. (2011) Democracy through Technocracy? Reflections on Technocratic Assumptions in EU Democracy Promotion Discourse. *Journal of Intervention and Statebuilding.* 5(2). pp. 211–234.

Langbein, J. and Wolczuk, K. (2012) Convergence without Membership? The Impact of the European Union in the Neighbourhood: Evidence from Ukraine. *Journal of European Public Policy.* 19(6). pp. 863–881.

Larsen, H. (2014) The EU as a Normative Power and the Research on External Perceptions: The Missing Link. *Journal of Common Market Studies.* 52(4). pp. 896–910.

Lawrence, R.Z. (1996) *Regionalism, Multilateralism, and Deeper Integration.* Washington: The Brookings Institutions Press. Available online at www.brookings.edu/research/books/1996/regional (accessed 5 October 2015).

Lehne, S. (2014) Time to Reset the European Neighbourhood Policy. *Carnegie Europe.* Available online at http://carnegieeurope.eu/publications/?fa=54420 (accessed 5 October 2015).

Leino, P. and Petrov, R. (2009) Between 'Common Values' and Competing Universals – The Promotion of the EU's Common Values through the European Neighbourhood Policy. *ELJ.* 15(5). pp. 654–671.

Leonard, M. (2014) Seven Reasons Why the Arab Uprisings Are Eclipsing Western Values. *European Council on Foreign Relations.* 23 January 2014. Available online at www.ecfr.eu/article/seven_reasons_why_the_arab_uprisings_are_eclipsing_western_values (accessed 5 October 2015).

Manners, I. (2002) Normative Power Europe: A Contradiction in Terms? *Journal of Common Market Studies.* 40(2). pp. 235–258.

Messerlin, P. *et al.* (2011) An Appraisal of the EU's Trade Policy towards its Eastern Neighbours: The Case of Georgia. *CEPS.* Available online at www.ceps.eu/publications/appraisal-eu%E2%80%99s-trade-policy-towards-its-eastern-neighbours-case-georgia (accessed 5 October 2015).

Orbie, J. and Babarinde, O. (2008) The Social Dimension of Globalization and EU Development Policy: Promoting Labour Standards and Corporate Social Responsibility. *Journal of European Integration.* 30(3). pp. 459–477.

Pace, M. (2007) Norm Shifting from EMP to ENP: The EU as a Norm Entrepreneur in the South? *Cambridge Review of International Affairs.* 20(4). pp. 659–675.

Panebianco, S. (2006) The Constraints on EU Action as a 'Norm Exporter' in the Mediterranean. In Elgström, O. and Smith, M. (eds) *The European Union's Roles in International Politics: Concepts and Analysis.* London: Routledge.

Pew Research Center, *The World's Muslims: Religion, Politics and Society.* 30 April 2013. Available online at www.pewforum.org/2013/04/30/the-worlds-muslims-religion-politics-society-overview (accessed 5 October 2015).

Popescu, N. (2014) Eurasian Union: The Real, the Imaginary and the Likely. *EUISS Chaillot Papers.* 132. 9 September 2014. Available online at www.iss.europa.eu/publications/detail/article/eurasian-union-the-real-the-imaginary-and-the-likely (accessed 5 October 2015).

Schimmelfennig, F. and Sedelmeier, U. (2004) Governance by Conditionality: EU Rule Transfer to the Candidate Countries of Central and Eastern Europe. *Journal of European Public Policy*. 11(4). pp. 661–679.

Shlapentokh, D. (2013) The Death of the Byzantine Empire and Construction of Historical/Political Identities in Late Putin Russia. *Journal of Balkan and Near Eastern Studies*. 15(1). pp. 69–96.

Van der Loo, G., Van Elsuwege P. and Petrov, R. (2014) The EU-Ukraine Association Agreement: Assessment of an Innovative Legal Instrument. *EUI Working Papers*, Law. n. 9.

Part II

Techniques to promote EU values

4 The ENP and multilateralism

Marise Cremona

Introduction: multilateralism as a principle of EU external policy

Multilateralism is at the heart of the EU's external mandate. The TEU directs the EU, working in partnership with countries and organizations which share its principles and values, to 'promote multilateral solutions to common problems, in particular in the framework of the United Nations' and to 'promote an international system based on stronger multilateral cooperation and good global governance.'[1] The European Security Strategy (ESS), which predates the Lisbon Treaty and whose influence can be seen in the text of Art. 21 TEU, also identifies multilateralism – 'effective multilateralism' – as one the EU's three strategic objectives.[2] The ESS gives us an idea of what is meant by multilateralism in this context:

> In a world of global threats, global markets and global media, our security and prosperity increasingly depend on an effective multilateral system. The development of a stronger international society, well-functioning international institutions and a rule-based international order is our objective. We are committed to upholding and developing International Law ... We want international organisations, regimes and treaties to be effective in confronting threats to international peace and security, and must therefore be ready to act when their rules are broken ... It should be an objective for us to widen the membership of [key institutions in the international system] while maintaining their high standards.[3]

The EU's concept of multilateralism as evidenced here conforms to a widely accepted understanding of multilateralism as inclusive, institutionalized,

---

[1] Article 21 TEU.
[2] European Council, European Security Strategy, 9, 12 December 2003. Available online at www.consilium.europa.eu/uedocs/cmsUpload/78367.pdf (accessed 5 September 2015). The second of the three identified strategic objectives is 'Building Security in our Neighbourhood', thereby bringing together the two themes of this chapter.
[3] Ibid.

rule-based cooperation.[4] More specifically, a clear link exists between the EU's concept of multilateralism and its commitment to international law, defined as both a principle of the EU's external action in Art. 21(1) TEU[5] and as an objective in Art. 3(5) TEU: 'In its relations with the wider world, the Union shall … contribute to … the strict observance and the development of international law, including respect for the principles of the United Nations Charter.' The principles which guide the EU's external action are those 'which have inspired its own creation, development and enlargement'; the EU seeks to project the values which underpin its own identity, and among these a multilateral approach to problem-solving certainly has an important place. This helps us to understand the two roles which multilateralism plays in EU external policy-making: as a principle underpinning its own policy choices (how the EU prefers to act at a global level), and as an objective of its external policy (what it is trying to achieve).[6]

The European Neighbourhood Policy (ENP) clearly demonstrates both these dimensions. The ENP is a paradigm of an external policy based on, and aiming to promote, the EU's values. According to Art. 8 TEU, the EU's 'special relationship' with its neighbours is to be 'founded on the values of the Union and characterised by close and peaceful relations based on cooperation.' As expressed by the Commission in 2014, reiterating the Communication relaunching the ENP in 2011[7]:

> the values upon which the European Union is built – freedom, democracy, respect for human rights and fundamental freedoms, and the rule of law – are also at the heart of the process of political association and economic integration. These are the same values that are enshrined in Article 2 of the Treaty on European Union and on which Articles 8 and 49 are based.[8]

The relationships of cooperation, association and integration which characterize the ENP are intended to reflect the EU's own experience of multilateral cooperation, including through enlargement. And although in its earlier years the emphasis was on the bilateral relationship between each ENP partner and the EU, more recently the regional, multilateral dimension has received more attention.

---

[4] R.O. Keohane, 'The Contingent Legitimacy of Multilateralism', GARNET Working Paper No. 09/06; J. Petersen, M. Aspinwall, C. Damro and C. Boswell, 'The Consequences of Europe: Multilateralism and the New Security Agenda,' Edinburgh Europa Institute, Mitchell Working Paper Series 3/2008.

[5] 'The Union's action on the international scene shall be guided by the principles which have inspired its own creation, development and enlargement, and which it seeks to advance in the wider world: democracy, the rule of law, the universality and indivisibility of human rights and fundamental freedoms, respect for human dignity, the principles of equality and solidarity, and respect for the principles of the United Nations Charter and international law.' Article 21(1) TEU.

[6] Petersen et al. (n 4) 11–12.

[7] European Commission/High Representative, 'A New Response to a Changing Neighbourhood', COM (2011) 303, 14, 25 March 2011.

[8] European Commission/High Representative, 'Neighbourhood at the Crossroads: Implementation of the European Neighbourhood Policy in 2013', JOIN (2014) 12, 15, 27 March 2014.

The creation of the Union for the Mediterranean in 2008[9] and the Eastern Partnership in 2009 with its 'multilateral track'[10] are evidence of this shift.[11] We also see it in the new financial instrument for the ENP, which includes among the objectives of EU support 'enhancing sub-regional, regional and European Neighbourhood-wide collaboration as well as cross-border cooperation.'[12] It can be seen also in a greater willingness on the part of the EU to get involved in trying to resolve regional disputes, including frozen conflicts.[13]

Within the ENP, the EU's regionalism should be seen as a component of, not as a rival to, multilateralism: the EU builds regional relations through a joint commitment to multilateral norms and uses its regional relations to help build support for the development of such norms. The focus of this chapter is on the interplay between the regional (represented by the ENP) and the multilateral in EU external policy-making. In particular, the chapter will examine three aspects of this relationship.

The first aspect reflects the Lisbon Treaty's injunction to 'promote multilateral solutions to common problems' (Art. 21(1) TEU), the ENP as a policy framework within which, through law, the EU seeks to address common problems and shared threats. This includes promoting the ratification of key international conventions by ENP partners, supporting international institutions and enlisting the support of the ENP partners for the EU's own multilateral legal agendas.

The second dimension involves collaboration to ensure effective enforcement of the law and reflects the EU objective to 'promote an international system based on stronger multilateral cooperation and good global governance' (Art. 21(2) TEU). This includes supporting the implementation and enforcement of ratified conventions, collaborating with the Council of Europe and other international bodies and organizations and using the EU's sanctions regimes to enforce international anti-corruption conventions.

The third dimension involves building active support among the ENP partners for the EU's own multilateral security agenda, especially but not exclusively

---

[9] 'Barcelona Process: Union for the Mediterranean', Communication from the Commission to the European Parliament and the Council, COM (2008) 319, 20 May 2008.

[10] 'Eastern Partnership' Communication from the Commission to the European Parliament and the Council, COM (2008) 823 final, 3 December 2008; Joint Declaration of the Prague Eastern Partnership Summit, 8435/09 (Presse 78), 7 May 2009. The multilateral track of the EaP is built around four thematic 'platforms', on good governance, economic integration and convergence with EU sectoral policies, energy security, and people-to-people contacts.

[11] See 'A New Response to a Changing Neighbourhood', COM (2011) 303 (n 7) 2, which refers to 'strengthen[ing] the two regional dimensions of the European Neighbourhood Policy, covering respectively the Eastern Partnership and the Southern Mediterranean, so that we can work out consistent regional initiatives in areas such as trade, energy, transport or migration and mobility, complementing and strengthening our bilateral co-operation.'

[12] Regulation n. 232/2014/EU establishing a European Neighbourhood Instrument [2014] OJ L 77/27, Art 2(2)(f).

[13] The Joint Declaration of the Eastern Partnership Summit (Riga, 21–22 May 2015) welcomed the EU's 'strengthened role in conflict resolution and confidence building efforts in the framework or in support of existing agreed formats and processes.' See www.consilium.europa.eu/en/meetings/international-summit/2015/05/21-22 (accessed 10 June 2015).

within the framework of the United Nations. Here the EU is building relationships with the aim, inter alia, of 'safeguard[ing] its values, fundamental interests, security, independence and integrity' (Art. 21(2) TEU). These mechanisms include seeking support from the ENP partners for the EU's sanctions regimes and seeking the participation of ENP states in EU-led crisis missions.

Promoting multilateral solutions to common problems

As we have seen, the EU's promotion of 'effective multilateralism' as a way of tackling common threats was a theme of the European Security Strategy, adopted in the year in which the ENP was first launched, and it is now enshrined in the Treaties. This is perhaps the most obvious way in which the ENP and multilateralism are joined in EU policy. The ENP consists of a group of states with whom the EU is building a close economic and increasingly political relationship, a relationship which is overtly based on the concept of 'shared values' (Art. 8 TEU). For the EU, the promotion of multilateral institutions and conventions ('a rule-based international order') is one way in which it can create a neighbourhood of shared values which reflect its own. In the following sections we use a few examples to illustrate a wider phenomenon.

Promoting the ratification of multilateral conventions

The promotion of multilateral conventions is a noticeable part of the EU's ENP agenda. The EU will report regularly on the state of ratification of key human rights conventions by ENP partners, for example.[14] Here we will take one example, the EU's strategy on weapons of mass destruction (WMD), to illustrate the 'shared values' of the ENP operating in a multilateral context.[15]

In June 2003, in the context of discussion of the European Security Strategy, the EU Council of Ministers adopted a Declaration on the non-proliferation of WMD and endorsed both a statement of '[B]asic principles for an EU strategy against proliferation of Weapons of Mass Destruction' and an Action Plan for the implementation of these 'basic principles'.[16] The EU Strategy against the proliferation of WMD was adopted in December 2003.[17] The priorities in the

---

[14] For a recent example, see SWD (2014) 98, 27 March 2014, on the implementation of the ENP in 2013, which tabulates the state of ratification and signature of the International Covenants on Civil and Political, and Economic, Social and Cultural Rights, the Convention on Elimination of Discrimination Against Women, the Convention Against Torture, the Convention on the Rights of the Child.

[15] For a full discussion of the EU's policy on non-proliferation, see P. Koutrakos, 'The Non-Proliferation Policy of the European Union' in M. Evans and P. Koutrakos (eds) *Beyond the Established Legal Orders: Policy Interconnections between the EU and the Rest of the World* (Oxford, Hart Publishing 2011).

[16] Basic Principles for an EU Strategy against Proliferation of Weapons of Mass Destruction, Council Doc 10352/03. Earlier conclusions were adopted in November 2001 on the link between terrorism and WMD: Council Conclusions on implications of the terrorist threat on the non-proliferation, disarmament and arms control policy of the European Union, Doc. 14732/01, 29 November 2001.

[17] EU Strategy against proliferation of Weapons of Mass Destruction, Council Doc 15708/03. For the most recent six-monthly report on the implementation of the Strategy, covering the second half of 2014, see [2015] OJ C 41/1.

Action Plan included: the ratification by all EU Member States and accession states of all International Atomic Energy Agency (IAEA) Additional Protocols, and the adoption of the necessary implementing legislation within the framework of Euratom; improving the efficiency of EU export controls in the light of enlargement;[18] and a new Directive to harmonize and strengthen Member State controls of radioactive sources.[19] In such ways the EU's commitment to and promotion of 'the multilateral treaty regime, which provides the normative basis for all non-proliferation efforts',[20] is directed both at its own Member States and at third countries.

In December 2008 the Council adopted Conclusions on 'new lines' for action by the EU in combating the proliferation of WMD, which again combine action by Member States (dissemination of national best practice, coordination of national policies) and cooperation with third countries and international organizations.[21] The mechanisms envisaged in the EU Strategy on WMD directed at third countries include diplomatic action (including the use of political dialogue and diplomatic pressure) and the adoption of a Common Position to formalize the EU's position on the universalization of a number of key international agreements.[22]

When it comes to the ENP states, the EU uses both binding and non-binding instruments. Prominent among the first are the 'WMD clauses'. These clauses have been included in agreements with third countries since 2003 and contain two elements.[23] First is the 'essential element': an obligation to comply with

---

[18] See, most recently, Communication from the Commission, 'Review of export control policy: ensuring security and competitiveness in a changing world' COM (2014) 244 final, 24 April 2014 and Council Conclusions on the Review of Export Control Policy, 21 November 2014.

[19] The Directive was adopted later the same year: Council Directive 2003/122/Euratom of 22 December 2003 on the control of high-activity sealed radioactive sources and orphan sources [2003] OJ L 346/57.

[20] Basic Principles (n 16) para 6.

[21] The 'New Lines' were extended in December 2010; see also Foreign Affairs Council Conclusions on ensuring the continued pursuit of an effective EU policy on the new challenges presented by the proliferation of WMD and their delivery systems, 21 October 2013.

[22] Common Position 2003/805/CFSP on 'The universalisation and reinforcement of multilateral agreements in the field of non-proliferation of weapons of mass destruction and means of delivery' [2003] OJ L 302/34. The Common Position commits the EU and Member States to urge and encourage third states to ratify a number of key conventions: the Nuclear Non-Proliferation Treaty and Safeguards Agreements (NPT), the IAEA Additional Protocols, the Chemical Weapons Convention, the Biological and Toxin Weapons Convention, the (non-binding) Hague Code of Conduct against Ballistic Missile Proliferation (Art. 1), and the Comprehensive Nuclear Test Ban Treaty. The six-monthly reports on the implementation of the WMD Strategy give details of the EU's efforts and their results.

[23] Council Conclusions of 17 November 2003 on 'The fight against the proliferation of weapons of mass destruction – Mainstreaming non-proliferation policies into the EU's wider relations with third countries', Council Doc. 14997/03. The Conclusions include a standard form of clause:

'Countering proliferation of weapons of mass destruction

The Parties consider that the proliferation of weapons of mass destruction and their means of delivery, both to state and non-state actors, represents one of the most serious threats to international stability and security. The Parties therefore agree to cooperate and to contribute to countering the

and implement existing commitments under international disarmament and non-proliferation treaties. Since this part of the clause is an 'essential element' of the agreement, it may lead to consultations and ultimately to suspension of the agreement in the case of a serious failure to comply. Second, there is a commitment to cooperate in order to promote accession to and implementation of further instruments, and to strengthen export controls. Examples include the new Association Agreements with Ukraine, Georgia and Moldova, which each contain a WMD clause.[24] The Association Agendas with these countries then each contain a section on 'co-operation in addressing common security threats, including combating terrorism, non-proliferation of weapons of mass destruction and illegal arms exports.' For example, Ukraine's Association Agenda, agreed in June 2013, contains a relatively detailed section which includes the following commitments:

- continue cooperation in the fight against non-proliferation of weapons of mass destruction, including on aspects related to the accession to and national implementation of relevant international instruments, such as CWC, BTWC and NPT, and export control regimes;
- further improve an effective system of national export control, controlling export and transit of WMD related goods, including WMD end use control on dual use technologies, in light of the EU regulation on export controls on dual use goods adopted in 2000 and on its updated version, further cooperate on the development of national lists of dual-use goods, controls over intangible transfer of technologies, enforcement of the export control system, including prevention and sanctions of breaches, and outreach to industry;
- continue cooperation in the fight against the trafficking of nuclear materials.

For those ENP states with agreements concluded before the practice of including a WMD clause, similar commitments are included in the Action Plans, all of which contain references to non-proliferation and WMD with a similar focus on cooperation

> proliferation of weapons of mass destruction and their means of delivery through full compliance with and national implementation of their existing obligations under international disarmament and non-proliferation treaties and agreements and other relevant international obligations. The parties agree that this provision constitutes an essential element of this agreement.
>
> The parties furthermore agree to cooperate and to contribute to countering the proliferation of weapons of mass destruction and their means of delivery by:
>
> - taking steps to sign, ratify, or accede to, as appropriate, and fully implement all other relevant international instruments;
> - the establishment of an effective system of national export controls, controlling the export as well as transit of WMD related goods, including a WMD end-use control on dual use technologies and containing effective sanctions for breaches of export controls.
>
> The Parties agree to establish a regular political dialogue that will accompany and consolidate these elements.'

[24] Article 11 of the Association Agreement with Ukraine [2014] OJ L 161/3; Article 9 of the Association Agreement with Moldova [2014] OJ L 260/4; Article 10 of the Association Agreement with Georgia [2014] OJ L 261/4.

and dialogue, implementation of international commitments and implementation of UNSC Resolution 1540 (2004).

Support for international institutions

A second way in which the EU encourages a multilateral approach to addressing common problems is through direct and indirect support for international (multilateral) institutions. This can be rather general in nature. In the EU–Jordan ENP Action Plan, for example, there are references to cooperation on issues of shared interest within the United Nations, as well as to cooperation with a view to enhancing the efficiency of multilateral institutions. But it can be more specific. In the context of the WMD strategy already mentioned, the EU has supported the IAEA through a series of Joint Actions (now known simply as Decisions) on nuclear security covering ENP states, among others.[25]

The EU and the International Criminal Court (ICC) concluded a cooperation agreement in 2006.[26] This agreement builds upon a 2003 Common Position which committed the EU and its Member States to promoting the ratification and implementation of the Rome Statute of the ICC.[27] The ICC is also included in the financial instrument for democracy and human rights worldwide, as part of the objective of strengthening international and regional frameworks for the promotion and protection of human rights, justice, the rule of law and democracy.[28] As a result, the EU has inserted references to the ICC into its agreements with third states,[29] including the more recent ENP Association Agreements.[30] The Association Agenda with Ukraine of June 2013 includes the establishment of a consultation mechanism on the ICC's activities and functioning and the implementation of the necessary measures for the entry into force of the Rome Statute in Ukraine. The Action Plans for Moldova, Georgia, Azerbaijan and Lebanon stipulate the ratification of the Rome Statute.

---

[25] Most recently Council Decision 2013/517/CFSP of 21 October 2013 on the Union support for the activities of the International Atomic Energy Agency in the areas of nuclear security and verification and in the framework of the implementation of the EU Strategy against Proliferation of Weapons of Mass Destruction [2014] OJ L 281/6. For a report of earlier activities covering the period 2005–2011, see 'IAEA – EU Joint Action – Partnership in Improving Nuclear Security'. Available online at http://eeas.europa.eu/non-proliferation-and-disarmament/pdf/iaea-eu-joint-action-booklet_en.pdf (accessed 27 August 2015).

[26] Agreement between the International Criminal Court and the European Union on cooperation and assistance [2006] OJ L 115/50.

[27] Council Common Position 2003/444/CFSP of 16 June 2003 on the International Criminal Court [2003] OJ L 150/67. This Common Position was replaced in 2011 by Council Decision 2011/168/CFSP [2011] OJ L 76/56.

[28] Regulation 235/2014/EU establishing a financing instrument for democracy and human rights worldwide [2014] OJ L 77/85, Art. 2 and Annex.

[29] For a recent example, see the Agreement establishing an Association between the European Union and its Member States, on the one hand, and Central America on the other [2012] OJ L 346/3, Art. 17.

[30] Association Agreement with Ukraine, Art. 8; Association Agreement with Georgia, Article 6; Association Agreement with Moldova, Art. 6.

Enlisting support for the EU's own multilateral agenda

The types of activity mentioned so far are essentially concerned with ensuring that the EU's ENP partners are integrated into, and fully participating in, a number of existing multilateral regimes and institutions which the EU sees as important for global governance and security (including its own security). However, the EU also sees the ENP as an opportunity to enlist the support of third states for its own multilateral legal agendas. In its Communication on the relaunching of the ENP in 2011, the Commission said that 'this vision includes ... joint initiatives in international fora on issues of common interest'[31] and that the envisaged increase in political and security cooperation would include a commitment to 'promote joint action with European Neighbourhood Policy partners in international fora on key security issues'.[32] This may involve coordination in advance of international negotiations: the 2014 ENP Communication suggested the need for policy cooperation on the negotiations on a new international climate agreement taking place in Paris in 2015.[33] It may also include inviting the ENP states to align themselves to EU public statements, the degree to which they do so being noted in the regular ENP Progress Reports.

An example of the use of different types of 'norm building' activities by the EU is the Arms Trade Treaty (ATT), which was strongly supported as an initiative by the EU and which has formed part of the EU's policy on disarmament and small arms and light weapons (SALW),[34] linked to its own code of conduct on arms exports.[35] Action was launched by the EU in 2005, with Council Conclusions affirming EU support for an international treaty to be negotiated under the aegis of the UN with a view to establishing common standards for the global trade in conventional arms.[36] In the next decade the Council regularly reverted to the issue, its Conclusions timed to coincide with developments within the UN,[37] and the ATT was included among the EU's priorities in the UN General Assembly

---

[31] COM (2011) 303 (n 7) 2.
[32] Ibid. 5.
[33] JOIN (2014) 12 (n 8) 12–13.
[34] EU Strategy to combat illicit accumulation and trafficking of SALW and their ammunition adopted by the European Council 15–16 December 2005, Council Doc 5319/06; Council Joint Action 2002/589/CFSP on the European Union's contribution to combating the destabilising accumulation and spread of small arms and light weapons [2002] OJ L 191/1.
[35] The 1998 Code of Conduct on Arms Exports was replaced in 2008 by Council Common Position 2008/944/CFSP defining common rules governing control of exports of military technology and equipment [2008] OJ L 335/99. See also Council Joint Action 2008/230/CFSP on support for EU activities in order to promote the control of arms exports and the principles and criteria of the EU Code of Conduct on Arms Exports among third countries [2008] OJ L 75/81.
[36] Council Conclusions 3 October 2005, Council Doc 12529/05.
[37] Council Conclusions 11 December 2006, Council Doc 16692/06, welcoming the formal start of the process towards the elaboration of a legally binding international Arms Trade Treaty through the adoption by the UN General Assembly of the resolution 'Towards an arms trade treaty: establishing common international standards for the import, export and transfer of conventional arms' on 6 December 2006; Council Conclusions 17–18 June 2007, Doc 10605/07; Council Conclusions 10 December 2007, Council Doc 15850/07.

(UNGA).[38] The EU adopted a Council Decision aimed at promoting the ATT process[39] and used its regular meetings with third countries to reaffirm its support for the ATT process.[40] On 30 October 2009, a UNGA Resolution,[41] with support from the EU Member States and the US but with abstentions from Russia and China, set in motion a process of negotiation which resulted in a text being adopted by the UNGA in April 2013[42] and being opened for signature in June the same year. Although some aspects of the ATT fall within the EU's exclusive external competence, the ATT is open only to states so the EU itself cannot become a party (somewhat ironically, perhaps, given the EU's championship). As a result, the EU has authorized Member States to sign and ratify the ATT on its behalf.[43] The Union's priority now 'is to support the early entry into force and full implementation of the Treaty.'[44] Assistance with implementation through strengthening arms control systems builds upon the EU's programmes on WMD and dual-use export controls supporting UNSCR 1540(2004).

During the campaign for the ATT, the EU included the ATT in meetings with ENP partners.[45] Earlier Action Plans focused on ratification and implementation of the existing UN Convention against Transnational Organized Crime (Palermo Convention) and its three protocols on trafficking of persons, smuggling of migrants and illicit trafficking in firearms. The more recent Association Agenda with Ukraine includes 'jointly supporting the process of ratification and implementation of the Arms Trade Treaty.'

---

[38] See e.g. the EU priorities for the 64th United Nations General Assembly, adopted by the Council 15 June 2009, Council Doc 10809/09.

[39] Council Decision 2009/42/CFSP on support for EU activities in order to promote among third countries the process leading towards an Arms Trade Treaty, in the framework of the European Security Strategy [2009] OJ L 17/39. See also Council Decision 2010/336/CFSP [2010] OJ L 152/14, adopted to support the negotiation process and (in the lead-up to the final negotiating conference) Council Decision 2013/43/CFSP [2013] OJ L 20/53.

[40] For example, in the Final Communiqué of the 15th ECOWAS–EU Ministerial Troika Meeting held in Luxembourg, 16 June 2009, 'The EU and ECOWAS reaffirmed their interest for a successful process leading to the adoption of an Arms Trade Treaty (ATT)', Council Doc 11146/09 (Presse 183). See also the EU–US Summit in Washington, 3 November 2009, Declaration on Non-Proliferation and Disarmament, Council Doc 15351/1/09, REV 1.

[41] UNGA First Committee, 30 October 2009. Available online at www.un.org/News/Press/docs/2009/gadis3402.doc.htm (accessed 27 August 2015).

[42] GA Resolution A/RES/67/234 B.

[43] Council Decision 2013/269/CFSP [sic] authorising Member States to sign, in the interests of the European Union, the Arms Trade Treaty [2013] OJ L 155/9 (note that the substantive legal bases for this Decision are Articles 114 and 207(3) TFEU); Council Decision 2014/165/EU authorising Member States to ratify, in the interests of the European Union, the Arms Trade Treaty, [2014] OJ L 89/44.

[44] Council Decision 2013/768/CFSP on EU activities in support of the implementation of the Arms Trade Treaty, in the framework of the European Security Strategy, [2013] OJ L 341/56, Preamble recital 5.

[45] See e.g. the European Union's position for the EU–Egypt Association Council's fifth meeting, 27 April 2009, para 68, Council Doc 8725/1/09 REV 1.

Collaboration to ensure effective enforcement of the law

The second dimension of multilateralism that we will address concerns the effective enforcement of international legal norms. This dimension of EU policy can be seen as an expression of its objective to 'promote an international system based on stronger multilateral cooperation and good global governance' (Art. 21(2) TEU). By seeking to enforce multilaterally agreed international law, and by working together with multilateral (including regional) organizations to achieve these goals, the link to multilateralism is two-fold. When compared to the promotion of multilateral instruments and institutions discussed in the previous section, here the link to the ENP is closer and more specific. Ensuring the effective enforcement of international law within the ENP states is part of the EU's vision of the ENP as transformative of these states both internally and as members of the international community; the international norms provide a point of reference in the implementation of a body of law seen as essential to a modern state, in particular a state that subscribes to the international rule of law. This aspect of multilateralism is therefore a distinctive part of the ENP and depends crucially on the ENP states' commitment to an internal reform process. The EU seeks to achieve these goals in a number of different ways.

Implementation and enforcement of international commitments

As we have already seen, the EU seeks from its ENP partners a commitment not only to ratify but to implement certain key international conventions, and is prepared to offer assistance targeted at implementation and enforcement. This has been the case with the WMD conventions and export controls, combating terrorism, anti-corruption and international crime (for example, the Palermo Convention) and other conventions which may be said to form a core of global governance.

To take just one example which demonstrates the range of the EU's interest, the 2014 Association Agreement with Ukraine expressly mentions the implementation of a wide range of international instruments or uses them as reference points for standards to be adopted by Ukraine. These include: the European Convention on Human Rights (ECHR); the Rome Statute of the ICC; 'international disarmament and non-proliferation treaties and agreements'; international instruments on 'arms controls, arms export controls and the fight against illicit trafficking of arms, including small arms and light weapons'; implementation of relevant United Nations Security Council Resolutions; the 'practical implementation' of the UN Refugee Convention; Council of Europe instruments on the protection of personal data; implementation of international standards on money laundering, in particular those of the Financial Action Task Force (FATF); 'relevant international conventions' on illicit drugs; the UN Convention against Transnational Organized Crime and its three Protocols on trafficking, smuggling and illegal firearms; the UN Convention against Corruption; the full implementation of Resolution 1373(2001) of the UN Security Council, the United Nations Global Counter-Terrorism Strategy and other relevant UN instruments; the Conventions of the Hague Conference on Private International Law in the field of International Legal Cooperation and Litigation as well as the Protection of Children; ILO Conventions on core labour standards; international treaties on intellectual property including TRIPS and the Paris and Berne Conventions; and the Kyoto Protocol to the UN Framework Convention on Climate Change.

These references are strikingly numerous, but the Agreement itself does not go into detail. The EU–Ukraine Association Agenda, agreed in June 2013, then picks up on a number of these as priorities for implementation efforts as well as adding new ones (e.g. the UN Disability Convention). It can be seen that although approximation to (effectively, implementation of) EU law is at the core of the new ENP Association Agreements (in particular the Deep and Comprehensive Free Trade Areas that they include), the Agreements also place a notable emphasis on implementation of international legal norms.

Not all these efforts are based on the bilateral agreements, Action Plans/Agendas; they may also be tackled by regionally oriented technical assistance projects. For example, over many years both eastern and southern ENP states (together with the Western Balkans) have been targeted for technical assistance and training aimed at improving export control mechanisms for arms and dual-use goods based on the EU's Code of Conduct on Arms Exports.[46] More recently, the Clima East and Clima South projects support the ENP partners' efforts 'to make the transition towards low carbon development and climate resilience.'[47]

Collaboration with the Council of Europe

Although this focus on implementation of international commitments, including capacity building, is a distinctive element of the ENP, the EU sees itself as part of a wider international effort and emphasizes its readiness to collaborate with other organizations. This emphasis has been more evident since 2011, and represents a more multilateral approach to the ENP, especially in the context of crisis prevention and conflict resolution: 'The EU is co-operating closely with other donor countries and international institutions to respond to humanitarian crises, to promote democratic transition and to foster economic development in partner countries.'[48] 'The ENP should serve as a catalyst for the wider international community to support democratic change and economic and social development in the region.'[49]

An example of such collaboration is that between the EU and the Council of Europe aimed at improving effective enforcement of the ECHR. The 2011

---

[46] Council Joint Action 2008/230/CFSP on support for EU activities in order to promote the control of arms exports and the principles and criteria of the EU Code of Conduct on Arms Exports among third countries [2008] OJ L 75/81. See also Council Decision 2009/1012/CFSP [2009] OJ L 348/16; Council Decision 2012/711/CFSP [2012] OJ L 321/62.
[47] JOIN (2014) 12 (n 8) 13.
[48] European Commission/High Representative 'Delivering on a new European Neighbourhood Policy', JOIN (2012) 14, 15, 14 May 2012.
[49] COM (2011) 303 (n 7) 1.

Commission Communication on the ENP mentioned the possibility of increased cooperation with the Council of Europe with a view to promoting compliance with human rights norms.[50] The EU and the Council of Europe have developed joint programmes for both the eastern and the southern neighbourhoods, focusing on judicial reform, electoral standards and the fight against corruption.[51] In April 2014 the European Commission and Council of Europe signed a 'Statement of Intent' covering cooperation in relation to EU enlargement countries (Turkey and the Western Balkans) and the Neighbourhood countries,[52] with EU funding allocated for a new series of Joint Programmes under the European Instrument for Democracy and Human Rights,[53] the Neighbourhood Instrument[54] and the Enlargement Instrument.[55] Evidence of this cooperation can also be seen in the Association Agendas for Ukraine and Moldova, which refer frequently to Council of Europe recommendations as a basis for reform, as well as to consultations with the Council of Europe over, for example, judicial reform.

Use of EU sanctions regimes to assist anti-corruption investigations

The third type of EU action designed to assist ENP states in the implementation and enforcement of international legal norms is a somewhat special case. Action against corruption has long been an important element of EU ENP programmes (also in cooperation with the Council of Europe Group of States against Corruption, GRECO) and is now included as part of the process of building 'sustainable democracy'.[56] Implementation of the UN Convention against Corruption and the Council of Europe Criminal Law Convention on Corruption is included in Action Plans/Association Agendas. However, in addition to these familiar measures, in a few cases following regime change the EU has used targeted sanctions to freeze the assets of individuals under investigation or indicted in a neighbourhood state for misappropriation of public funds. Such measures have been adopted in relation to Tunisia, Egypt and Ukraine. In the case of Tunisia, the Council 'decided to adopt restrictive measures against persons responsible for misappropriation of Tunisian State funds and who are thus depriving the Tunisian people of the benefits of the sustainable development of their economy and society and undermining the development of democracy in the country' and in Decision 2011/72/CFSP

---

[50] COM (2011) 303 (n 7) 5.
[51] JOIN (2012) 14 (n 48) 11.
[52] Press Release IP/14/356. This follows a Joint Declaration in 2001 and a Memorandum of Understanding signed in 2007. See further www.jp.coe.int/default.asp (accessed 27 August 2015).
[53] Regulation 235/2014/EU establishing a financing instrument for democracy and human rights worldwide [2014] OJ L 77/85.
[54] Regulation 232/2014/EU establishing a European Neighbourhood Instrument [2014] OJ L 77/27.
[55] Regulation 231/2014/EU establishing an Instrument for Pre-Accession Assistance (IPA II) [2014] OJ L 77/11.
[56] JOIN (2012) 14 (n 48) 7.

imposed an asset freeze on a number of persons, initially only former President Ben Ali and his wife, but subsequently on a longer list of persons.[57] As expressed in a representative statement of grounds for designating each targeted individual:

> Person subject to judicial investigations by the Tunisian authorities for complicity in the misappropriation of public monies by a public office-holder, complicity in the misuse of office by a public office-holder to procure an unjustified advantage for a third party and to cause a loss to the administration, and complicity in exerting wrongful influence over a public office-holder with a view to obtaining directly or indirectly an advantage for another person.[58]

In *Al Matri*, unlike the above example, the grounds for including the applicant's name in the Council Decision did not actually mention misappropriation of state funds but instead referred to actions which were under investigation 'as part of money laundering operations.' The applicant argued that as a result there was a lack of coincidence between the grounds given for including the applicant's name and the objective of the restrictive measures as defined in the Decision.[59] The Court agreed that money laundering was not necessarily the same as misappropriation of public funds and annulled the particular decision as far as it concerned the applicant. However, the Court did not question the appropriateness of the Council using restrictive measures to target those responsible, or under investigation, for misappropriation of state funds.

In the Egyptian case, the Council Decision states that in order to support 'the peaceful and orderly transition to a civilian and democratic government in Egypt based on the rule of law', restrictive measures would be adopted 'against persons having been identified as responsible for misappropriation of Egyptian State funds and who are thus depriving the Egyptian people of the benefits of the sustainable development of their economy and society and undermining the development of democracy in the country.'[60] Unlike Tunisia, the grounds for designation explicitly state that the individual is subject to judicial proceedings in respect of the misappropriation of state funds 'on the basis of the United Nations Convention against Corruption.' The applicant in *Ezz* argued that the situation was more properly a case of mutual judicial assistance rather than the common foreign and security policy (CFSP).[61] The General Court disagreed and found that the Decision

---

[57] Decision 2011/72/CFSP concerning restrictive measures directed against certain persons and entities in view of the situation in Tunisia [2011] OJ L 28/6; Implementing Decision 2011/79/CFSP implementing Decision 2011/72 [2011] OJ L 31/40; Council Regulation 101/2011/EU concerning restrictive measures directed against certain persons, entities and bodies in view of the situation in Tunisia [2011] OJ L 31/1.
[58] Decision 2011/72/CFSP (n 57), Annex para 1.
[59] Case T200/11 *Al Matri v. Council*, ECLI:EU:T:2013:275.
[60] Council Decision 2011/172/CFSP concerning restrictive measures directed against certain persons, entities and bodies in view of the situation in Egypt [2011] OJ L 76/63.
[61] Case T-256/11 *Ezz and Others v. Council*, ECLI:EU:T:2014:93.

could properly be adopted as a CFSP measure: it 'forms part of a policy of supporting the new Egyptian authorities, intended to promote both the economic and political stability of Egypt and, in particular, to assist the authorities of that country in their fight against the misappropriation of State funds. It is therefore fully based on the CFSP and satisfies the objectives referred to in Art. 21(2)(b) and (d) TEU.'[62] Further, although the judicial proceedings in Egypt formed the grounds for the listing, the restrictive measures imposed by the EU were, the Court held, a CFSP measure and not an administrative penalty which would be subject to the principle of legality found in Art. 49(1) of the Charter of Fundamental Rights and Art. 7(1) ECHR. The Court of Justice did not disagree with this assessment. In this case, then, the UN Convention was the basis of a request for assistance by the Egyptian authorities, so the EU was not simply encouraging its implementation by Egypt but offering assistance by responding to a specific request.[63]

In the case of Ukraine, too, a number of different types of restrictive measures have been adopted; among them those aimed at members of the former government who are now accused of misappropriation of state funds. As the Preamble to the Council's Decision says, 'the Council agreed to focus restrictive measures on the freezing and recovery of assets of persons identified as responsible for the misappropriation of Ukrainian State funds and persons responsible for human rights violations, with a view to consolidating and supporting the rule of law and respect for human rights in Ukraine.'[64] A typical statement of reasons describes the persons identified as a '[P]erson subject to criminal proceedings in Ukraine to investigate crimes in connection with the embezzlement of Ukrainian State funds and their illegal transfer outside Ukraine.'

We see here, therefore, the EU being prepared to use its CFSP powers to freeze assets belonging to nationals of third countries who are under investigation for offences linked to the UN and Council of Europe Conventions against corruption; in one instance, as a result of the way the request to the EU was framed, the UN Convention is explicitly mentioned. And although these are characterized as CFSP measures, they are clearly designed to assist the third country in a criminal investigation.

Co-opting ENP states into the EU's security agenda

The third dimension to multilateralism and the ENP is yet more specific to the ENP itself. It is linked to the EU's vision of the ENP as creating a 'ring of friends'

---

[62] Case T-256/11 *Ezz and Others v. Council*, ECLI:EU:T:2014:93, para 44.
[63] Judgment of 5 March 2015 in Case C-220/14 P *Ezz and others v. Council*, ECLI:EU:C:2015:147, para 79. Under Article 55(2) of the Convention parties are required, following a request, 'to identify, trace and freeze or seize proceeds of crime, property, equipment or other instrumentalities … for the purpose of eventual confiscation.'
[64] Council Decision 2014/119/CFSP concerning restrictive measures directed against certain persons, entities and bodies in view of the situation in Ukraine [2014] OJ L 66/26; Council Regulation 208/2014/EU concerning restrictive measures directed against certain persons, entities and bodies in view of the situation in Ukraine [2014] OJ L 66/1.

around the EU,[65] the furtherance of the EU's interests as well as its values (Art. 3(5) TEU) and the EU's objective of safeguarding 'its values, fundamental interests, security, independence and integrity' (Art. 21(2) TEU). We see in the revised ENP an increased emphasis on the convergence of the ENP partners not only with the EU's regulatory standards but also with its foreign policy objectives. The language varies depending on the position of each partner. In the case of Jordan, for example, which started a mandate as a non-permanent member of the UN Security Council in January 2014, the language of its Action Plan stresses UN-based cooperation 'as a way to promote effective multilateralism.' The new Association Agreements with Georgia, Moldova and Ukraine include the promotion of 'international stability and security based on effective multilateralism' among their objectives, and 'cooperation between the Parties for achieving peace, security and stability on the European continent.'[66] As well as a general provision for political dialogue, they also contain provisions on cooperation and 'gradual convergence' in foreign and security policy.[67] Here, we look at two examples of this policy convergence, essentially a co-option of willing ENP states into the EU's multilateral security agenda, both of which predate the new generation of Association Agreements, which in this respect give expression to an existing reality. In both instances the ENP state's support is sought and given on a case-by-case basis and there is no commitment in advance to further specific EU interests, only a general commitment to 'convergence'. However, the level of commitment is included in Progress Reports and provides evidence of the ENP state's willingness to develop closer relations with the EU.[68]

Seeking support for EU sanctions regimes

The first example relates to the EU's sanction regimes. The practice of accession states associating themselves with EU sanctions also extends to some ENP states. The degree of commitment evidenced by the Action Plans varies considerably among the ENP partners. The Action Plan for Tunisia does not go beyond dialogue and cooperation on security issues and does not mention sanctions regimes. In the Action Plan for Jordan there is no explicit mention of sanctions either, but 'Jordan is invited to align itself, on a case-by-case basis, with relevant EU CFSP declarations.' The Action Plan for Azerbaijan, on the other hand, includes 'consultations on sanctions issued by the EU, including arms embargoes.' The Action Plans for Armenia, Georgia and Moldova contain a similar commitment to

---

[65] Commission Communication 'Wider Europe – Neighbourhood: A New Framework for Relations with our Eastern and Southern Neighbours', COM (2003)104, 4, 11 April 2003.
[66] Association Agreements with Georgia and Moldova, Art. 3; Association Agreement with Ukraine, Art. 4.
[67] Association Agreements with Georgia and Moldova, Art. 5; Association Agreement with Ukraine, Art. 7.
[68] As an example, the progress report on Armenia for 2014 states that it aligned itself with 15 out of 49 EU CFSP declarations it was invited to subscribe to (SWD (2015) 63, 9); Georgia, with 23 out of 49 (SWD (2015) 66, 9). Azerbaijan, on the other hand, aligned itself with none (SWD (2015) 64, 8).

'develop cooperation' on EU sanctions, and the Association Agenda with Ukraine mentions continued 'consultations on sanctions applied by the EU.'

What does this mean in practice? Ukraine, Moldova and Georgia (as well as Albania, Liechtenstein, Macedonia, Montenegro, Serbia and Norway) have aligned themselves with EU sanctions against Syria.[69] Ukraine and Georgia (with a number of candidate, potential candidate and EFTA states) have aligned themselves with sanctions relating to the annexation of Crimea,[70] and Ukraine and Moldova (with others) have aligned themselves with the sanctions already mentioned relating to the misappropriation of state funds in Ukraine.[71] Moldova and Armenia (and others) have aligned themselves with the EU's sanctions against Burma.[72] Clearly, the decisions of each ENP partner will depend on their own positions and interests, and the incidence of alignment by candidate and potential candidate states is predictably higher than among ENP partner states.

Seeking participation of ENP states in EU-led missions

A number of ENP Action Plans envisage the possibility of involving ENP partners in EU Common Security and Defence Policy (CSDP) missions. Possible involvement in EU-led peacekeeping missions conducted under UN auspices, as well as participation in training activities on conflict prevention and crisis management, is included in the Action Plans for Tunisia and Jordan.[73] Where regular participation is envisaged, a framework agreement may be concluded defining the modalities of participation, including the status of seconded personnel; such agreements have been concluded with Ukraine, Moldova and Georgia.[74] Georgia and Moldova have taken part in the EU Training Mission in Mali, and Georgia participated in the military mission in the Central African Republic (EUFOR RCA). The Eastern Partnership's 'multilateral track' has included a panel on CSDP cooperation since 2013. According to the EU '[this] panel will focus on CSDP matters in

---

[69] Declaration by the High Representative on behalf of the European Union on the alignment of certain third countries with Council Decision 2014/309/CFSP amending Council Decision 2013/255/CFSP concerning restrictive measures against Syria, Presse 390/14, 7 July 2014.

[70] Declaration by the High Representative on behalf of the EU on the alignment of certain third countries concerning restrictive measures in response to the illegal annexation of Crimea and Sevastopol, Presse 622/14, 28 July 2015.

[71] Declaration by the High Representative on behalf of the EU on the alignment of certain third countries concerning restrictive measures in view of the situation in Ukraine, Presse 620/15, 28 July 2015.

[72] Declaration by the High Representative on behalf of the EU on the alignment of certain third countries concerning restrictive measures against Myanmar/Burma, Presse 576/15, 10 July 2015.

[73] See also JOIN (2014) 12 (n 8) 7.

[74] Agreement between the European Union and Ukraine establishing a framework for the participation of Ukraine in the European Union crisis management operations [2005] OJ L 182/29; Agreement between the European Union and the Republic of Moldova establishing a framework for the participation of the Republic of Moldova in European Union crisis management operations [2013] OJ L 8/2; Agreement between the European Union and Georgia establishing a framework for the participation of Georgia in European Union crisis management operations [2014] OJ L 14/2.

order to help eastern partners improve their capacity and their contributions to CSDP missions and operations, and to share information among EaP countries, Member States and EU institutions.'[75] It is with Ukraine that this cooperation is most developed; the framework agreement dates from 2005 and Ukraine has participated in a number of missions (in Macedonia and Bosnia Herzegovina, and in the anti-piracy mission, Operation Atalanta). The Association Agenda for Ukraine, agreed in June 2013, contains a series of provisions indicating the objective of a more structured form of CSDP cooperation:

> continue the practice of jointly identifying opportunities for Ukraine to participate in current and future CSDP operations, building on the good experience of Ukraine's participation in EU operations in the Balkans, as well as other EU operations (e.g. Atalanta); further implement 'Seville' Arrangements for Consultation and Co-operation between the EU and Ukraine in EU-led crisis management operations, including continued participation of Ukraine in relevant crisis management exercises and CSDP-related training activities; increase interoperability where appropriate between Ukrainian peacekeeping units and EU Member States forces through lessons learned from relevant EU crisis management operations to which Ukraine participated, and through involvement of the units of the Armed Forces of Ukraine into the formation of EU Multinational Tactical Battle Groups.

It is in these forms of participation in the EU's own security policy, via its CSDP missions, that we can see most clearly the ENP extending the EU's vision of multilateral action beyond its borders. Here, the EU is not simply encouraging the ENP states to sign up to multilateral commitments, or even seeking to ensure that those commitments are integrated into domestic reform programmes. We see (some of) its ENP partners actively supporting the EU in its attempts to resolve crises through multilateral mechanisms, especially but not only under the aegis of the United Nations. It is here that the partnership potential of the ENP is most clearly in evidence.

Conclusions

We have seen that multilateralism is both a principle and an objective of EU external policy – it is both one way in which the EU conducts its external policy and an objective of that policy – and this applies also to the ENP. In fact, the ENP demonstrates that, for the EU, its regional and multilateral agendas are not in conflict but support each other. We looked at three ways in which the ENP and the EU's policy of multilateralism interact. The first dimension, which we characterized as seeking multilateral solutions to common problems, includes supporting the ratification of multilateral conventions, supporting multilateral organizations and institutions of global governance, such as the IAEA and the

---

[75] JOIN (2014) 12 (n 8) 14.

ICC, and campaigning for the formalization of new multilaterally agreed norms on issues ranging from climate change to the arms trade. Although the concept of shared values underpinning the ENP provides a rhetorical basis for engaging the ENP states in these activities, and although the ENP offers some useful instruments such as Action Plans, it is clear that for this type of activity the specificity of the ENP is limited. The EU engages with ENP states in the same way in which it engages with other partners.

When we turned to the second dimension – ensuring the enforcement of multilateral legal norms – the specificity of the ENP became more evident. This is not simply a matter of enlisting the support of ENP states, along with others; it is more a case of seeking to ensure that agreed international norms (representing shared values) are embedded and operative in the legal orders of the ENP states. It is part of the EU's transformative, modernizing agenda for the ENP.

The third dimension – enlisting the active participation of the ENP states in the EU's own security activities, including its sanctions regimes – is a form of multilateralism which denotes a higher level of commitment; the ENP states here, where they take part, are acting alongside other close partners of the EU: the candidate and potential candidate states of the Western Balkans, Turkey and the EEA and EFTA partners. The vision of multilateralism which this represents is one based on safeguarding the 'values, fundamental interests, security, independence and integrity' of the EU.[76]

Each of these three dimensions, in different ways, brings together the regional and multilateral in EU policy-making: the EU is seeking to ensure that its neighbours in the 'wider Europe' espouse its interest in supporting a rules-based international order, its idea of global 'good citizenship'. This is a question of securing its interests as much as of promoting its values.

Bibliography

Keohane, R.O. The Contingent Legitimacy of Multilateralism. *GARNET Working Paper* No. 09/06.

Koutrakos, P. (2011) The Non-Proliferation Policy of the European Union. In Evans, M. and Koutrakos, P. *Beyond the Established Legal Orders: Policy Interconnections between the EU and the Rest of the World*. Oxford: Hart Publishing.

Petersen, J., Aspinwall, M., Damro, C. and Boswell, C. *The Consequences of Europe: Multilateralism and the New Security Agenda*. Edinburgh Europa Institute. *Mitchell Working Paper Series* 3/2008.

---

[76] Article 21(2) TEU.

5 EU values in integration-oriented agreements with Ukraine, Moldova and Georgia

Roman Petrov

Introduction

Association agreements between the EU and third countries have become one of the most recognizable brands of the EU's external policy. Treaties of this kind were signed by the EU Heads of State and governments with three of the EU's Eastern Neighbourhood countries (Ukraine, Moldova and Georgia) on 27 June 2014 and were followed by ratifications by national parliaments in Moldova, Georgia and Ukraine.[1] This was the culmination of a very long negotiation and signature process that had begun in 2008. This new generation of EU Association Agreements (AAs) will substitute outdated partnerships and association agreements, which were concluded in 1994–1998.[2]

Ukraine's road towards the signature of its AA was the most dramatic. Due to mounting economic and political pressure from Russia, the government of Ukraine decided to suspend the preparation for signature of the EU–Ukraine AA on 21

---

[1] The Moldovan Parliament expediently ratified the Association Agreement on 2 July 2014. It was followed by the Georgian Parliament on 18 July 2014 and by the Ukrainian Parliament on 16 September 2014. On the same date, the European Parliament approved the three agreements. The latter agreements are now subject to a lengthy process of ratification by the parliaments of the EU Member States. Therefore the interim application of the Association Agreements was authorized by the Council (see Council Decision 2014/295/EU of 17 March 2014 on the signing, on behalf of the European Union, and provisional application of the Association Agreement between the European Union and the European Atomic Energy Community and their Member States, of the one part, and Ukraine, of the other part, as regards the Preamble, Article 1, and Titles I, II and VII thereof [2014] OJ L161/1). However, the application of Title IV (deep and comprehensive free trade area) of the EU–Ukraine Association Agreement has been postponed until 1 January 2016 due to political and security pressure of the Russian Federation. See COM (2014) 609 Proposal for a Council Decision amending the Council Decision on the signing, on behalf of the European Union, and provisional application of the Association Agreement between the European Union and the European Atomic Energy Community and their Member States, of the one part, and Ukraine, of the other part, as regards Title III (with the exception of the provisions relating to the treatment of third-country nationals legally employed as workers in the territory of the other Party) and Titles IV, V, VI and VII thereof, as well as the related Annexes and Protocols, 23 September 2014.

[2] R. Petrov, 'The Partnership and Cooperation Agreements with the Newly Independent States' in A. Ott and K. Inglis (eds), *European Enlargement Handbook* (The Hague, Asser Press 2002) 175–194.

November 2013.[3] Following this news, hundreds of thousands of Ukrainians took to the streets. The 'Maidan' revolution, which claimed more than 100 casualties, resulted in the dismissal of President Victor Yanukovich on 22 February 2014 and the election of pro-European President Petro Poroshenko on 25 May 2014. As a consequence, the 'most ambitious agreement the EU has ever offered to a partner country'[4] was back on the agenda and was signed, along with the Moldovan and Georgian AAs, on 27 June 2014.[5]

As it is stressed by the Joint Declaration of the Eastern Partnership Summit of 21–22 May 2015, 'democracy, respect for human rights and fundamental freedoms, and the rule of law lie at the heart of political association and economic integration as envisaged in the Association Agreements.'[6] Their entry into force will pose the question of how the legal systems of Ukraine, Moldova and Georgia should be changed to reflect EU common values. However, there are no straightforward means to clarify this issue, given that the AAs represent the first international agreements in the modern history of these three countries, which signify their far-reaching integration into the legal order of a supranational international organization. Promoting EU common values is a key objective of the AAs. EU common values underpin mutual 'close and lasting relationships', and the parties share a 'common history and common values' and are 'committed to implementing and promoting' them.[7]

In this chapter we consider four issues. First, we look at the objectives and specific features of the AAs between the EU and Ukraine, Moldova and Georgia. Second, we focus on the scope of the EU policy of enhanced conditionality applied within these AAs. Third, we explore the techniques used to promote EU common values within the legal systems of Ukraine, Moldova and Georgia. Fourth, we examine how the EU defends principles of international law, such as national sovereignty and territorial integrity, by the use of restrictive measures towards Russia.

Objectives and specific features of the Association Agreements with Ukraine, Moldova and Georgia

The AAs between the EU and Ukraine, Moldova and Georgia are the most voluminous and ambitious of all the EU Association Agreements with third

---

[3] The Ukrainian government's decision cannot be disconnected from the Russian proposal to establish a Eurasian Union building upon the already existing customs union between Russia, Belarus and Kazakhstan. On the background of this initiative and its implications for EU–Ukraine relations, see G. Van der Loo and P. Van Elsuwege, 'Competing Paths of Regional Economic Integration in the Post-Soviet Space: Legal and Political Dilemmas for Ukraine' (2012) 37 *Review of Central and East European Law* 421–447.

[4] H. Van Rompuy, Press remarks by the President of the European Council following the EU–Ukraine Summit, Brussels, 25 February 2013, EUCO 48/13.

[5] European Council, 'Statement at the signing ceremony of the Association Agreements with Georgia, Republic of Moldova and Ukraine', Brussels, 27 June 2014, EUCO 137/14. Available online at www.consilium.europa.eu/uedocs/cms_data/docs/pressdata/en/ec/143415.pdf (accessed 10 June 2015).

[6] See Joint Declaration of the Eastern Partnership Summit (Riga, 21–22 May 2015). Available online at www.consilium.europa.eu/en/meetings/international-summit/2015/05/21-22 (accessed 10 June 2015).

[7] Preamble to the EU–Ukraine, EU–Moldova and EU–Georgia AAs.

countries.[8] They are comprehensive mixed agreements based on Art. 217 TFEU (association agreements) and Arts. 31(1) and 37 TEU (EU action in the area of Common Foreign and Security Policy).[9] There are many novel aspects in these agreements. The most prominent ones are, on the one hand, the strong emphasis on the comprehensive regulatory convergence between the parties and, on the other hand, the possibility to apply and implement most of the EU *acquis* within the Ukrainian, Moldovan and Georgian legal orders.

Of particular significance is the ambition to set up Deep and Comprehensive Free Trade Areas (DCFTAs), leading to the gradual and partial integration of Ukraine, Moldova and Georgia into the EU internal market. Accordingly, the AAs belong to the selected group of 'integration-oriented agreements', i.e. agreements including principles, concepts and provisions which are to be interpreted and applied as if the third country was part of the EU. It is argued that the AAs are unique in many respects and, therefore, provide a new model of integration without membership.

The AAs with Ukraine, Moldova and Georgia are characterized by three specific features: comprehensiveness, complexity and conditionality.[10] The AAs are comprehensive framework agreements which embrace the whole spectrum of EU activities and envisage cooperation in the fields of trade (through the setting up DCFTAs), Common Foreign and Security Policy, and justice and home affairs.[11]

The complexity of the AAs reflects the high level of ambition of Ukraine, Moldova and Georgia to achieve economic integration in the EU internal market through the establishment of the DCFTAs and to share principles of the EU's common policies. This requires comprehensive legislative and regulatory approximation, including advanced mechanisms to secure the uniform interpretation and effective implementation of relevant EU legislation into the national legal orders of Ukraine, Moldova and Georgia. In order to achieve this objective, the AAs are equipped with multiple specific provisions on legislative and regulatory approximation, including more than 40 detailed annexes. These annexes specify the procedure and pace of the approximation process for different policy areas and are based on specific commitments and mechanisms.

The AAs are also founded on a strict conditionality approach, which links the third country's performance and the deepening of its integration with the EU.[12] In addition to the standard reference to democratic principles, human

---

[8] For example, the EU–Ukraine AA comprises 7 titles, 28 chapters, 486 articles and 43 annexes on about 1,000 pages.

[9] EU–Ukraine Association Agreement [2014] OJ L161/3; EU–Moldova Association Agreement [2014] OJ L260/4; EU–Georgia Association Agreement [2014] OJ L261/4.

[10] For the first time these features of the AAs were described by G. Van der Loo, P. Van Elsuwege and R. Petrov, 'The EU-Ukraine Association Agreement: Assessment of an Innovative Legal Instrument' (2014) *EUI Working Papers* (Law) 2014/09.

[11] See Titles II and III of the AAs.

[12] For example, the preamble to the EU–Ukraine AA explicitly states that 'political association and economic integration of Ukraine within the European Union will depend on progress in the implementation of the current agreement as well as *Ukraine's track record in ensuring respect for common values, and progress in achieving convergence with the EU in political, economic and legal areas*' (emphasis added).

rights and fundamental freedoms as defined by international legal instruments (Helsinki Final Act, the Charter of Paris for a New Europe, the UN Universal Declaration on Human Rights, and the European Convention on Human Rights and Fundamental Freedoms),[13] the AAs contain common values that go beyond classical human rights and also include very strong security elements, such as the 'promotion of respect for the principles of sovereignty and territorial integrity, inviolability of borders and independence, as well as countering the proliferation of weapons of mass destruction, related materials and their means of delivery.'[14]

Enhanced conditionality in the Association Agreements with Ukraine, Moldova and Georgia

Conditionality is one of the key strategic tools of the ENP and it is, therefore, no surprise that this instrument also occupies a prominent place in the AAs. Two different forms of conditionality can be distinguished in these agreements. On the one hand, the AAs include several provisions related to Ukraine's, Moldova's and Georgia's commitment to the common European values of democracy, the rule of law and respect for human rights and fundamental freedoms ('common values' conditionality). On the other hand, the provisions of the DCFTAs are based on an explicit 'market access' conditionality, implying that Ukraine, Moldova and Georgia will only be granted additional access to a section of the EU's internal market if the EU decides, after a strict monitoring procedure, that these countries have successfully implemented its legislative approximation commitments. Both forms of conditionality bear some revolutionary features in comparison to other external agreements concluded between the EU and third countries.[15]

'Common values' conditionality

International agreements concluded by the EU after the 1990s are inspired by the principle of conditionality. This means that, in general, the text of the agreement contains a clause that defines the core common values of the relationship. This is the 'essential element clause' and is combined with a 'suspension' clause, which sets up a procedure to suspend the agreement in case these essential elements of the agreement are violated.

The AAs also include such clauses.[16] However, they differ from similar provisions included in, for instance, the Stabilisation and Association Agreements with the Western Balkans. First, in addition to the standard reference to democratic principles, human rights and fundamental freedoms as defined by international legal instruments (Helsinki Final Act, the Charter of Paris for a New Europe,

---

[13] Art. 2 EU–Ukraine, EU–Moldova and EU–Georgia AAs.
[14] Art. 2 EU–Ukraine AA and Art. 3 EU–Moldova and EU–Georgia AAs.
[15] L. Bartels, *Human Rights Conditionality in the EU's International Agreements* (Oxford, Oxford University Press 2005).
[16] Art. 2 in conjunction with Art. 478 EU–Ukraine AA; Art. 2 in conjunction with Art. 455 EU–Moldova AA; Art. 2 in conjunction with Art. 422 EU–Georgia AA.

the UN Universal Declaration on Human Rights, and the European Convention on Human Rights and Fundamental Freedoms),[17] a specific reference to human rights and fundamental freedoms is included in the AA provisions on 'dialogue and cooperation on domestic reform'[18] and in the AA provisions dealing with EU cooperation with Ukraine, Moldova and Georgia on justice, freedom and security.[19]

Second, the essential elements of the AAs contain security elements and are broader in scope since they include the 'promotion of respect for the principles of sovereignty and territorial integrity, inviolability of borders and independence, as well as countering the proliferation of weapons of mass destruction, related materials and their means of delivery.'[20]

Third, 'the principles of free market economy', as well as a list of other issues such as 'rule of law, the fight against corruption, the fight against the different forms of trans-national organized crime and terrorism, the promotion of sustainable development and effective multilateralism' are not included in the definition of essential elements.[21] Rather, they are considered to 'underpin' the relationship between the parties and are 'central to enhancing' this relationship.[22]

In other words, a distinction is made between hard-core common values related to fundamental rights and security, and a range of other general principles that are deemed crucial for developing closer relations but which cannot trigger the suspension of the entire agreement.[23]

'Market access' conditionality

Apart from the more general 'common values' conditionality, the AAs entail a specific form of 'market access' conditionality, which is explicitly linked to the process of legislative approximation in Ukraine, Moldova and Georgia. Hence, it is one of the specific mechanisms introduced to tackle the challenges of integration

---

[17] Art. 2 EU–Ukraine, EU–Moldova and EU–Georgia AAs. The same principles and legal instruments are mentioned in Art. 2 of the SAA with Serbia.
[18] Art. 6 EU–Ukraine AA, Art. 4 EU–Moldova and EU–Georgia AAs. This dialogue foresees that the parties 'shall cooperate in order to ensure that their internal policies are based on principles common to the parties in particular stability and effectiveness of democratic institutions and the rule of law and on respect of human rights and fundamental freedoms.'
[19] Art. 7 EU–Ukraine AA, Art. 5 EU–Moldova and EU–Georgia AAs.
[20] Art. 2 EU–Ukraine AA. In comparison, Arts. 2 and 3 of the SAA with Serbia only include full cooperation with the International Criminal Tribunal for the former Yugoslavia (ICTY) and non-proliferation of weapons of mass destruction as essential elements of the agreement. On the other hand, Art. 2 of the SAA includes a general reference to 'respect for principles of international law', which is not in Art. 2 of the EU–Ukraine AA.
[21] Art. 3 EU–Ukraine AA, Art. 2 EU–Moldova and EU–Georgia AAs. In contrast, Art. 2 of the SAA with Serbia includes the principles of the market economy in the list of essential elements.
[22] Ibid.
[23] Art. 478 EU–Ukraine AA, Art. 455 EU–Moldova AA and Art. 422 EU–Georgia AA foresee that a suspension of the entire agreement, including the part on Trade and Trade-related measures, is only possible in case of violation of the essential elements or in accordance with the general rules of international law.

without membership. Of particular significance is the far-reaching monitoring of these countries' efforts to approximate national legislation to EU law, including aspects of implementation and enforcement.[24] To facilitate the assessment process, the Ukrainian, Moldovan and Georgian governments are obliged to provide reports to the EU in line with approximation deadlines specified in the Agreement.[25] In addition to the drafting of Progress Reports, which is a common practice within the EU's pre-accession strategy and the ENP, the monitoring procedure may include 'on-the-spot missions, with the participation of EU institutions, bodies and agencies, non-governmental bodies, supervisory authorities, independent experts and others as needed.'[26] Arguably, this is a new mechanism that was introduced precisely to guarantee that legislative approximation goes beyond a formal adaptation of national legislation and, as such, it may have a far-reaching effect on the domestic legal orders of the countries concerned.

Means to promote EU values into the legal systems of Ukraine, Moldova and Georgia via Association Agreements

Exporting the EU *acquis*[27] into the legal orders of third countries is indispensable to ensuring that the EU is seen as a global actor on the international scene.[28] Indeed, the adoption of the EU *acquis* encourages third countries to revisit their national rules and standards and make them compatible with those of the EU. This is a way of sharing 'the Union's common values'.[29] In addition, the export of the EU *acquis* contributes to the establishment of a friendly legal environment between the EU and third countries, therefore encouraging the flow of investment and the mutual liberalization of markets.

A deeper examination of the legal and procedural instruments involved could clarify many problems which are relevant for the promotion of EU common values via the AAs. The simple question 'how does the EU export its *acquis*?' could help us understand the rationale behind many tools of the EU's external policy

---

[24] Art. 475(2) EU–Ukraine AA, Arts. 451 and 452 EU–Moldova AA and Art. 419(2) EU–Georgia AA.
[25] Ibid.
[26] Art. 475(3) EU–Ukraine AA, Art. 451(2) EU–Moldova AA and Art. 419(3) EU–Georgia AA.
[27] See R. Petrov, 'Exporting the *acquis communautaire* through EU External Agreements' (Baden-Baden, Nomos 2011) 313; R. Petrov and P. Leino, 'Between "Common Values" and Competing Universals: The Promotion of the EU's Common Values through the European Neighbourhood Policy' (2009) 15(5) *European Law Journal* 654–671; R. Petrov, 'Exporting the Acquis Communautaire into the Legal Systems of Third Countries' (2008) 13(1) *European Foreign Affairs Review* 33–52; C. Gialdino, 'Some Reflections on the Acquis Communautaire' (1995) 32 *CML Rev* 1089–1121; C. Delcourt, 'The *Acquis Communautaire:* Has the Concept Had Its Day?' (2001) 38 *CML Rev* 829–870; L. Auzolai, 'The *Acquis* of the European Union and International Organisations' (2005) 11(2) *ELJ* 196–231; R. Petrov, 'The External Dimension of the Acquis Communautaire' (2002) *EUI Working Paper* 07/2002.
[28] On this matter, see M. Cremona, 'The Union as a Global Actor: Roles, Models and Identity' (2004) 41 *CML Rev* 553–573.
[29] Art. 2 TEU.

towards third countries, in particular, the impact of the EU external agreements on exporting EU *acquis*.

We will thus consider the techniques used in the association agreements to reflect EU common values, placing special emphasis on that of legislative approximation.

Legislative approximation in the Association Agreements with Ukraine, Moldova and Georgia

The promotion of EU common values takes place through the legislative and regulatory approximation of the legal systems of Ukraine, Moldova and Georgia in line with the EU *acquis*. The AAs with these countries contain multiple specific provisions dealing with legislative and regulatory approximation, including detailed annexes specifying the procedure and pace of the approximation process for different policy areas.[30] The various approximation clauses differ from one another because in some areas the annexes contain detailed lists of relevant EU legislation, whereas in others they are more general in nature or even lack a clear legal obligation to approximate. To a certain extent, the variation between these approximation provisions is the result of the different objectives of each chapter.

Not surprisingly, the most advanced mechanisms of legislative approximation are to be found in the chapters related to the establishment of the DCFTA. The AAs also include several mechanisms to deal with the dynamic evolution of the incorporated EU *acquis*, as well as sophisticated forms of dispute settlement.

The procedures to amend or update the incorporated EU acquis *in the AAs*

The procedures to amend or update the incorporated EU *acquis* in the AAs deserve special attention. Due to the constant evolution of EU law, a crucial challenge for the AAs is to keep up to date and in line with evolving EU legislation. This can be based on either 'dynamic' or 'static' mechanisms depending on whether or not there is an obligation to automatically adopt every amendment to the EU *acquis* that is covered under the agreement.[31] The AAs differ from other models of integration without membership.[32] There is no single mechanism to amend the incorporated EU *acquis* covering the entire agreement; rather, there are many different ones, varying from 'static' to 'dynamic' procedures. The Association Councils 'may' update or amend the Annexes to the Agreement '[to take] into account the evolution of EU law', without compromising any specific provisions

---

[30] By contrast to the EU–Moldova and EU–Georgia AAs, Art. 474 of the EU–Ukraine AA recapitulates the entire scope of Ukraine's legislative approximation commitments 'as referred to in Annexes I to XLIV to this Agreement, based on the commitments identified in Titles IV, V and VI of this Agreement, and according to the provisions of those Annexes.'

[31] For the difference between static and dynamic procedures, see A. Lazowski, 'Enhanced Multilateralism and Enhanced Bilateralism: Integration without Membership in the European Union' (2008) 45(2) *CML Rev* 1433–1445, at 1444.

[32] For example, as provided in Art. 102 EEA or the EU–Switzerland bilateral sectoral agreements.

included in the DCFTA.[33] In addition, the Association Council will also be the forum for exchange of information on EU and Ukrainian, Moldovan and Georgian legislative acts, 'both under preparation and in force.' Given that this allows the Ukrainian, Moldovan and Georgian administrations to be consulted and to express their opinions and concerns on draft amendments of relevant legislation, this procedure can be considered as a limited form of 'decision-shaping'. However, it can hardly be seen as dynamic, since the Association Councils are not obliged to update the Annexes regarding each and every modification of relevant EU legislation. Moreover, because the Association Councils, which comprise both the EU and other party's representatives, must take decisions 'by agreement', Ukraine, Moldova and Georgia can always veto this process.[34]

The role of the case law of the Court of Justice in the AAs

The AAs envisage a procedure of referrals to the EU Court of Justice (CJEU);[35] this is crucial to preserve the Court's exclusive jurisdiction to interpret the EU *acquis* and values.[36]

It is settled case law that the EU and its Member States are not bound by a particular interpretation of the rules of Union law, referred to in an agreement that 'extends' the EU *acquis* to third countries such as those of the EEA and the European Common Aviation Area (ECAA).[37] In Opinion 1/91 on the draft EEA Agreement, the Court of Justice also clarified that the interpretation of EU rules cannot be entrusted to bodies created on the basis of international agreements.[38] In order to avoid a repetition of the EEA saga, the AAs preclude the arbitration panel from giving a binding ruling on the interpretation of the agreement's provisions, which are essentially rules of EU law, by delegating disputes on 'a question of interpretation of a provision of EU law' to the Court of Justice by means of a preliminary ruling.[39] However, a preliminary ruling in the AAs must comply with the objective of 'interpretation and application of a provision of

---

[33] Art. 463(3) EU–Ukraine AA; Art. 436(3) EU–Moldova AA; Art. 406(3) EU–Georgia AA.
[34] For instance, combined reading of Arts. 462(1) and 463(1) EU–Ukraine AA.
[35] Art. 322 EU–Ukraine AA; Art. 403 EU–Moldova AA; Art. 267 EU–Georgia AA.
[36] Art. 19 TEU. For an analysis see I. Govaere, 'Beware of the Trojan Horse: Dispute Settlement in (Mixed) Agreements and the Autonomy of the EU Legal Order', in C. Hillion and P. Koutrakos (eds), *Mixed Agreements Revisited* (Oxford, Hart Publishing 2010) 192–199.
[37] Opinion 1/00, Proposed agreement between the European Community and non-Member States on the establishment of a European Common Aviation Area [2002] ECR 3493 (ECLI:EU:C:2002:231), paras 3 and 11.
[38] Opinion 1/91, Opinion delivered pursuant to the second subparagraph of Article 228(1) of the Treaty – Draft agreement between the Community, on the one hand, and the countries of the European Free Trade Association, on the other, relating to the creation of the European Economic Area [1991] ECR 06079 (ECLI:EU:C:1991:490), para. 42.
[39] However, due to the absence of the homogeneity objective in the AA, the arbitration panel would be able to rule only on AA provisions which are textually identical to provisions of EU law, and not on EU law as such. The inclusion of such an objective would have made it impossible to dissociate the AA provisions from identical provisions of EU law (ECJ, Opinion 1/91, ibid. para. 45).

[Agreement] relating to regulatory approximation' in the EU–Ukraine AA (Art. 322), 'interpretation and application of a provision of [Agreement] relating to gradual approximation' in the EU–Moldova AA, and 'interpretation and application of a provision of [Agreement] ... defined by a reference to a provision of Union law' in the EU–Georgia AA.

By contrast with other agreements, the procedure of referrals to the Court of Justice of the EU envisaged in the AAs does not make a distinction between pre-signature and post-signature case law.[40] Therefore, there will be numerous opportunities for the domestic courts of Ukraine, Moldova and Georgia to use this mechanism.

In addition to this preliminary ruling procedure, the EU–Ukraine AA (but not the EU–Moldova or EU–Georgia AAs) includes specific provisions guaranteeing the uniform interpretation of legal norms. It is well known that similar provisions in international agreements and in EU law do not automatically have the same meaning, but that the objective, purpose and context of the agreement need to be taken into account.[41] Of course, the situation is different when express provisions on identical interpretation are laid down in an agreement itself.[42] Several DCFTA chapters contain such explicit provisions. The most straightforward obligation can be found, somewhat hidden, in the annex to the Services and Establishment Chapter. Article 6 of Annex XVII states that:

> [I]nsofar as the provisions of this Annex and the applicable provisions specified in the Appendices are identical in substance to corresponding [EU provisions], those provisions shall, in their implementation and application, be interpreted in conformity with the relevant rulings of the Court of Justice of the European Union.

In the case of the EU–Ukraine AA, the obligation of a consistent interpretation only applies to a specific DCFTA chapter and not to the entire agreement.[43]

Protection of EU values in the Association Agreements with Ukraine, Moldova and Georgia via the EU's restrictive measures towards third countries

The principles of national sovereignty and territorial integrity, inviolability of borders and independence are considered as core values of the AAs and must

---

[40] See Art. 16 ECAA and Art. 16(2) EU–Switzerland Agreement on the free movement of persons [2002] OJ L114/6. An example of an integration agreement which does not make this difference is Art. 21(5) EU–Georgia Aviation Agreement [2012] OJ L321/3.

[41] Court of Justice, Opinion 1/91 (n 38) paras 14. See also Case 270/80 *Polydor* v. *Harlequin* [1982] ECR 329 (ECLI:EU:C:1982:43), paras. 15–19.

[42] Court of Justice, Case C-351/08, *Christian Grimme* v. *Deutsche Angestellten-Krankenkasse* [2009] ECR 10777 (ECLI:EU:C:2009:697), para. 29; Case C-547/10, *Swiss Confederation* v. *European Commission* (ECLI:EU:C:2013:139), para. 80.

[43] Two other DCFTA Chapters (public procurement and competition) contain a sort of duty of consistent interpretation, albeit drafted in less strict terms. Ukraine must respectively take 'due account' of (Art. 153(2)) or use 'as sources of inspiration' (Art. 264) the relevant case law of the Court of Justice.

be shared and respected by the EU and Ukraine, Moldova and Georgia.[44] Furthermore, in the case of the EU–Ukraine AA, these principles constitute essential elements of the agreement.[45]

The overall security situation in the EU's neighbouring countries has gradually deteriorated over the last decade. Currently, Moldova and Georgia have unresolved border security conflicts either with other neighbouring countries in the EU or with third countries (mainly with the Russian Federation).[46] The annexation of Crimea by Russia took place in March 2014. Ukraine has been engaged in a bloody military conflict with the Russian Federation since April 2014.

Moldova has experienced prolonged conflict with its breakaway part, Transnistria (the so-called Pridnestrovian Moldovan Republic). This territory is not recognized by any of the UN members and formally constitutes part of the Republic of Moldova (Transnistria autonomous territorial unit with special legal status). However, de facto, Transnistria is an independent state with a strong presence of Russian military troops. The EU is engaged in solving the Transnistrian conflict via the European Border Assistance Mission to Moldova and Ukraine (EUBAM).[47] As part of the EU Common Security and Defence Policy, the EUBAM helps to control traffic on borders between Moldova and Ukraine around Transnistria in order to prevent the illegal movement of people and goods from and to Transnistria.[48]

Georgia went through a military conflict with Russia over the breakaway areas of Abkhazia and South Ossetia. The conflict took place in August 2008 and led to many casualties and to Georgia losing control of Abkhazia and South Ossetia.[49] Currently, Russian military troops are stationed in Abkhazia and South Ossetia with de facto control of their territories.

The EU played a modest role in settling the conflict in the Caucasus, allowing some EU Member States to lead the peace process in the region.[50] No sanctions were applied by the EU in the aftermath of the Georgia–Russia conflict.

However, the next security challenge within the country, which was on the road to signing its AA, compelled the EU to act and to apply sanctions against one of the

---

[44] Art. 2 EU–Ukraine AA; Art. 3(g) EU–Moldova AA; Art. 2(3) EU–Georgia AA.
[45] Art. 2 EU–Ukraine AA.
[46] These are: the dispute between Armenia and Azerbaijan over status of the self-proclaimed and unrecognized Nagorno-Karabakh Republic; the conflict between Georgia and Russia over the breakaway areas of Abkhazia and South Ossetia; the conflict between Moldova and its breakaway part, Transnistria; and, finally, the annexation of Crimea by Russia.
[47] Memorandum of Understanding between the European Commission, the Government of the Republic of Moldova and the Government of Ukraine on the European Commission Border Assistance Mission to the Republic of Moldova and to Ukraine of 7 October 2005. Available online at www.eubam.org/files/memorandum_of_understanding_en.pdf (accessed 17 June 2015).
[48] X. Kurowska and B. Tallis, 'Border Assistance Mission: Beyond Border Monitoring?' (2009) 14(1) *EFARev* 47–64.
[49] For more details, see Independent International Fact-Finding Mission on the Conflict in Georgia. Available online at www.ceiig.ch (accessed 30 May 2015).
[50] S. Vasilyan, 'The External Legitimacy of the EU in the South Caucasus' (2011) 16(3) *EFARev* 341–357; R.G. Whitman and S. Wolff, 'The EU as a Conflict Manager? The Case of Georgia and Its Implications' (2010) 86(1) *International Affairs* 87–107; G. Christou, 'Multilateralism, Conflict Prevention, and the Eastern Partnership' (2011) 16(3) *EFARev* 207–225.

leading geopolitical players on the European continent – the Russian Federation. This happened after the self-proclaimed authorities of the Autonomous Republic of Crimea held an unrecognized referendum under Russian military presence in March 2014. As a result, part of Ukraine's territory – the Autonomous Republic of Crimea and the city of Sevastopol – were annexed by the Russian Federation and incorporated by the Russian Federation as its own federal subjects on 21 March 2014. The annexation was not recognized by Ukraine or the United Nations General Assembly[51] and is universally considered as a blatant violation by the Russian Federation of international public law.[52]

Following turbulent events in Crimea, the EU decided to react against Russia. First of all, bilateral talks on visa matters and on a new EU–Russia agreement were suspended and the EU–Russia summit was cancelled. In addition, travel bans and asset freezes were enacted against 'certain persons responsible for actions which undermine or threaten the territorial integrity, sovereignty and independence of Ukraine.'[53] The list of these persons is constantly increasing and covers leading Ukrainian, Russian and Crimean politicians who favoured Crimea's annexation.

The EU had to extend the scope of its sanctions against Russia after the security situation in Ukraine drastically deteriorated towards the end of the summer of 2014. The world was shocked when Malaysia Airlines Flight 17 (MH17) was shot down above the part of Eastern Ukraine controlled by pro-Russian separatists, leading to the loss of 298 lives. The bloodshed between Ukraine and the armies of the self-proclaimed 'people's republics' of Donetsk and Lugansk led to several thousand casualties and about a million refugees from the east of Ukraine.[54] EU Member States had to speak with one voice in order to show their solidarity

---

[51] UN General Assembly Resolution 68/262 adopted on 27 March 2014 'Territorial Integrity of Ukraine'. In the meantime, only six countries (Afganistan, Cuba, Nicaragua, Russia, Syria and Venezuela) recognized the Republic of Crimea and Sevastopol as federal subjects of the Russian Federation.

[52] For legal assessment of the annexation of Crimea by the Russian Federation, see C. Marxsen, 'The Crimea Crisis – An International Law Perspective' (2014) 74(2) *Zeitschrift für ausländisches öffentliches Recht und Völkerrecht* 367–391.

[53] Council Regulation (EU) No 269/2014 of 17 March 2014 concerning restrictive measures in respect of actions undermining or threatening the territorial integrity, sovereignty and independence of Ukraine [2014] OJ L78/6 amended by Council Regulation (EU) No 476/2014 of 12 May 2014 [2014] OJ L137, Council Regulation (EU) No 783/2014 of 18 July 2014 [2014] OJ L214/2, Council Regulations (EU) No 810/2014 and No 811/2014 of 25 July 2014 [2014] OJ L221/11, Council Regulation (EU) No 959/2014 of 8 September 2014 [2014] OJ L271/1, Council Implementing Regulation (EU) No 961/2014 of 12 May 2014 [2014] OJ L271/8, Council Decision 2014/145/CFSP concerning restrictive measures in respect of actions undermining or threatening the territorial integrity, sovereignty and independence of Ukraine [2014] OJ L78/16 amended by Council Decision 2014/265/CFSP of 12 May 2014 [2014] OJ L137/9, Council Decision 2014/119/CFSP concerning restrictive measures directed against certain persons, entities and bodies in view of the situation in Ukraine [2014] OJ L66/26. Council Regulation (EU) No. 833/2014 of 31 July 2014 concerning restrictive measures in view of Russia's actions destabilising the situation in Ukraine [2014] OJ L229/1, amended by Council Regulation (EU) No. 960/2014 of 8 September 2014 [2014] OJ L271/2.

[54] UN Report on the human rights situation in Ukraine of 17 August 2014. Available online at www.ohchr.org/Documents/Countries/UA/UkraineReport28August2014.pdf (accessed 20 May 2015).

against the direct Russian involvement in the civil conflict in Ukraine. As a result, they agreed on a new level of sanctions against Russian and Ukrainian officials and nationals involved in supporting the separatists' movement in the Donbass region of Ukraine. For example, 'economic' sanctions against Russia (the prohibition of exports of arms, energy and military-related technologies and dual-use goods; the freezing of economic cooperation) were added to the list of restrictions.

It is too early to judge the effectiveness of the EU sanctions at the time of writing of this chapter. The fact that they were adopted by unanimity provides a promising picture of the EU's solidarity against violations of international law and in particular of the territorial integrity of one of its nearest neighbours, which was about to enter into an integration-oriented AA. The threat of wide-ranging retaliatory measures by the Russian Federation against the EU did not prevent the adoption of sanctions against this country. However, the EU cannot afford to impose immediate, large-scale sanctions against its third largest trading partner – Russia – due to the adverse effect that this might have on the EU's economy, especially in the field of energy.

It is to be hoped that the procedure of political dialogue and the institutional framework of the AAs will be effectively used to protect the principles of sovereignty and territorial integrity, inviolability of borders and independence, which are considered as core values of the AAs.

Concluding remarks

Taking into account the comprehensive nature of the agreement and the underlying conditionality approach, the AAs occupy a unique position within the network of bilateral agreements concluded between the EU and third countries.

The AAs are innovative legal instruments in the EU's external relations, based as they are on comprehensiveness, complexity and conditionality. These three features are central to ensuring effective and successful integration of EU values into the legal systems of Ukraine, Moldova and Georgia.[55] The AAs employ various substantive and procedural means of promoting and protecting EU values. The security challenges of Ukraine, Moldova and Georgia highlight the urgent need not only to declare and promote EU values (such as the principles of sovereignty and territorial integrity, inviolability of borders and independence), but also to protect them (by enforcing restrictive measures against third countries) and to deepen cooperation between the EU and Ukraine, Moldova and Georgia in the area of the CFSP.

Bibliography

Auzolai, L. (2005) The *Acquis* of the European Union and International Organisations. *ELJ*. 11(2). pp. 196–231.

Bartels, L. (2005) *Human Rights Conditionality in the EU's International Agreements*. Oxford: Oxford University Press.

---

[55] As confirmed in Joint Declaration of the Eastern Partnership Summit (n 6).

Christou, G. (2011) Multilateralism, Conflict Prevention, and the Eastern Partnership. *EFARev.* 16(3). pp. 207–225.

Cremona, M. (2004) The Union as a Global Actor: Roles, Models and Identity. *CML Rev.* 41(2). pp. 553–573.

Delcourt, C. (2001) The *Acquis Communautaire:* Has the Concept Had Its Day? *CML Rev.* 38 (4). pp. 829–870.

Gialdino, C. (1995) Some Reflections on the Acquis Communautaire. *CML Rev.* 32(5). pp. 1089–1121.

Govaere, I. (2010) Beware of the Trojan Horse: Dispute Settlement in (Mixed) Agreements and the Autonomy of the EU Legal Order. In Hillion, C. and Koutrakos, P. *Mixed Agreements Revisited.* Oxford: Hart Publishing.

Kurowska, X. and Tallis, B. (2009) Border Assistance Mission: Beyond Border Monitoring? *EFARev.* 14(1). pp. 47–64.

Lazowski, A. (2008) Enhanced Multilateralism and Enhanced Bilateralism: Integration without Membership in the European Union. *CML Rev.* 45(2). pp. 1433–1445.

Marxsen, C. (2014) The Crimea Crisis – An International Law Perspective. *Zeitschrift für ausländisches öffentliches Recht und Völkerrecht.* 74(2). pp. 367–391.

Petrov, R. (2002) The External Dimension of the Acquis Communautaire. *EUI Working Papers, Max Weber Programme.* n. 07.

—(2002) The Partnership and Cooperation Agreements with the Newly Independent States. In Ott, A. and Inglis, K. *European Enlargement Handbook.* The Hague: Asser Press. pp. 175–194.

—(2008) Exporting the Acquis Communautaire into the Legal Systems of Third Countries. *EFARev.* 13(1). pp. 33–52.

—(2011) *Exporting the Acquis Communautaire Through EU External Agreements.* Baden-Baden: Nomos.

Petrov, R. and Leino, P. (2009) Between 'Common Values' and Competing Universals – The Promotion of the EU's Common Values through the European Neighbourhood Policy. *European Law Journal.* 15(5). pp. 654–671.

Van der Loo, G., Van Elsuwege, P. and Petrov, R. (2014) The EU-Ukraine Association Agreement: Assessment of an Innovative Legal Instrument. *EUI Working Papers, Law.* n. 09.

Vasilyan, S. (2011) The External Legitimacy of the EU in the South Caucasus. *EFARev.* 16(3). pp. 341–357.

Whitman, R.G. and Wolff, S. (2010) The EU as a Conflict Manager? The Case of Georgia and its Implications. *International Affairs.* 86(1). pp. 87–107.

Part III
The EU's values in EU–Russia relations

6 Shared values and interests in the conflictual relationship between the EU and Russia

Paul Kalinichenko

Introduction

EU–Russia relations have never been simple. On the one hand, these two international actors have common values and interests. On the other, they have a conflictual relationship, which has become particularly acute after the Ukrainian crisis which started in 2014.

Evidence of the EU and Russia's common foundational values is demonstrated by the Russian Constitution, which was adopted by referendum on 12 December 1993 and was the result of radical changes in Russian society which had started in the era of the Soviet perestroika. The Constitution provides a real legal basis for the Europeanization of Russian law[1] and reflects the common values of Europe's cultural and civilizational system.[2] The EU Treaty framework and the Russian Constitution are absolutely comparable, both in letter and in spirit.[3]

The EU and Russia also have common interests and concerns. Given that they share frontiers, they cooperate in order to regulate local border traffic[4] and to facilitate people's transfrontier movements.[5] They also have common transborder

---

[1] P. Kalinichenko, *European Union: Law and Relations with Russia* (in Russian) (Moscow, Norma 2012) 172. The Russian Constitution was built in accordance with European standards. A.E. Kellermann, 'Impact of the EU Enlargement on the Russian Federation' (in Russian) (2005) 61(1) *Police and Law* 116–118.

[2] J.J. Hesse and V. Wright (eds), *Federalizing Europe? The Costs, Benefits, and Preconditions of Federal Political Systems* (Oxford, Oxford University Press 1996) 353; S.E. Finner, V. Bogdanor and B. Rudden (eds), *Comparing Constitutions* (Oxford, Clarendon Press 1995) 17.

[3] For example, Art. 2 of the Russian primary law and Art. F of the Maastricht Treaty (adopted in the same year of the Russian Constitution) consider respect for human rights and freedoms as the main organizing principle of political power. This means that Russia is open from a normative point of view to the values of the European legal order. However, the positions of Russia and the EU differ with respect to the 'universality', 'export' and 'methods' of implementing these principles in the international arena. See P. Leino and R. Petrov, 'Between "Common Values" and Competing Universals – The Promotion of the EU's Common Values through the European Neighbourhood Policy' (2009) 5(15) *ELJ* 669–670.

[4] Regulation (EC) No 1931/2006 of the European Parliament and of the Council of 20 December 2006 laying down rules on local border traffic at the external land borders of the Member States and amending the provisions of the Schengen Convention [2007] OJ L 29/3.

[5] The EU created the Facilitated Transit Documents for Russian citizens who cross the EU territory from the Kaliningrad region to the other part of Russia and back. Council Regulation (EC)

problems that affect their security as well as that of all the international community. Migration and cross-border crimes are a case in point. More significantly, threats of a global nature, such as terrorism, the Islamic State, civil wars in Syria and in Libya, Iran's nuclear program[6] and the proliferation of weapons of mass destruction, are common concerns that can only be tackled by joint efforts. Finally, the two parties are also interdependent in the global economy.[7]

Despite common values and interests, the two international actors have gradually become 'distant neighbours'.[8] The competition entered into by the EU with the Russia-led initiatives to develop multilateral economic cooperation with its neighbours has contributed to a deterioration in these relations. Following its refusal to participate in the ENP, Russia favoured the setting up of various special supranational structures, such as the Eurasian Economic Community (2000), and enhanced forms of economic cooperation, called the Single Economic Area and the Custom Union (2010).

The Treaty on Eurasian Economic Union (EAEU), signed in Astana on 28 May 2014,[9] can be viewed within this context. It sets up an international organization of regional economic integration, whose ambitions are limited.[10] The aim of this agreement is the codification of the most important provisions of previous treaties concluded by EAEU Member States within the Single Economic Area and the Custom Union. By concluding Association Agreements with Ukraine, Georgia and Moldova,[11] the EU has entered into a sort of unwelcome competition with the

---

No 693/2003 of 14 April 2003 establishing a specific Facilitated Transit Document (FTD), a Facilitated Rail Transit Document (FRTD) and amending the Common Consular Instructions and the Common Manual [2003] OJ L 99/8.

[6] Most recently, Russia was one of the countries that eased the negotiation of Joint Comprehensive Plan of Action (JCPOA) concluded on 14 July 2015 between the United States and Iran and approved by the UNSC on 20 July 2015 (see Resolution 2231 (2015)). 'U.N. Security Council endorses Iran nuclear deal with 6 world powers', Chicago Tribune, 20 July 2015. Available online at www.chicagotribune.com/news/nationworld/ct-un-approves-iran-nuclear-deal-20150720-story.html (accessed 24 July 2015).

[7] According to data of 2013, Russia is the EU's third most important trading partner (after the US and China), with €123 billion in exported goods to Russia (7.3% of all EU exports) and €213 billion in imported goods in 2012 (11.9% of all EU imports, second after China). The EU is thus by far the largest market for Russian goods, accounting for roughly half of Russian exports in 2012. The EU is also the main supplier for Russia, with a 43% market share, followed by China and Ukraine. See Memo 'EU Russia Summit' (Yekaterinburg, 3–4 June 2013).

[8] See E. Dundovich's chapter in this volume.

[9] Treaty on Eurasian Economic Union. Available online at www.eurasiancommission.org (accessed 24 June 2015).

[10] A superficial examination of this document could give the impression that it takes the European integration as a model. Indeed, the EU single market principles (free movement of goods, persons, services and capitals) clearly inspires the EAEU Treaty. Yet on closer inspection, the latter Treaty differs from those founding the EU, both in spirit and content; indeed, it does not aim at political cooperation amongst the parties, is not based on common values and does not intend to be the 'Constitution' of Eurasia.

[11] See 'EU forges closer ties with Ukraine, Georgia and Moldova'. Available online at http://eeas.europa.eu/top_stories/2014/270614_association_agreement_en.htm (accessed 24 June 2015).

Eurasian projects.[12] Indeed, these projects and the Association Agreements are not compatible with each other as far as the economic aspects are concerned. Since the EU is the main trading partner of both Russia and Ukraine, by establishing a free trade area with Ukraine but not with Russia, the EU has affected Russia's economic interests. It is natural that the prospect of closer economic ties between Ukraine (and other eastern neighbours) and the EU is not regarded favourably by Russia.

With the Ukrainian crisis, the deterioration in EU–Russia relations has reached its lowest point. This was clearly expressed by EU High Representative Mogherini in 2014[13] and more recently by the European Parliament in a Resolution of 10 June 2015. The European Parliament stressed that the EU cannot envisage a return to 'business as usual' and has no choice but to conduct a critical reassessment of its relations with Russia. It highlighted that due to its actions in Crimea and in Eastern Ukraine, Russia can no longer be treated or considered as a 'strategic partner'.[14]

Against this backdrop, this chapter discusses the conflictual relationship between the EU and Russia from a legal perspective. First, a short description of the legal foundations of these relations will be provided. Special emphasis will be placed on the judicial practice of the Partnership and Cooperation Agreement (PCA)[15] of 1998 in order to highlight the common values and how these are implemented in practice. Second, an account is given of the state of EU–Russia trade relations in the context of the WTO and of the EU's reaction to the Ukrainian conflict in the context of the EU Common Foreign and Security Policy (CFSP). The aim is to show that after the Ukrainian crisis of 2014 the EU and Russia entered a new era of confrontation and brinkmanship. The conclusion of this chapter is that since Russia and the EU need each other, this conflictual relationship is not tenable. Restrictive measures against Russia should be abolished. In order to revitalize their relations, the legal framework underpinning EU–Russia relations should be replaced. The two partners should not compete with each other in their projects of economic integration and should find a way to conduct their foreign affairs in a mutually acceptable manner.

Legal background of EU–Russia relations

EU–Russia relations rest upon three legal layers. The first consists of the EU–Russia PCA and other bilateral agreements, including the facilitation of the issuance of visas to the citizens of the European Union and the Russian

---

[12] It should be stressed that the EU has not officially recognized any of the Eurasian bodies.
[13] https://euobserver.com/enlargement/125442 2 September 2014 (accessed 24 August 2015).
[14] European Parliament resolution of 10 June 2015 on the state of the EU-Russia relations, 2015/2001/INI, point 2.
[15] Agreement on partnership and cooperation establishing a partnership between the European Communities and their Member States, of one part, and the Russian Federation, of the other part, 1997; Sobraniye Zakonodatelstva Rosiyskoy Federatsii (Compilation of legislation of the Russian Federation – SZ RF), 1998, N 16, st. 1802; [1997] OJ L 327/1.

Federation,[16] which is the first of its kind for the EU. The second consists of soft law, such as 'roadmaps' for the establishment of four EU–Russia Common Spaces. The third covers the Russian legislation and the EU *acquis* within the EU–Russia sectoral cooperation.[17]

The PCA constitutes the core of the first layer of EU–Russia relations. This agreement, which was signed on 24 June 1994 in Corfu and entered into force on 1 December 1997, formed a firm foundation for EU–Russia political dialogue and economic, social and cultural cooperation, including legislative approximation. It is an 'entry-level' and 'framework' agreement and a basis for other bilateral agreements.[18]

The PCA is aimed at establishing a market economy in Russia in preparation for its accession to the WTO. The *finalité* of the agreement is Russia's integration into the world economy and, in the longer term, the creation of a free trade area.[19] In Art. 2, the PCA also refers to respect for human rights and other democratic principles of the Helsinki Act of 1975 and the Charter of Paris for a New Europe 1990 as essential elements of the partnership. Although these provisions do not take into account Russian membership in the Council of Europe or the European Convention on the Protection of Human Rights and Fundamental Freedoms of 1950, or even its adoption of the EU Charter of Fundamental Rights in 2000, they constitute an important aspect of 'shared values' between Russia and the EU.[20]

The second layer of EU–Russia relations is made up of various soft law instruments.[21] Such acts contain a list of practical actions that are necessary for the evolution of EU–Russia relations. However, there is no time frame to implement these actions, nor have any mechanisms or instruments of control been set up to oversee the implementation process. Given that these documents are not legally binding,[22] in themselves they do not represent a sufficient legal basis to deepen EU–Russia relations.

---

[16] Agreement between the European Community and the Russian Federation on the facilitation of the issuance of visas to the citizens of the European Union and the Russian Federation OJ [2007] L 129/27.

[17] P. Kalinichenko, 'Legislative Approximation and Application of EU Law in Russia', in P. Van Elsuwege and R. Petrov (eds), *Legislative Approximation and Application of EU Law in the Eastern Neighbourhood of the European Union: Towards a Common Regulatory Space?* (London, Routledge 2014) 247.

[18] R. Petrov, 'The Partnership and Co-operation Agreements with the Newly Independent States', in A. Ott and K. Inglis (eds), *Handbook on European Enlargement. A Commentary on the Enlargement Process* (The Hague, Asser Press 2002) 177.

[19] See A.E. Kellermann, 'Impact of the EU Enlargement on the Russian Federation' (in Russian) (2005) 61(1) *Police and Law* 117.

[20] P. Leino and R. Petrov (n 3) 669–670.

[21] E.g. the EU–Russia roadmaps of 2005. There are roadmaps on a Common Economic Space; a Common Space of Freedom, Security and Justice; a Common Space of External Security; and a Common Space of Research and Education, including Cultural Aspects. Available online at www.eeas.europa.eu/russia/common_spaces (accessed 12 June 2015). In 2010, the EU–Russia roadmaps were supplemented by another soft law initiative – the 'Partnership for Modernisation', which includes a workplan with cooperation activities and common projects. See Joint Statement of the EU–Russia Summit of 31 May 2010 and Working Plan on Partnership for Modernisation of December 2010. See also http://formodernisation.com (accessed 12 June 2015).

[22] See P. Van Elsuwege, 'The Four Common Spaces: New Impetus to the EU-Russia Strategic Partnership?' in M. Maresceau (ed.), *Law and Practice of EU External Relations: Salient Features of a Changing Landscape* (Cambridge, Cambridge University Press 2008) 334–359.

Finally, the third layer of the bilateral relationship is based on a number of sectoral trade agreements concluded in 2011.[23] However, their effective implementation is problematic due to the lack of a new EU–Russia framework agreement.[24]

It is interesting to examine how the PCA has been applied by the Russian judiciary. In accordance with Art. 15(4)[25] of the Russian Constitution, the EU–Russia PCA forms part of the national legal order. The Russian judiciary treats the PCA as an international agreement, which contains self-executing rules within the domestic legal order. In case of conflict, Russian judges prefer to acknowledge the priority of the EU–Russia PCA over national legislation.[26] This makes the EU–Russia PCA an efficient instrument for bilateral cooperation without further implementation into the Russian legal system. Russian courts consider the EU–Russia PCA to be an international agreement that guarantees the protection of the rights and interests of Russian nationals and subjects in their economic relations with the EU. Since 1997, more than 20 judgments have been delivered regarding the application of this and other bilateral agreements (e.g. the 2000 EU–Russia agreement on cooperation in science and technology)[27] within the Russian legal order.

Russian courts have developed considerable experience in applying provisions of the EU–Russia PCA in their decisions, though mainly in fields related to the economy (trade, customs and tax). By contrast, there has been limited experience regarding the democratic and human rights clauses of the EU–Russia PCA in Russian judicial practice. This is not surprising since the agreement focuses more on economic relations than on political cooperation. Nonetheless, the Russian judiciary has acknowledged the importance of respecting democratic principles

---

[23] These agreements are: Agreement in the form of an Exchange of Letters between the European Union and the Russian Federation relating to the introduction or increase of export duties on raw materials [2012] OJ L 57/52; Agreement in the form of an Exchange of Letters between the European Union and the Government of the Russian Federation relating to the preservation of commitments on trade in services contained in the current EU-Russia Partnership and Cooperation Agreement [2012] OJ L 57/43; Agreement between the European Union and the Government of the Russian Federation on trade in parts and components of motor vehicles between the European Union and the Russian Federation [2012] OJ L 57/14; Agreement in the form of an Exchange of Letters between the European Union and the Russian Federation relating to the administration of tariff-rate quotas applying to exports of wood from the Russian Federation to the European Union [2012] OJ L 57/1.

[24] 'EU and Russia sign bilateral agreements ahead of Russia's WTO accession ceremony'. Available online at http://eeas.europa.eu/delegations/wto/press_corner/all_news/news/2011/20111216_kdg_rf_signature.htm (accessed 14 June 2015).

[25] 'Universally recognized principles and norms of international law as well as international agreements of the Russian Federation should be an integral part of its legal system. If an international agreement of the Russian Federation establishes rules, which differ from those stipulated by law, then the rules of the international agreement shall be applied.'

[26] More than 20 cases on applying the PCA and about 100 cases with links to EU law are known in Russian judicial practice today. See R. Petrov and P. Kalinichenko, 'The Europeanization of Third Country Judiciaries through the Application of the EU Acquis: the Cases of Russia and Ukraine' (2011) 60 *International and Comparative Law Quarterly* 337–339.

[27] [2000] OJ L 299/15.

and human rights for the partnership between Russia and the EU, as enshrined in Art. 2 of the EU–Russia PCA. The obligation on the Russian courts to respect these principles is rooted in the provisions of the Russian Constitution, which are reflected in the PCA.

The Russian judiciary also holds that that these principles are legally binding and form the basis of values shared by the EU, its Member States and Russia. For example, in the *YUKOS* case,[28] the Federal Commercial Court of Moscow District acknowledged that the obligation of Russian courts to recognize foreign judicial decisions, which can serve as the legal basis for the execution of judgments of any national court of an EU Member State,[29] stems from the general objectives of the EU–Russia PCA governing sincere cooperation between the parties to the agreement.[30] The Court stated: 'This provision of the Agreement corresponds to the constitutional principle of the rule of law, which obliges the Russian Federation to recognize, to comply and to protect human and citizen's rights and freedoms as a supreme value'.[31]

The PCA provisions also pay special attention to the principles of non-discrimination and access to justice. The corresponding provisions of the agreement have been the focus of judicial proceedings in the EU and in Russia. For instance, in the *Simutenkov*[32] case in 2005, the European Court of Justice held that the PCA's provision dealing with the principle of non-discrimination on the basis of nationality for legally employed workers had direct effect. The implication of the case is that Russian nationals can protect their rights provided by the PCA in EU domestic courts. This interpretation encouraged the Russian judiciary to confer direct effect on the selected provisions of the agreement on the basis of Art. 5(3) of the Federal Law of the Russian Federation 'On International Treaties of the Russian Federation'.[33] For example, in the *British Bank* v. *the Svyatoslav Fyodorov 'Eye Microsurgery' clinic* case,[34] the Russian Supreme Court considered that Art. 98 of the PCA, concerning access to justice, could form the legal grounds for the execution of a judgment by a British court in Russia. In the *Topol* case,[35] the High Arbitration Court of Russia confirmed the direct effect of that provision in the domestic legal order, which was an important guarantee for foreign investments.

The PCA has thus been a useful instrument of economic cooperation between the parties. In 2014 the EU and Russia celebrated the twentieth anniversary of this agreement. However, the agreement has become obsolete. Indeed, Russia's

---

[28] Judgment of the Federal Commercial Court of Moscow District of 2 March 2006 (KG-A40/698-06-P).
[29] Art. 98 of the EU–Russia PCA.
[30] Art. 2 of the EU–Russia PCA.
[31] Item 19 of the Judgment of the Federal Commercial Court of Moscow District of 2 March 2006.
[32] Case C-265/03 *Igor Simutenkov* v. *Ministerio de Educación y Cultura, Real Federación Española de Fútbol* [2005] ECR I-2579.
[33] See Federal Law of 15 July 1995 101-FZ 'On International Treaties of the Russian Federation' *SZ RF*, 1995, No 29, Art. 2757.
[34] Judgment of the Supreme Court of Russia of 7 June 2002 (5-G02-64).
[35] See Judgment of the Supreme Commercial Court of the Russian Federation of 1 October 2012 *Topol* v. *Rospatent* (BAC-6474/12).

accession to the WTO in 2012 made many of its provisions outdated.[36] In 2006, Russia initiated negotiations concerning a New Basic Agreement between itself and the EU to replace the PCA. This initiative was supported by the EU and negotiations started in 2008. Between 2008 and 2011, the parties agreed on several key points of the future agreement, but in December 2011 they decided to delay the negotiations. The EU–Russia summit of 2013 continued the talks on the New Basic Agreement, which aimed 'to provide a solid legal basis for EU-Russia relations, covering all areas of our relationship, most importantly trade, investment and energy';[37] however, no concrete results were achieved. In a speech on 27 September 2014 at the UN General Assembly, the Russian Foreign Minister[38] stated that the European partners had agreed to open negotiations on a free trade agreement between the EU and the EEU in the nearest future. Yet, regrettably, this announcement was not followed through. The Ukrainian crisis has removed the New Basic Agreement negotiations from the EU–Russia agenda and has prevented negotiations for a free trade agreement.

Trade disputes between the EU and Russia within the WTO

EU–Russia relations in the WTO context are useful in gauging trade tensions between the parties and are also an indication that the WTO partners have confidence that the WTO dispute settlement mechanism will be able to diffuse tensions between the parties.[39] Since its accession to the WTO in 2012, Russia has requested four consultations with WTO partners: three were addressed to the EU and one to Ukraine.[40] In parallel, the European Commission has requested consultation with Russia on five cases. Interestingly, with the development of the Ukrainian crisis, the number of requests has increased. In 2013 the EU requested consultation with Russia for the first time on recycling fees on motor vehicles.[41] Between late December 2013 and May 2015 the two parties in total submitted six requests for consultation (three each).

In December 2013, Russia submitted a request for consultation concerning cost adjustment methodologies and certain anti-dumping measures on imports from its

---

[36] P. Van Elsuwege, 'Towards a Modernisation of EU-Russia Legal Relations?' *CEURUS EU-Russia Papers* 5(2). Available online at http://ceurus.ut.ee/wp-content/uploads/2011/06/EU-Russia-Paper-51.pdf (accessed 2 June 2015).

[37] See the Memo 'EU Russia Summit' (Yekaterinburg, 3–4 June 2013).

[38] Address by Russian Foreign Minister Sergey Lavrov to the 69th session of the UN General Assembly, New York, 27 September 2014. Available online at www.mid.ru/brp_4.nsf/0/CDEA7854FF002B5A44257D62004F7236 (accessed 30 September 2014).

[39] For a full description of the disputes involving Russia in the WTO context, see P. Kalinichenko, 'Some Legal Issues of the EU-Russia Relations in the Post-Crimea Era: From Good Neighbourliness to Crisis and Back', in D. Kochenov and E. Basheska (eds), *Good Neighbourliness in the European Legal Context* (Leiden and Boston, Brill 2015) 348–351.

[40] See Ukraine – Anti-Dumping Measures on Ammonium Nitrate–Request for consultations by the Russian Federation, WT/DS 493 (7 May 2015).

[41] Russian Federation – Recycling Fee on Motor Vehicles – Request for consultations by the European Union, WT/DS 462/1 (11 July 2013). On 29 July 2013, the European Union and Ukraine requested

territory.[42] Russia claimed that the provisions of Arts. 2.1 and 2.5 of the EU Basic Anti-Dumping Regulation 2009[43] are incompatible with the WTO Anti-Dumping Code 1994.[44] The EU General Court's judgments of 7 February 2013 in cases involving several Russian chemical exporters were the basis of this request for consultation.[45] The judicature refused to admit differences between the WTO rules and the EU anti-dumping legislation concerning cost adjustment methodologies. Moreover, the Court pointed out that this methodology was a 'principle of law'.[46] In practice, the judicature repeated the EU position on dual prices on gas and therefore justified the main reason for anti-dumping sanctions against Russian exports.[47] However, this conclusion is questionable from a legal point of view; indeed, WTO rules do not allow such reasons for anti-dumping sanctions. This is why after the parties' consultations failed, Russia requested the establishment of a panel of arbitrators in June 2014.[48] This dispute shows that although the EU tries to formulate new principles in EU–Russia relations, Russia refuses to recognize them.

Russia submitted two further requests for consultation with the EU in May 2015. The first concerns the cost adjustment methodologies used by the European Union for the calculation of dumping margins in anti-dumping investigations.[49] The second is related to the EU Third Energy Package and its compliance with the rules of the GATT,[50] GATS,[51] TRIMs[52] and TBT Agreements.[53] More specifically, Russia questions the legality of provisions of 'the natural gas' Directive of 2009[54] and the implementation of the Directive in a number of Member States,

to join the consultations requested by Japan with Russia regarding the latter country's measures relating to a charge, the so-called recycling fee, imposed on motor vehicles. For more information, see www.wto.org/english/tratop_e/dispu_e/cases_e/ds463_e.htm (accessed 20 August 2015).

[42] European Union – Cost Adjustment Methodologies and Certain Anti-Dumping Measures on Imports from Russia – Request for consultations by the Russian Federation, WT/DS474/1 (9 January 2014).

[43] Council Regulation (EC) No 1225/2009 of 30 November 2009 on protection against dumped imports from countries not members of the European Community [2009] OJ L 343/51.

[44] Agreement on Implementation of Article VI of the General Agreement on Tariffs and Trade 1994 (Anti-Dumping Agreement).

[45] Case T-235/08, *Acron OAO and Dorogobuzh OAO* v. *Council of the EU* [2013] OJ C 101/15; Case T-459/08, *EuroChem MCC* v. *Council of the EU* [2009] OJ C 220/31.

[46] Case T-459/08 (n 45) para. 86.

[47] Concerning the dual price on gas problem in the EU-Russia relations, see G. Van der Loo, 'EU-Russia Trade Relations: It Takes WTO to Tango?' (2013) 40(1) *Legal Issues of Economic Integration* 7–32.

[48] European Union – Cost Adjustment Methodologies and Certain Anti-Dumping Measures on Imports from Russia – Request for the establishment of a panel by the Russian Federation, WT/DS474/4 (6 June 2015).

[49] European Union – Cost Adjustment Methodologies and Certain Anti-Dumping Measures on Imports from Russia – Second complaint, WT/DS494 (7 May 2015).

[50] The General Agreement on Tariffs and Trade.

[51] The General Agreement on Trade in Services.

[52] The Agreement on Trade-Related Investment Measures.

[53] The Agreement on Technical Barriers to Trade.

[54] Directive 2009/73/EC of the European Parliament and of the Council of 13 July 2009 concerning common rules for the internal market in natural gas and repealing Directive 2003/55/EC [2009] OJ L 211/94.

as well as the exceptions granted by the European Commission for certain projects and companies concerning the investment climate and competition within the internal gas market of the EU.[55]

Between April and October 2014 the EU also requested consultations with Russia in three cases, none of which prevented the start of a trade dispute.

The first request concerned certain Russian measures related to adopting, maintaining or applying an import ban or import restrictions on live pigs and other pig products from Lithuania and Poland. These measures prevent the importation of the products at issue from the EU into Russia and breach the Sanitary and Phytosanitary agreement.[56]

In May 2014 the European Commission submitted a new request for consultation with Russia within the scope of the WTO dispute settlement mechanism. This concerned the anti-dumping duties imposed by the Eurasian Economic Commission on light commercial vehicles from Germany and Italy. Short-term consultations among the parties achieved nothing, and the EU therefore requested the establishment of a panel of arbitrators.

In October 2014 the EU requested consultation with Russia over their excessive import duties on a number of products across various sectors. 'Those higher duties have a clear negative impact on European exports of paper products, refrigerators and palm oil that are worth approximately €600 million a year.'[57] Since the consultations failed, the EU proceeded with the next step in the WTO dispute settlement procedure.

Although the above-mentioned trade disputes were not the first between Russia and the EU, the increase in trade tensions between the EU and Russia at the start of the Ukrainian crisis cannot be accidental. This shows that this conflict impacted on EU–Russia trade relations.

Legal aspects of modern confrontation in EU–Russia relations

The Maidan protests and the ensuing conflict within the territory of Ukraine, including Russia's annexation of Crimea, have clearly poisoned both Ukraine–Russia and EU–Russia relations.

As a result of the Ukrainian crisis, the years of 'strategic partnership' seem to have been forgotten. The EU has isolated Russia by blocking the negotiation of its accession to international organizations (the OECD and the International Energy Agency). It has suspended bilateral summits, the implementation of regional cooperation programmes and negotiations on the liberalization of

---

[55] European Union and its Member States – Certain Measures Relating to the Energy Sector – Request for consultations by the Russian Federation, WT/DS476/1 (8 May 2015).
[56] Russian Federation – Measures on the Importation of Live Pigs, Pork and Other Pig Products from the European Union – Request for consultations by the European Union, WT/DS475/1 (14 April 2014).
[57] For more information, see http://trade.ec.europa.eu/doclib/press/index.cfm?id=1265 (accessed 20 August 2015).

visas,[58] as well as negotiations for a new bilateral agreement. In addition to these diplomatic measures, the EU introduced targeted sanctions of a political (i.e. visa bans) and economic nature in four waves between March 2014 and September 2014. Sanctions against Russia were introduced in the form of restrictions on the import and export of goods and services, and an arms embargo.[59] Restrictive measures against individuals,[60] in the form of travel bans and asset freezes, were imposed. Other entities – such as state-owned Russian banks and energy and defence companies – became the subject of access restrictions to the EU's capital markets. Restrictions on certain services required for oil projects (oil companies) were also introduced.[61]

How did Russia react? The State Duma and the Federal Council adopted Statements in which they condemned the EU for the sanctions against Russian officials.[62] However, it was not until the summer of 2014 that Russia responded to the EU restrictions. In accordance with the Russian Presidential Decree of 6 August 2014,[63] the Russian government introduced special economic measures

---

[58] http://europa.eu/newsroom/highlights/special-coverage/eu_sanctions/index_en.htm#2 (accessed 2 June 2015).

[59] Council Decision 2014/145/CFSP of 17 March 2014 concerning restrictive measures in respect of actions undermining or threatening the territorial integrity, sovereignty and independence of Ukraine [2014] OJ L 078/16; Council Regulation (EU) No 269/2014 of 17 March 2014 concerning restrictive measures in respect of actions undermining or threatening the territorial integrity, sovereignty and independence of Ukraine [2014] OJ L 078/6; Council Decision 2014/386/CFSP of 23 June 2014 concerning restrictions on goods originating in Crimea or Sevastopol, in response to the illegal annexation of Crimea and Sevastopol [2014] OJ L 183/70; Council Regulation (EU) No 692/2014 of 23 June 2014 concerning restrictions on the import into the Union of goods originating in Crimea or Sevastopol, in response to the illegal annexation of Crimea and Sevastopol [2014] OJ L 183/9; Council Decision 2014/512/CFSP of 31 July 2014 concerning restrictive measures in view of Russia's actions destabilising the situation in Ukraine [2014] OJ L 229/13; Council Regulation (EU) No 833/2014 of 31 July 2014 concerning restrictive measures in view of Russia's actions destabilising the situation in Ukraine [2014] OJ L 229/1.

[60] The political and military leadership of Crimea, those of the Luhansk and Donetsk regions and members of the Federation Council and of the Duma of the Russian Federation.

[61] For a full account of the EU's restrictive measures, see P. Kalinichenko, 'Some Legal Issues of the EU-Russia Relations in the Post-Crimea Era: From Good Neighbourliness to Crisis and Back' (n 39).

[62] Заявление Государственной Думы Федерального Собрания Российской Федерации от 18 марта 2014 г. 'О санкциях Соединенных Штатов Америки и Европейского Союза' (Zayavleniye Gosudarstvennoy Dumy Federalnogo Sobraniya Rossiyskoy Federatsii ot 18 marta 2014 g. 'O sanktsiyakh Soyedinennykh Shtatov Ameriki i Evropeyskogo Soyuza' – Statement of the State Duma of the Federal Assembly of the Russian Federation of 18 March 2014 'On the United States of America and the European Union Sanctions'), SZ RF, 24 March 2014, N 12 Article 1226; Заявление Совета Федервции Федерального Собрания Российской Федерации от 21 марта 2014 г. (Zayavleniye Sovieta Federatsii Federalnogo Sobraniya Rossiyskoy Federatsii ot 21 marta 2014 g. 'O sanktsiyakh Soyedinennykh Shtatov Ameriki i Evropeyskogo Soyuza' – Statement of the Federal Council of the Federal Assembly of the Russian Federation of 21 March 2014 'Concerning the United States of America and the European Union Sanctions'), SZ RF, 24 March 2014, N 12 Article 1205.

[63] Указ Президента Российской Федерации от 6 августа 2014 г. № 560 'О применении отдельных специальных экономических мер в целях обеспечения безопасности Российской Федерации'

aimed at providing security.⁶⁴ These measures included a ban on the import of agricultural products and food from countries implementing sanctions against Russia. Russia thus blocked European agriculture exports to Russia worth €11.8 billion.⁶⁵

More recently, in May 2015 Russia imposed travel bans on 89 EU citizens, including politicians and officials from EU Member States such as Germany, Poland, the Baltic states, the UK and Sweden who criticized Moscow's annexation of Crimea. The decision was taken in response to hostile acts against the Russian Federation, including the blacklisting of Russian citizens.⁶⁶

The sanctions imposed by the EU are questionable due to their unilateral nature. In fact, they were adopted outside of the UN Security Council. They may also be incompatible with EU legal standards. As stated by the conference of the representatives of the Member State governments:

> respect for fundamental rights and freedoms implies, in particular that proper attention is given to the observance and the due process rights of the individuals or entities concerned [by restrictive measures]. For this purpose and in order to guarantee a thorough judicial review of decisions subjecting an individual or entity to restrictive measures, such decisions must be based on clear and distinct criteria. These criteria should be tailored to the specifics of each restrictive measure.⁶⁷

(Ukaz Prezidenta Rossiyskoy Federatsii ot 6 avgusta 2014 No 560 'O priminenii otdelnykh specialnykh economicheskikh mer v tselyakh obespecheniya besopasnosti Rossiyskoy Federatsii' – Decree of the President of the Russian Federation of 6 August 2014 No 560 'On Application of Certain Special Economic Measures Aimed to Provide Security of the Russian Federation'), SZ RF, 11 August 2014, N 32, Article 4470.

[64] Постановление Правительства Российской Федерации от 7 августа 2014 г. № 778 'О мерах по реализации Указа Президента Российской Федерации' от 6 августа 2014 г. N 560 'О применении отдельных специальных экономических мер в целях обеспечения безопасности Российской Федерации' (Postanovleniye Pravitelstva Rossiyskoy Federatsii ot 7 avgusta 2014 g. No 778 'O merakh po realizatsii Ukaza Prezidenta Rossiyskoy Federatsii' ot 6 avgusta 2014 No 560 'O priminenii otdelnykh specialnykh economicheskikh mer v tselyakh obespecheniya besopasnosti Rossiyskoy Federatsii' – Ordinance of the Government of the Russian Federation of 7 August 2014 No 778; 'On Measures to Implement the Decree of the President of the Russia Federation' of 6 August 2014 No 560; 'On Application of Certain Special Economic Measures Aimed to Provide Security of the Russian Federation'), SZ RF, 11 August 2014, N 32, Article 4543. However, the Russian Government mitigated the sanction later. See Постановление Правительства Российской Федерации от 20 августа 2014 г. № 830 (Postanovleniye Pravitelstva Rossiyskoy Federatsii ot 20 avgusta 2014 g. No 830 – Ordinance of the Government of the Russian Federation of 20 August 2014 No 830), SZ RF, 25 August 2014, N 34, Article 4685.

[65] Delphine d'Amora, 'Putin Strikes Back Against Sanctions With Food Import Bans', *The Moscow Times*, 6 August 2014. Available online at www.themoscowtimes.com/business/article/putin-orders-agricultural-import-bans-on-countries-that-sanctioned-russia/504675.html (accessed 24 October 2014).

[66] www.ft.com/intl/cms/s/0/d2fee02a-077b-11e5-a58f-00144feabdc0.html?siteedition=intl (accessed 2 June 2015).

[67] See Declaration n. 25 on Arts. 61 H and 188 K of the Treaty on the Functioning of the European Union, included in the Final Act of the Intergovernmental Conference.

Although the Council has a broad discretion to adopt CFSP decisions, including those freezing the assets of individuals, the Court of Justice has the authority to review these decisions, and where blacklisting an individual is based on facts that are materially inaccurate and there is a manifest error in the assessment of facts, the Court can annul that decision, as has happened in several cases, the most recent of which was *Mazen Al-Tabbaa*.[68]

Several Russian nationals have introduced annulment actions before the EU General Court contesting the EU's restrictive measures on human rights and other grounds (including breach of the PCA)[69] or in terms of their legal basis.[70] A preliminary ruling before the Court of Justice is also pending. This was raised in the UK by an oil company, Rosneft, owned in part by the British company BP and in part by the Russian state, which was affected by the sanctions against Russia. The UK Divisional Court referred questions on the validity of the CFSP decision regarding the restrictive measures against Russia[71] and on the interpretation of the EU Regulation implementing the measures.[72] Although the Court considered the measures to be illegal, this has not prevented the Council from re-enacting them, after amending the statement of reasons at the basis of the listing. This is what happened in the *Ternavsky* case[73] concerning a Belarusian national. The applicant brought an annulment action against a number of measures adopted between 2012–13[74] and 2014[75] that included him in a list of people whose assets were frozen on account of the benefits received from Lukashenka's regime. The reasons originally justifying the listing were modified in 2014. The Court found that in 2012 the Council did not sufficiently show that Ternavsky had close ties with the president of Belarus and annulled the challenged acts. However, the applicant lost the case insofar as the measures adopted in 2014, which had the effect of re-listing him, were considered legal. Indeed, this time in the opinion of the Court, the reasons offered by the

---

[68] Judgment of 9 July 2014 in Joined Cases T-329/12 and T-74/13 *Mazen Al-Tabbaa* v. *Council of the European Union*, nyr. See also judgment of 16 July 2014 in case T-572/11 *Hassan* v. *Council of the European Union*, of 16 July 2014, nyr.

[69] See the pending cases, T-715/14 *NK Rosneft and Others* v. *Council* [2014] OJ C 431/40; T-720/14 *Rotenberg* v. *Council* [2015] OJ C 7/37; and T-734/14, *VTB Bank* v. *Council* [2015] OJ C 16/43.

[70] T-732/14 *Sberbank of Russia* v. *Council* [2015] OJ C 16/41.

[71] Council Decision 2014/145/CFSP of 17 March 2014 (n 59).

[72] Case C-72/15 *Rosneft* [2015] OJ C 155/12.

[73] See judgment of 21 May 2015 in case T-163/12 *Ternavsky* v. *Council*, nyr.

[74] These are: Implementing Decision 2012/171/CFSP of 23 March 2012 implementing Decision 2010/639/CFSP concerning restrictive measures against Belarus [2012] OJ L 87/95; the Council Implementing Regulation (EU) No 265/2012 of 23 March 2012 implementing Article 8a(1) of Regulation (EC) No 765/2006 concerning restrictive measures in respect of Belarus [2012] OJ L 87/37; Council Decision 2013/534/CFSP of 29 October 2013 amending Decision 2012/642/CFSP concerning restrictive measures against Belarus [2013] OJ L 288/69; Council Implementing Regulation (EU) No 1054/2013 of 29 October 2013 implementing Article 8a(1) of Regulation (EC) No 765/2006 concerning restrictive measures in respect of Belarus [2013] OJ L 288/1.

[75] Council Implementing Decision 2014/24/CFSP of 20 January 2014 implementing Decision 2012/642/CFSP concerning restrictive measures against Belarus [2014] OJ L 16/32 and of Council Implementing Regulation (EU) No 46/2014 of 20 January 2014 implementing Regulation (EC) No 765/2006 concerning restrictive measures in respect of Belarus [2014] OJ L 16/3.

Council convincingly showed that the applicant benefited from the support of the governmental regime.

Apart from the legal flows that the EU restrictive measures may have, the adoption of sanctions has not led Russia to change its behaviour and has attracted negative reactions from the business world.[76] Russian countersanctions have led to inflated food prices within the Russian domestic market and have come at great cost to the Russian people, even more so than have the EU sanctions.[77] If anything, the EU restrictive measures have exacerbated EU–Russia relations and have led Russia 'to cooperate more actively with Asian countries'.[78] It is to be hoped that these sanctions will be abolished.

Conclusions

Despite the Ukrainian crisis, the EU and Russia continue to share values and interests. Short-term political decisions cannot be allowed to lead to the termination of such an interdependence. New challenges and global threats demand closer cooperation and partnership rather than confrontation. Russia and the EU should be committed to working together in a long-term perspective. The idea of a 'common economic area from Lisbon to Vladivostok'[79] should be back on the agenda of Russia and other European countries.

However, all this can only happen by joint efforts. The reinforcement of ties between the EU and the USA on the one hand, and between Russia and a few BRICS countries on the other, are not viable strategies.

Both economic interdependency and common responsibility for European security impose a joint responsibility on the two parties for a mutual understanding. The EU also needs to cooperate with Russia in relation to the deep and comprehensive free trade area between the EU and Ukraine. It is not by chance that the so-called '[T]hree-party consultations on the EU–Ukraine Association Agreement/Deep and Comprehensive Free Trade Area' were established in 2014.[80] The parties to this Agreement have met Russian requests to suspend its entry into force until the end of 2015.

---

[76] See, for example, 'Association of European Businesses urges EU to refrain from sanctions against Russia', *ITAR-TASS*. Available online at http://en.itar-tass.com/economy/747335 (accessed 24 June 2015).

[77] Ben Kennedy, 'Who will Russia's food sanctions hurt more?', *CBS Moneywatch*, 7 September 2014. Available online at www.cbsnews.com/news/will-russian-food-sanctions-affect-western-agriculture (accessed 24 June 2015).

[78] See the speech of President Medvedev available online at www.presstv.ir/Detail/2015/06/12/415487/Russia-West-sanction-Ukraine (accessed 20 August 2015).

[79] Statement by President Barroso following the EU–Russia Summit, Brussels, 28 January 2014. Available online at europa.eu/rapid/press-release_SPEECH-14-66_en.htm (accessed 3 September 2015).

[80] The outcome of this consultation was published in May 2015 and concerns three hot topics of EU–Russia economic relations: a customs cooperation, technical barriers to trade and sanitary and phytosanitary issues. Joint Operational Conclusions by the European Commission, the Russian Federation and Ukraine. Available online at http://economy.gov.ru/wps/wcm/connect/economylib4/en/home/press/news/2015051901 (accessed 24 July 2015).

In addition to shared interests, Russia declares that it has values in common with the EU. Since the legal foundations underpinning their relations have become outdated, they could be revisited on the grounds of shared values, common interests and joint perspectives.

The 'war of sanctions', which has frozen official contacts and negotiations, and the halt in political cooperation between the NATO and Russia have not achieved anything. This crisis can only be overcome through dialogue. However, at the moment the main critics of the EU sanctions amongst EU Member States (Austria, Greece, Finland, Italy and Spain) are too weak to convince the other members to lift them.

The EU and Russia will have to overcome numerous hurdles to ensure that their relations return to the status of 'business as usual'. This largely depends on solving practical problems around the future of Ukraine. New formulas for European security are needed. The establishment of contacts and relations between the EU and Eurasian organizations for economic and security cooperation, such as the EAEU, the Collective Security Treaty Organization and the Shanghai Cooperation Organization, may be a promising start for the renewal of EU–Russia relations.

Bibliography

Alisievich, E.S. (2008) Russian Court Practice of Applying Legal Views of the European Court of Human Rights. In Hober, K. *The Uppsala Yearbook of East European Law 2006*. London: Wildy, Simmonds & Hill Publ. pp. 81–91.

Burkov, A. (2006) Implementatsia Konventsii po zashite prav cheloveka i fundamentalnykh svobod v rosiskikhsudakh. *Pravo Rossii; teoria is praktika*. 1. pp. 69–75.

Danilenko, G. (1999) Implementation of International Law in the CIS States: Theory and Practice. *European Journal of International Law*. 10(1). pp. 51–69.

Finner, S.E., Bogdanor, V. and Rudden B. (1995) Comparing Constitutions. In Hesse, J.J. and Wright, V. (1996) *Federalizing Europe? The Costs, Benefits, and Preconditions of Federal Political Systems*. Oxford: Claredon University Press.

Kalinichenko, P. (2011) The Court of Justice of the EU: The Case Law for Companies and Individuals from the C.I.S. Countries. *Baltic Horizons*. 17(114). pp. 101–106.

—(2012) *European Union: Law and Relations with Russia* (in Russian). Moscow: Norma.

—(2014) Legislative Approximation and Application of EU Law in Russia. In Van Elsuwege, P. and Petrov, R. *Legislative Approximation and Application of EU Law in the Eastern Neighbourhood of the European Union: Towards a Common Regulatory Space?* London: Routlege.

—(2015) Some Legal Issues of the EU-Russia Relations in the Post Crimea Era: From Good Neighbourliness to Crisis and Back. In Kochenov, D. and Basheska, E. *Good Neighbourliness in the European Legal Context*. Leiden and Boston: Brill.

Kellermann, A.E. (2005) Impact of the EU Enlargement on the Russian Federation. *Police and Law*. 61(1). pp. 94–120.

—(2005) The Impact of EU Enlargement on the Russian Federation. *Azerbaijani-Russian Journal of International and Comparative Law*. 2(1). pp. 157–204.

Leino, P. and Petrov, R. (2009) Between 'Common Values' and Competing Universals – The Promotion of the EU's Common Values through the European Neighbourhood Policy. *European Law Journal*. 15(5). pp. 654–671.

Maresceau, M. (2004) Bilateral Agreements Concluded by the European Community. *Collected Courses of the Hague Academy of International Law.* The Hague: Martinus Nijoff. 309.

Marochkin, S. (2007) International Law in the Courts of the Russian Federation: Practice of Application. *Chinese Journal of International Law.* 6(2). pp. 329–244.

Müllersson, R. (2014) Ukraine: Victim of Geopolitics. *Chinese Journal of International Law.* 13(1). pp. 133–145.

Petrov, R. (2002) The Partnership and Co-Operation Agreements with the Newly Independent States. In Ott, A. and Inglis, K. *Handbook on European Enlargement. A Commentary on the Enlargement Process.* The Hague: TMC Asser Press.

Petrov, R. and Kalinichenko, P. (2011) The Europeanization of Third Country Judiciaries through the Application of the EU Acquis: The Cases of Russia and Ukraine. *International and Comparative Law Quarterly.* 60(2). pp. 325–353.

Salikov, M. (2006) Aspects of Protection of Citizens of the Russian Federation in the European Court of Human Rights. *Uppsala Yearbook of East European Law.* pp. 92–106.

Van Elsuwege, P. (2008) The Four Common Spaces: New Impetus to the EU-Russia Strategic Partnership? In Maresceau, M. and Dashwood, A. *Law and Practice of EU External Relations: Salient Features of a Changing Landscape.* Cambridge: Cambridge University Press.

—(2012) Towards a Modernisation of EU-Russia Legal Relations? *CEURUS EU-Russia Papers.* 5(2). pp. 1–30. Available online at http://ceurus.ut.ee/wp content/uploads/2011/06/EU-Russia-Paper-51.pdf (accessed 2 June 2015).

7 'New values' for a new 'Great Russia'

Elena Dundovich

The West is rotting, the West is dying. Everything is collapsing and falling apart in a general ruin; Charlemagne's Europe, the Europe of 1815, the dominance of the Pope of Rome, all the thrones of the West, Catholicism, Protestantism, faith, long since lost, they will in reason fall into chaos. It will be a gigantic shipwreck, but on this wreck will float like the Holy Ark, bigger than ever, the Russian Empire.[1]

Introduction

Since 2000, Putin's presidencies have set out to create a new image of a 'Great Russia', both at home and abroad. His goals are to educate the new generations in patriotism and nationalism, and to achieve international recognition of Russia as a global actor. This chapter describes the strategy chosen by Putin to achieve these aims. The focus will be on Putin's determination to revive the Russian identity, reshape the historical memory, defend the Orthodox Church and the traditional family, and use rituals to celebrate the grandeur of Russia. The promotion of these 'new values' has led to clashes with the European Union on several occasions. The Ukraine crisis has strained EU–Russia relations to such an extent that the two international actors have become 'distant neighbours'.

The origin of Russian identity

During his presidencies, Putin has taken a series of initiatives aimed at reconsidering traditional Slavophile thought and its evolution up to the concept of Eurasism. The most prominent promoters of the tradition of the 'Russian identity', such as Berdyaev, Ilyin and Leont'ev, are exalted.

In the middle of the nineteenth century, 'Russian identity' was based on two essential points: first, that Russian civilization is distinct from Western civilization and follows its own special and original way. The second is that the Russian people have a world-historical mission. This concept finds its root in the upheaval caused in the Russian Empire by the Napoleonic campaign. The 'westernization' of the country, which was imposed by Peter the Great from 1682 and continued

---

[1] F.I. Tjutčev, '1849' in F. Herre (ed.), *Francesco Giuseppe* (Milan, Fabbri Editori 1998) 125.

until Alexander I, suffered a decisive setback following the invasion of Russia by Napoleon's Grand Army. This is when the 'Russian identity', conceived as something completely different from Western Europe, started to take root.[2]

The most important of all the changes concerned the use of the language. The nobility and the court had to quickly abandon French, which at that time had almost achieved the status of the first language. Russian was revived in its place. The use of the mother tongue led the intelligentsia of the country to rediscover the rural world, which had continued to speak Russian and which, at the same time, had preserved the characteristic elements of the traditional pre-Petrine Russia.[3]

The westernizers, who continued to think that it was necessary to encourage 'Europeanization' by taking the Western monarchies as a model, were opposed by the Slavophiles, who favoured the model of the old Muscovy,[4] which had been rejected at the time of the Petrine reforms.

Later, Slavophile thought evolved in the pan-Slavic ideal, which advocated the unification of all Slavic peoples, overlooking religious, linguistic and geopolitical differences. The ultimate goal was to create a great pan-Slavic empire that would have stretched from the Adriatic Sea to the Pacific Ocean and from the Aegean Sea to the Arctic Sea, under Moscow's hegemony as the Third Rome.

With the fall of the Empire and the October Revolution, more than two million Russians left the country. Although their political tendencies were very different, they were all united by a strong anti-Bolshevism. Most moved to Paris where, over the years, alternative political movements to communism began to take shape. It is in this context that the precursor to the Eurasist ideology found fertile ground.[5] This movement has its roots in Slavophile and pan-Slavic thought since it is based on the idea of 'Russian otherness' as opposed to the West. However, Russia's historical relationship with Asia is central for the supporters of this line of thought. It should be noted that in the second half of the nineteenth century, Asia was the centre of renewed attention by Russia, which had penetrated deep into the Caucasus, in Persia, Turkestan, Mongolia and Manchuria, clashing with British interests in Afghanistan and Tibet and with the Japanese in Korea. Like the proponents of the Slavic idea, the Eurasists saw Peter the Great as the main enemy of Russia, while they looked favourably on the Tartar and Mongolian world.[6]

Russian nationalism had mixed fortunes throughout the Soviet period. In the communist vision, a worker's nationality did not matter, only his or her class membership. On the basis of this assumption, Lenin had given birth to a new form of state community based on class solidarity rather than on nationalism. Thus the new Soviet Union, established in 1922, was also able to give minorities the

---

[2] D. Groh, *La Russia e l'autocoscienza d'Europa* (Torino, Einaudi 1980).
[3] V.O. Ključevskij, *Kurs Russkoi Istorii* (Izdat. Političeskoj Literatury, Moscow 1956) 242.
[4] The Grand Duchy of Moscow, also generally known simply as Muscovy, was a late medieval Rus' principality centred on Moscow and the predecessor state of the early modern Tsardom of Russia.
[5] N.S. Trubezkoj, *My i drugie* (Novikova & Sizemskaja, Moscow 1995) 97–110.
[6] C. Scocozza, *Un'identità difficile. Occidentalisti e slavofili russi tra passato e presente* (Naples, La Città del Sole 2007) 110–117.

right to self-determination with the conviction that this could prevent the onset of nationalism.[7]

In this historical context, the national feeling of minorities was encouraged, while the Russian feeling was not only ignored but even deterred where not directly fought against. The Bolshevik leadership saw the Great Russian chauvinism as a real enemy, as its traditional interests were in sharp conflict with the need to safeguard the fruits of the revolution. Precisely for this reason, after the creation of the USSR, the malaise of Russians (Русский – russki – as opposed to Российский – rossiski – or the inhabitants of Soviet Russia, without ethnic distinction) became increasingly evident as they saw their sense of national belonging repeatedly eroded.

This state of affairs changed radically with the start of the German attack aimed at the total destruction of the Soviet Union. Policies for the development of independent national-cultural identities, widely encouraged in the 1920s, were finally abandoned in favour of a decisive Russification of the peoples of the Union.[8] As the great leader of the Party, Stalin was converted into a heroic defender of the revived Holy Mother Russia.[9] On 3 July 1941, in his first wartime speech to the Union, he used the words 'brothers and sisters' or 'my friends', instead of the usual 'comrades', and launched his appeal in the name of his 'motherland' (and not in the name of the Communist Party as he had done previously). The myth of the first Great Patriotic War of 1812[10] was revived; the biographies of the generals who fought Napoleon were reprinted.

After the collapse of the USSR, many Russian scholars, encouraged by the presidency, began to do extensive research to redefine Russian identity. At first, it was imagined that Russia would evolve into a new form of national state, along the lines of Western Europe. However, soon the frustrations borne by the Russians in the early 1990s[11] led them to regret the ancient imperial dimension. Its loss was considered as one of the determining causes of its diminished international status.

The early 1990s were also witness to the onset of the neo-Eurasists, led by the political theorist Aleksandr Dugin. The model of the Eurasist vision was obviously the Great Russian Empire, promoting the incorporation of the Russian-speaking populations that had remained outside the borders of Federal Russia (about 25 million people). While in the 1920s the Eurasists' main enemy had been the Roman-Germanic world, currently the Anglo-Saxon world, with its libertines and libertarian lifestyle, is the antagonist.[12]

---

[7] A. Graziosi, *L'Urss di Lenin e Stalin. Storia dell'Unione Sovietica 1914–1945* (Bologna, Il Mulino 2007) 183–185, 202–208.

[8] T. Martin, *The Affirmative Action Empire: Nations and Nationalism in the Soviet Union, 1923–1939* (Ithaca, Cornell University Press 2004) 25.

[9] J. Gooding, *Rulers and Subjects* (London, Arnold 1996) 192.

[10] The Second World War would later become the Second Great Patriotic War.

[11] F. Benvenuti, *Russia Oggi* (Roma, Carocci 2013) 35.

[12] G. Celestino, 'Entrevista con Alexander Dugin: Un Largo Camino. La Quarta Teoría Política (4Tpes)'. Available online at https://4tpes.wordpress.com/2014/06/11/entrevista-con-alexander-dugin-un-largo-camino (accessed 16 May 2015).

Putin's attitudes toward the West and its values

In the late 1990s, the end of Yeltsin's era left a difficult legacy for Putin.[13] The regime abruptly lost its authoritarian-oligarchic connotation to become an authoritarian-bureaucratic system, thanks to the harsh offensive against the oligarchs. The most important key to the success of the first two Putin presidencies, characterized by strong pragmatism, resided in the economic recovery of the country. The economic well-being and private freedom that Russians began to enjoy in those years legitimized the president's authoritarianism.

The early years of Putin's regime were characterized by an attitude of strong openness towards Europe and the West. Following the attack on the Twin Towers in 2001, Putin was among the first world leaders to give open support to the United States in the war against Islamic terrorism. Indeed, in those years Russia was facing the harsh attack of the Chechen fundamentalist irredentists. The president referred on several occasions to the commonality of the roots (especially Christian) of the European peoples, with the declared hope of being able to create a Eurasian union from Lisbon to Vladivostok.[14] However, with the worsening of diplomatic relations, as a result of Western support for the so-called coloured revolutions, the Russian government changed its attitude.

The outcome was the 'patriotic involution' of Putin's third presidency. Whereas in the previous decade, the performance of the Russian economy had been the president's main source of legitimacy, after 2012 patriotism became a genuine glue for the country.[15]

A clear distinction between nationalism and patriotism is essential in order to understand this change.[16] Nationalism, as the Eurasists had been claiming since the 1990s, was responsible for Russia's greatest debacles in recent times, because with its illusion of a nation-state based on the European model, it had threatened to hamper the country's hegemonic ambitions. Patriotism was instead seen as instrumental to the rebirth of a 'new Russia'.[17] The West, after nearly twenty years, ceased to be a model. In the inaugural speech of his third term, addressed to the Federal Assembly, Putin declared: 'In patriotism I see the foundations of our policy being consolidated.' The official definition, accepted and proposed by the government, is to 'love your country', keeping in mind that 'true patriotism,

---

[13] L. Šestova, *Russia: Lost in Transition: The Yeltsin and Putin Legacies* (Washington, Carnegie Endowment for International Peace 2007) 38.

[14] A. Janov, 'Putin and the "Russian Idea"' (2013) Institute of Modern Russia. Available online at http://imrussia.org/en/analysis/nation/504-putin-and-the russian-idea (accessed 16 May 2015).

[15] R. Toscano, 'From KGB to Reactionary Nostalgia for Imperial Russia. Who is Vladimir Putin?' (2014) 1 ResetDOC. Available online at www.resetdoc.org/story/00000022461 (accessed 14 April 2015).

[16] O. Melnikova, 'The Spread of Russian Chauvinism' (2013) Institute of Modern Russia. Available online at http://imrussia.org/en/opinions/795-the-virus-of-the-russian-chauvinism (accessed 14 May 2015).

[17] N.A. Naročniskaja, 'On ne peut interdire aux Russes de s'appeler Russes' (2007) RSG. Available online at www.russiesujetgeopolitique.ru/on-ne-peut-interdire-aux-russes-de-sappeler-russes (accessed 19 April 2015).

as a particular expression of love for all mankind, cannot coexist with hatred against other nationalities.'[18] This definition, according to statistics compiled by the Levada Center, is the one currently accepted by the vast majority of Russians (68 per cent).[19]

It is not by chance that as of 2012 Dugin's political thought,[20] which was once considered extremist, has been adopted by the ruling political leadership, which often refers to the 'greatness, the exceptional nature and the moral paradigm of Russia.'[21] Dugin's writings[22] were included in the programmes of studies of Russian military academies. The Eurasist Movement (founded in 2001) and the Izborsk Club (an organization with the patriotic orientation of Eurasist inspiration, founded in 2012) have many politicians, intellectuals and high-ranking Orthodox clergy in their ranks.

The keystone of Putin's ideological project has become the 'grandeur of the country', without showing any preference for the communist or pre-revolutionary model. The president has become imbued with the nationalist thinking of the nineteenth century, whereby Russia has a natural vocation to power on a global scale. After more than a decade of confusion, any attempt to create a nation-state must be rejected. Putin's idea of Russia is that of a multinational empire where various nationalities live together under the common roof of Russian culture.[23] The imperial ambition of the country justifies Putin's authoritarian grip and the cult of the strong and charismatic leader (references to the 'great reformers' such as Ivan the Terrible, Peter the Great and Stalin, but also to Stolypin and Kolchak, are very frequent).[24]

The role of the Orthodox Church in forging Russian identity is crucial. Since taking office in the Kremlin, Putin has started assiduously attending churches and monasteries, as well as meeting frequently with Patriarch Alexy II. Under his presidency, the Church has acquired even greater strength. European states are accused of having betrayed their Christian roots, of having given way to moral relativism and of no longer being able to distinguish between good and evil in the name of political correctness.[25] Conversely, the support of the Church for Putin's

---

[18] Translated by the author.
[19] Data from a survey carried out by the Levada Center in Moscow on 21–25 February 2014 in B. Bruk, 'Has Patriotism in Russia Been Hijacked?' (2014) Institute of Modern Russia. Available online at http://imrussia.org/en/analysis/nation/735 (accessed 11 March 2015).
[20] A. Dugin, 'Geopolitique de la Novorossie: sauver Poutine' (2014) RSG. Available online at www.russiesujetgeopolitique.ru/le-renversement-de-poutine (accessed 1 March 2015).
[21] D. Remnik, 'Watching the Eclipse' (2014) NYM. Available online at www.newyorker.com/magazine/2014/08/11/watching-eclipse (accessed 13 April 2015).
[22] A. Dugin, *Fondements de la Géopolitique. L'avenir géopolitique de la Russie* (Moscow, Arkotgeia 1997) 100.
[23] Then as today, ethnic nationalism finds little support in Russia. The idea of Russification, which culminated in the twilight of the nineteenth century without finding any success, is not at the moment seriously considered, so that, out of 53 nationalist organizations existing today in Russia, only 7 have an underlying ethnic principle.
[24] V.V. Putin, *Memorie d'oltrecortina* (Roma, Carocci 2001) 209.
[25] D. Trenin, 'A Practical Approach to EU-Russian Relations' (2014) ROPV. Available online at www.russiaotherpointsofview.com/2014/01/a-practical-approach-to-eu-russian-relations.htlm (accessed 16 April 2015).

regime has been absolute,[26] especially after he distanced himself from Europe. The conservative policies of the current leadership, displayed in the laws against blasphemy and the homosexual and libertarian propaganda of the Western press, perfectly match the Church's ideals. An emblematic case is that of Pussy Riot (2012), a punk band and the creators of a blasphemous anti-Putin performance in a cathedral in Moscow for which its members were arrested.

Putin has made himself the champion of 'traditional European values' as opposed to the 'new European values' based on 'boundless tolerance', which leads to rampant perversion and immorality. Europe has abandoned and disowned its Christian roots in the name of an 'ultra-liberal' vision. During the second presidential campaign, Putin benefited from the support of the Orthodox Church and turned his attention to the defence of key elements of society, such as religion, patriotism and the traditional family. The rejection of Europe as a 'moral power' unleashed a series of repressions against the so-called foreign agents (i.e. the various NGOs operating in Russia). They are seen as 'fifth columns' operating on behalf of the corrupt West, aimed at undermining the foundations of Russian society itself and spreading a distorted image of the country abroad.

The historical memory

In a speech in November 2003, Putin stressed that it was necessary to purify Russian history of its negative aspects. The past is considered only as a series of victories, heroism and enormous achievements. His words were: 'Our duty is to remind our young generations – the "naši" – that Russia has always been a great power.'[27]

Since Putin's rise to power, great attention has been devoted to the question of historical memory. Emphasis was placed on the 'First Great Patriotic War'[28] and efforts were made to dismiss the crimes of Stalinism. Any voice outside the chorus was silenced. This was the case of the Center for Research and Information (NITs) of the Memorial Association, which in 2008 was accused of wanting to spread a distorted image of the past and of damaging the international image of Russia. The Center's archives were searched and a series of documents on the history of terror and the Gulag were confiscated.[29]

In 2009 the authorities' interference became even more oppressive, with a series of legislative proposals whose aim was to discourage historical narratives which were different from those emerging from the official historiography. In addition,

---

[26] G. Galeazzi, 'Putin, the Last Tsar: The Orthodox Church's Approval' (2012) VI. Available online at http://vaticaninsider.lastampa.it/en/world-news/detail/articolo/russia-15048 (accessed 19 April 2015).

[27] A. Roginiskij, 'Mantenere viva la memoria del Gulag nella Russia d'oggi' in G. Nissim (ed.), *Storie di uomini giusti nel Gulag* (Milan, Mondadori 2004) 320.

[28] L. Giannotti, *Putin e la Russia* (Roma, Editori Riuniti-University Press 2014) 105 and I. Torbakov, 'History, Memory and National Identity' in M. Laruelle (ed.), *Russian Nationalism, Foreign Policy and Identity Debates in Putin's Russia: New Ideological Patterns after the Orange Revolution* (Stuttgart, Ibidem-Verlag 2014) 61.

[29] Available online at www.fidh.org/IMG/pdf/Ru2412en.pdf (accessed 10 July 2015).

the government reached its goal in setting up a 'Commission to counter attempts to falsify history against the interests of Russia.'[30]

In this context, while during the Soviet age the rulers of the Imperial era were denigrated, today they enjoy general support. Indeed, they are greeted as the founders of the Great Empire and the defenders of their country from the enemy. For example, whereas in 1994 only 4 per cent of the population recognized Nicholas II as a true patriot, in 2013 48 per cent of Russians considered him among the most esteemed heads of state in the history of the twentieth century.[31]

As to Lenin and the early revolutionaries, they are accused of encouraging exasperated defeatism among the troops. They were forced to sign the most humiliating and harsh peace treaty in Russian history. Finally, they stirred up a civil war in the name of a doctrine that had nothing to do with the Russian tradition.

The rehabilitation of the First World War, which had been labelled as imperialist between 1914 and 2014, also needs highlighting. Putin recently inaugurated the first monument to this 'forgotten war' on Poklonnaya Hill in Moscow.[32] This conflict has become part of Russian military glory, together with the war against Napoleon and the Second World War. Heroes and glorious actions of the war must be celebrated with movies, documentaries and monuments in cities throughout the entire Federation. The first museum dedicated to the Great War was recently opened in St. Petersburg.[33]

The greatest focus, however, has been devoted to the memory of Stalin's dictatorship. He is seen, on the one hand, as the person responsible for unprecedented mass atrocities but, on the other, as the leader who brought the USSR to the level of world superpower.

To sum up, as in the previous era history proves to be a powerful ideological weapon. It is not a coincidence that in 2013 a new plan was passed to use unified textbooks in the Federation. In these manuals Stalinism is extensively rehabilitated (especially the NKVD, the predecessor of the KGB, Putin's former employer), and the dissolution of the USSR (as a geopolitical entity, not as an ideological power) is presented as a catastrophe.[34]

Rituals and symbols

In recent years, special attention has also been devoted to rituals, symbols and ceremonies to celebrate the grandeur of the president and his close union with

---

[30] H. Blanc and R. Lesnik, *Les prédateurs du Kremlin* (Paris, Seuil 2009) 200–201.

[31] A. Morozov, 'Post-Soviet Russia Has Mixed Feelings for Tsar Nicholas II' (2013) 1 RBTH. Available online at http://in.rbth.com/society/2013/07/17/post-soviet_russia_has_mixed_feelings_for_tsar_nicholas_ii_27185.html (accessed 25 May 2015).

[32] V.V. Putin, 'Speech for the inauguration of the Monument to the Heroes of the Great War' (2014). Available online at www.youtube.com/watch?v=K81T66P7MGg (accessed 28 May 2015).

[33] A. Janov, 'The Lessons of the First World War, or Why Putin's Regime Is Doomed' (2014) Institute of Modern Russia. Available online at http://imrussia.org/en/analysis/nation/800-the-lessons-of-the-first-world-war-or-why-putins-regime-is-doomed (accessed 30 March 2015).

[34] V. Kara-Murza, 'The Approved Past: How History Will Be Taught to Russia's Children' (2013) Institute of Modern Russia. Available online at http://imrussia.org/en/analysis /nation/600-the-approved-past-how-history-will-be-taught-to-russias-children (accessed 19 April 2015).

the various institutions and the population of the country. Since his appearance in 2000 at the inauguration of Putin's presidency, the presence of Patriarch Alexy II behind the president has been very prominent, together with the Presidential Regiment (heir of the Kremlin Regiment, responsible for the safety of the palaces of the Citadel and the Lenin mausoleum), with their new nineteenth century-style uniforms, explicitly reminiscent of the models of the late empire. Since 2000 the inauguration of Putin's presidencies has taken place in the Grand Kremlin Palace (formerly the imperial residence in Moscow), in the rich halls of St. George and St. Andrew's, where the new president, cheered on by two wings of the crowd made up of the country's highest dignitaries, holds a keynote talk. He attends a parade in his honour at the foot of the steps of the Palace of the Facets, from where the tsars used to be acclaimed by the crowds during their coronations.

In addition, Putin has also instigated other changes reminiscent of Soviet aesthetics by reintroducing school uniforms and the title of 'labour hero'. As in the Soviet era, youth organizations have attracted renewed interest.[35] The two main active organizations at the moment are the Young Guards (a name that clearly refers to the Soviet precedent), which is part of the United Russia Party, and the nashi (Наши, ours), which is directly connected to the president. Both organizations emphasize the value of 'brotherhood among peoples' and anti-fascism and glorify the Second Great Patriotic War (World War II). In a similar fashion, they both support traditional forms of marriages and the family in general (possibly large in size), religion and the army. They also promote anti-abortion campaigns and strive to protect the foreign image of Russia, especially in former Soviet countries, thus counteracting all forms of historical revisionism. As with any organization of this type, they are also seen as forms of social elevation or as springboards for political careers, and are often promoters of defamatory campaigns against the opposition to the regime.

A special mention should be made regarding the revival of the Cossacks. Originating from Little Russia, they had always been loyal servants of the Imperial Crown. Putin's presidencies have witnessed the reopening of military academies that preserve the characteristic elements of Cossack tradition and culture. The government used these special troops both in Transnistria (where the Cossacks reappeared in 1992) and in Georgia (2008) and, more recently, in Ukraine. Finally, a large detachment of Cossacks, charged with overseeing law and order, was deployed during the Olympic Games in Sochi (2014).[36]

The objectives of Putin's strategy could never have been achieved without tight control of the mass media. The first hint of Putin's media policy was given in his controversial speech of 26 October 2000, when he announced that he would not tolerate criticism from the media in the hands of the oligarchs. The opportunity

---

[35] A. Janov, 'The Young Guard, or "Russification of the Spirit"' (2013) Institute of Modern Russia. Available online at http://imrussia.org/en/analysis/nation/771-the-young-guard-or russification-of-the-spirit (accessed 16 April 2015).

[36] E. Barry, 'The Cossacks Are Back. May the Hills Tremble' (2013) NYT. Available online at www.nytimes.com/2013/03/17/world/europe/cossacks-are-back-in-russia-may-the-hills-tremble. (accessed 16 April 2015).

was thus opened up for new restrictive measures that in the West were considered as an attack against freedom of speech. Russia's population favoured Putin's fight against the oligarchs who controlled the media. Vladimir Guzinsky's media companies, such as NTV, the radio station Ekho Moskvy and the newspaper Segodnya, became the property of Gazprom. Berezovsky was forced to cede control of ORT, the most important Russian TV channel after the collapse of the Soviet regime. Today, state agencies control almost all the mass media. For example, in 2012, during the last presidential election, it was reported that 73 per cent of the population used state sources of information.[37]

Russia's foreign policy during Putin's presidencies

At the time of Putin's first election, Russia's status in the international arena was as appalling as its domestic one. The country was dominated by a strong sense of frustration. This sense of hopelessness was further increased by the perception of the West's betrayal regarding its commitments to the Soviet leadership. In February 1990 Western diplomats had indeed committed not to extend the Atlantic Pact to former Iron Curtain countries. However, this promise was blatantly violated in the course of the following years, when the former Warsaw Pact countries and later the Baltic Republics, once fully part of the USSR, were invited to accede to NATO.

Putin's first mandate was still characterized by his willingness to cooperate with the United States and its allies. This favourable attitude is revealed in his words in a BBC interview, in which he announced: 'I cannot imagine my own country as isolated from Europe and from what we often call the civilized world. This is why I can hardly look at NATO as an enemy.'[38] More concretely, the president provided support to US President George W. Bush following 9/11, within the anti-Afghanistan Coalition, and also agreed to the deployment of troops in Georgia and Central Asia. Finally, he gave his consent to the cancellation of the Anti-Ballistic Missile Treaty (ABMT) in force between 1972 and 2002.

The two countries were at that time brought very close by the common threat represented by terrorism. Indeed, these were the early years of the second Chechen war (1999–2009), involving a series of ferocious Islamist terrorist acts. However, the government in Moscow felt that the concessions made to the United States were not appreciated as an act of openness toward the West, but were rather considered as the result of the United States' leading role in the international community. In the following years, relations between Russia and the West deteriorated further after the manifest support shown by the West for the coloured revolutions (Georgia, 2003; Ukraine, 2004–2005; and Kyrgyzstan, 2005). Other geopolitical

---

[37] E. Vartanova, 'The Russian Media Model in the Context of Post-Soviet Dynamics' in D.C. Hallin and P. Mancini (eds), *Comparing Media Systems Beyond the Western World* (Cambridge, Cambridge University Press 2012) 119–142.
[38] D. Remink, 'Watching the Eclipse' (2014) NYT. Available online at www.newyorker.com/magazine/ 2014/08/11/watching-eclipse (accessed 23 April 2015).

events exacerbated these relations, giving the impression that the United States in particular was trying to expand its range of influence at the expense of its former enemy. This perception was very strong after it concluded bilateral agreements with Poland and the Czech Republic on the hosting of the anti-missile shield and after it supported Kosovo's secession from Serbia (2008). Russia reacted by using its energy policy strategically and by founding the Eurasian Customs Union with Belarus and Kazakhstan (2010), with the aim of gradually expanding it to other states of the former USSR.

The new values promoted by Putin naturally had an impact on his foreign policy.[39] Moscow's sharp change in attitude in the field of foreign policy was made very clear in the Russia–Georgia conflict in August 2008, where the response to the provocations of the small but aggressive Caucasian country was as immediate as it was tough and overwhelming.

As far as the European Union is concerned, Moscow did not willingly sit by during the 2004 enlargement of the Union. Despite this, during Putin's first and second presidencies, relations between the EU and Russia were decidedly less tense than those with the United States. Once again, the turning point was the Georgian war, when European support for Georgia enraged Russia's leaders. In 2009 the inauguration of the EU's Eastern Partnership strengthened the idea that the Europeans were pushing the limits of their natural and historic area of influence too far, directly threatening Russia's interests. This sense of being surrounded was further increased by trade initiatives such as the opening of the Trans-Pacific Partnership (TPP) negotiations between the United States and other partners, including some Asian countries, and the Transatlantic Trade and Investment Partnership (TTIP) with the European Union.

Although in 2010 Putin was still a promoter of a Eurasian Union that would reach from Lisbon to Vladivostok, the political climate deteriorated over a period of a few years. In fact, the Eurasian Union was created but only with a Russia-centric nature, without any EU countries. Relations between Moscow and Brussels progressively deteriorated during the association agreement negotiations with Ukraine. The situation reached a serious impasse with the secession of Crimea, the annexation by Russia and the ensuing imposition of sanctions.[40]

Over the past 15 years, and particularly during the first two terms of Putin's presidencies, in reality the Kremlin's foreign policy has sought to keep an equal distance from other world powers (the so-called multivectoralism). The aggressive and nationalist tones were basically used only for the purposes of internal mobilization, propaganda and legitimation. The two significant exceptions to this general trend are represented by the Georgian and Ukrainian crises. In both cases domestic and foreign policies were closely welded, significantly increasing the influence of the most intransigent fringes both in the population and the ruling political leadership itself.

---

[39] S. Giusti, *La proiezione esterna della Federazione russa* (Pisa, ETS 2012).
[40] See P. Kalinichenko's chapter in this volume.

In recent years, and especially since the outbreak of the crisis in Ukraine, Putin has on several occasions been accused by the West of being a leader who has lost a sense of proportion and is suffering from a complete detachment from reality. However, facts suggest that the situation is quite different. Patriotic feelings cement the country, and the president's power and popularity have been strengthened rather than weakened by the Western attitude. Indeed, competition with the West, and the resulting sense of being surrounded, reinforces Putin's position and diverts the population's attention from the difficult economic situation and other domestic issues that plague the country. The sanctions applied by the EU and the United States have been instrumentalized by the Kremlin administration. On the one hand, Putin can blame the West's sanctions for the poor state of the Russian economy. On the other, the sanctions have been used by the government as an opportunity to carry out the necessary reforms and modernization of the country.

Putin's speech to the Federal Assembly in December 2014 highlights the presidency's long-term objectives. These are consolidating Crimea's integration into the Russian Federation, advancing the programme of reforms and decreasing the country's economic dependence on the export of gas and oil.

Another central point is the strengthening of international relations with alternative partners to the Atlantic world. In the president's speech, there was a clear but measured condemnation of the attitude held by the West, primarily the United States. They are accused of preventing the revival of Russia as a great power and of trying to erode its traditional areas of influence. The discourse on national defence of 26 December 2014 confirmed this trend. In this presidential speech, emphasis was placed on the need to strengthen Russia's ties with the Asian allies of the Collective Security Treaty Organization (CSTO), whose members are Armenia, Belarus, Kazakhstan, Kyrgyzstan and Tajikistan, and with its partners of the Shanghai Cooperation Organization (SCO), BRICS and Arab countries.

Putin certainly cannot ignore Russia's Western partners. However, the only opportunity offered to the West by the Kremlin is that of an equal partnership. Therefore, although the West is not officially an opponent, it is still a powerful competitor, a keen rival and the source of the greatest risks and military threats.

Bibliography

Andolenko, S. (2013) *History of the Russian Army*. Bologna: Odoya.
Barry, E. (2013) The Cossacks Are Back. May the Hills Tremble. *New York Times*. 16 March 2013. Available online at www.nytimes.com/2013/03/17/world/europe/cossacks-are-back-in-russia-may-the-hills-tremble.html?_r=0 (accessed 16 April 2015).
Benvenuti, F. (2013) *Russia Oggi*. Roma: Carocci.
Blanc, H. and Lesnik, R. (2009) *Les prédateurs du Kremlin*. Paris: Seuil.
Bruk, B. (2014) Has Patriotism in Russia Been Hijacked? 8 May 2014. Available online at http://imrussia.org/en/analysis/nation/735 (accessed 11 March 2015).
Celestino, G. (2014) Entrevista con Alexander Dugin: Un Largo Camino. *La Quarta Teoria Politica (4Tpes)*. Available online at https://4tpes.wordpress.com/2014/06/11/entrevista-con-alexander-dugin-un-largo-camino (accessed 16 May 2015).

Dugin, A. (1997) *Fondements de la Géopolitique. L'Avenir Géopolitique de la Russie*. Moscow: Arkotgeia.
—(2014) Geopolitique de la Novorossie: Sauver Poutine. 7 October 2014. Available online at www.russiesujetgeopolitique.ru/le-renversement-de-poutine (accessed 1 March 2015).
Galeazzi, G. (2012) Putin, The Last Tsar: The Orthodox Church's Approval. 5 November 2012. Available online at (http://vaticaninsider.lastampa.it/en/news/detail/articolo/russia-rusia-15048 (accessed 19 April 2015).
Giannotti, L. (2014) *Putin e la Russia*. Roma: Editori Riuniti-University Press.
Giusti, S. (2012) *La proiezione esterna della Federazione russa*. Pisa: ETS.
Gooding, J. (1996) *Rulers & Subjects*. London: Arnold.
Graziosi, A. (2007) *L'Urss di Lenin e Stalin. Storia dell'Unione Sovietica 1914–1945*. Bologna: Il Mulino.
Groh, D. (1980) *La Russia e l'autocoscienza d'Europa*. Torino: Einaudi.
Janov, A. (2013) Putin and the 'Russian Idea'. 1 July 2013. Available online at http://imrussia.org/en/analysis/nation/504-putin-and-the russian-idea (accessed 16 May 2015).
—(2013) The Young Guard, or 'Russification of the Spirit'. 9 July 2014. Available online at http://imrussia.org/en/analysis /nation/771-the-young-guard-or russification-of-the-spirit (accessed 16 April 2015).
—(2014) The Lessons of the First World War, or Why Putin's Regime is Doomed. 5 September 2014. Available online at http://imrussia.org/en/analysis/nation/800-the-lessons-of-the-first-world-war-or-why-putins-regime-is-doomed (accessed 30 March 2015).
Kara-Murza, V. (2013) The Approved Past: How History Will be Taught to Russia's Children. Institute of Modern Russia. 7 November 2013. Available online at http://imrussia.org/en/analysis/nation/600-the-approved-past-how-history-will-be-t aught-to-russias-children (accessed 19 April 2015).
Ključevskij, V.O. (1956) *Kurs Russkoi Istorii*. Moscow: Progress.
March, L. (2014) Is Nationalism Rising in Russian Foreign Policy? In Laruelle, M. *Russian Nationalism, Foreign Policy and Identity Debates in Putin's Russia*. Stuttgart: Ibidem-Verlag.
Martin, T. (2004) *The Affirmative Action Empire. Nations and Nationalism in the Soviet Union, 1923–1939*. Ithaca: Cornell University Press.
Melnikova, O. (2013) The Spread of Russian Chauvinism. 28 August 2014. Available online at http://imrussia.org/en/opinions/795-the-virus-of-the-russian-chauvinism (accessed 14 May 2015).
Morozov, A. (2013) Post-Soviet Russia Has Mixed Feelings for Tsar Nicholas II. 17 July 2013. Available online at http://in.rbth.com/society/2013/07/17/post-soviet_russia_has_mixed_feelings_for_tsar_nicholas_ii_27185.html (accessed 25 May 2015).
Naročniskaja, N.A. (2015) *On ne peut interdire aux Russes de s'appeler Russes*. Available online at www.russiesujetgeopolitique.ru/on-ne-peut-interdire-aux-russes-de-sappeler-russes (accessed 19 April 2015).
Putin, V.V. (2011) *Memorie d'oltrecortina*. Roma: Carocci.
—(2014) Speech for the inauguration of the Monument to the Heroes of the Great War. YouTube. Available online at www.youtube.com/watch?v=K81T66P7MGg (accessed 28 May 2015).
Remnik, D. (2014) Watching the Eclipse. *The New Yorker.* 11 August 2014. Available online at www.newyorker.com/magazine/2014/08/11/watching-eclipse (accessed 13 April 2015).
Roginiskij, A. Mantenere viva la memoria del Gulag nella Russia d'oggi. In Nissim, G. (2004) *Storie di uomini giusti nel Gulag*. Milano: Mondadori.

Scocozza, C. (2007) *Un'identità difficile. Occidentalisti e slavofili russi tra passato e presente.* Napoli: La Città del Sole.
Šestova, L. (2007) *Russia: Lost in Transition: The Yeltsin and Putin Legacies.* Washington: Carnegie Endowment for International Peace.
Torbakov, I. (2014) History, Memory and National Identity. In Laruelle, M. *Russian Nationalism, Foreign Policy and Identity Debates in Putin's Russia.* Stuttgart: Ibidem-Verlag.
Toscano, R. (2014) From KGB to Reactionary Nostalgia for Imperial Russia. Who Is Vladimir Putin? 20 November 2014. Available online at www.resetdoc.org/story/00000022461 (accessed 14 April 2015).
Trenin, D. (2014) *A Practical Approach to EU-Russian Relations.* 23 January 2014. Available online at www.russiaotherpointsofview.com/2014/01/a-practical-approach-to-eu-russian-relations.htlm (accessed 16 April 2015).
Trubezkoj, N.S. (1995) *My i drugie.* Moscow: Novikova & Sizemskaja.
Tjutčev, F.I. (1998) 1849. In Herre, F. *Francesco Giuseppe.* Milano: Fabbri Editori.
Vartanova, E. (2012) The Russian Media Model in the Context of Post Soviet Dynamics. In Hallin, D.C. and Mancini, P. *Systems Beyond the Western World.* Cambridge: Cambridge University Press.

Part IV
The ENP and the principle of coherence

8 The European Neighbourhood Policy's value conditionality

From enlargements to post-Crimea

Dimitry Kochenov and Elena Basheska

Introduction

The European Neighbourhood Policy (ENP) story started with the idea of a 'Wider Europe', formulated shortly before the 2004 eastern enlargement as the first response to the challenge of the changing geopolitical reality.[1] The renewed Union emerged as a leading regional actor and was keen to capitalize on this potential.[2]

In dealing with the new neighbours the EU set out to create a 'ring of friends'[3] to ensure stability, prosperity and peace in the neighbouring countries engaged

---

[1] As presented in the letter (requested by GAERC) by Chris Patten and Javier Solana at an informal meeting of the Foreign Ministers in September 2002.

[2] Literature on the ENP is growing very fast. See, most importantly, N. Ghazaryan, *The European Neighbourhood Policy and the Democratic Values of the EU: A Legal Analysis* (Oxford, Hart Publishing 2014). See also R. Petrov and P. Van Elsuwege (eds), *Legislative Approximation and Application of EU Law in the Eastern Neighbourhood of the European Union: Towards a Common Regulatory Space?* (London, Routledge 2014); C. Kaunert and S. Léonard (eds), *European Security Governance and the European Neighbourhood After the Lisbon Treaty* (London, Routledge 2013); B. Van Vooren, *EU External Relations Law and the European Neighbourhood Policy: A Paradigm for Coherence* (London, Routledge: 2012); L. Delcour and E. Tulmets (eds), *Pioneer Europe? Testing EU Foreign Policy in the Neighbourhood* (Baden-Baden, Nomos 2008); R. Zaiotti, 'Of Friends and Fences: Europe's Neighbourhood Policy and the "Gated Community Syndrome"' (2007) 29(2) *European Integration* 143; G. Sasse, '"Conditionality-lite": The European Neighbourhood Policy and the EU's Eastern Neighbours' in N. Casarini and C. Musu (eds), *European Foreign Policy in an Evolving International System: The Road towards Convergence* (Basingstoke, Palgrave 2007) 163; M. Cremona and G. Meloni (eds), 'The European Neighbourhood Policy: A Framework for Modernisation?' (2007) 21 *EUI Working Paper Law*; R. Balfour and A. Missiroli, 'Reassessing the European Neighbourhood Policy' (2007) 54 *EPC Issue Paper*; M. Cremona and C. Hillion, 'L'Union fait la force? Potential and Limitations of the European Neighbourhood Policy as an Integrated EU Foreign and Security Policy' (2006) 39 *EUI Working Paper*; A. Magen, 'The Shadow of Enlargement: Can the European Neighbourhood Policy Achieve Compliance' (2006) 12 *Columbia Journal of European Law* 383; R. Dannreuter, 'Developing the Alternative to Enlargement: The European Neighbourhood Policy' (2006) 11 *European Foreign Affairs Review* 183; F. Attinà and R. Rossi (eds), *European Neighbourhood Policy: Political, Economic and Social Issues* (Catania, Catania University Press 2004).

[3] See Speech by José Manuel Barroso, President of the European Commission, on 'The European Union and the Emerging World Order – Perceptions and Strategies', at the 7th ECSA World Conference (Brussels, 30 November 2004), available at http://europa.eu/rapid/press-release_SPEECH-04-499_en.htm (accessed 17 July 2014). See also some of the key documents outlining

in the process of transformation to come closer to internalizing the goals set out in the Treaties.[4] While plentiful congratulatory accounts exist, EU pre-accession strategy aside,[5] prosperity, peace and other values cherished within the Union have not been guaranteed on the enforcement side.[6]

The ENP was to represent a new approach to the EU's neighbourhood, deeply rooted in international law. In particular, the principle of good neighbourly relations between states in international law designates a model of interstate relations or a certain type of tie between neighbouring states, providing for peaceful coexistence, dialogue and cooperation, and is based on the main principles in international law embodied in Art. 2 of the UN Charter.[7] Article 3(5) TEU imposes an obligation on the Union to contribute to the 'strict observance and the development of international law, including respect for the principles of the United Nations Charter' in its relations with the wider world.[8] In addition, Art. 21(1) TEU refers to 'respect for the principles of the United Nations Charter and international law.' Thus, the EU has committed to respect and promote international law in general, as well as the UN principle on which good neighbourly relations rests, in particular in its relations with the 'wider world', similar to what one would expect of individual states. New Association Agreements with ENP countries provide, for instance, that:

> [T]he respect for democratic principles, human rights and fundamental freedoms and respect for the principle of the rule of law, promotion of respect for

---

the basics of the ENP: Commission (EC), 'Wider Europe – Neighbourhood: A New Framework for Relations with our Eastern and Southern Neighbours', COM (2003) 104 final, 11 March 2003, 4; European Commission (EC), 'European Neighbourhood Policy: Strategy Paper', COM (2004) 373 final, 12 May 2004; European Commission, 'On Strengthening the European Neighbourhood Policy,' COM (2006) 726 final, 4 December 2006; European Commission, 'A Strong European Neighbourhood Policy', COM (2007) 774 final, 5 December 2007.

[4] Most broadly conceived, the goals are reflected in Art. 3 TEU and serve as a continuation and elaboration of the foundational values of Art. 2 TEU.

[5] M. Maresceau, 'Quelques réflexions sur l'application des principes fondamentaux dans la stratégie d'adhésion de l'UE' in *Le Droit de l'Union Européenne en Principes: Liber Amicorum en l'Honneur de Jean Raux*. (2006) *LCDJ* 69; M. Maresceau, 'The EU Pre-accession Strategies: A Political and Legal Analysis' in M. Maresceau and E. Lanon (eds), *The EU's Enlargement and Mediterranean Strategies, A Comparative Analysis* (Basingstoke/New York, Palgrave 2001) 18. Available online at www.palgraveconnect.com/pc/doifinder/10.1057/9780333977811 (accessed 5 October 2015).

[6] A. Williams, *The Ethos of Europe* (Cambridge, Cambridge University Press 2010). See especially Ch. 2.

[7] See E. Basheska, 'The Position of the Good Neighbourliness Principle in International and EU Law' in D. Kochenov and E. Basheska, *Good Neighbourliness in the European Legal Context* (Leiden, Martinus Nijhoff 2015) 24. See also, I. Pop, *Components of Good Neighbourliness Between States – Its Specific Legal Contents – Some Considerations Concerning the Reports of the Sub-Committee on Good-Neighbourliness Created by the Legal Committee of the General-Assembly of the United Nations* (Bucharest, Editura R.A.I., 1991); and Declaration on Principles of International Law Concerning Friendly Relations and Cooperation Among States in Accordance with the UN Charter, UNGA Res 2625 (XXV) (24 October 1970).

[8] For a meticulous analysis of the EU's objectives related to the shaping of the international order, see J. Larik, 'Shaping the International Order as an EU Objective' in D. Kochenov and F. Amtenbrink (eds), *European Union's Shaping of the International Legal Order* (Cambridge, Cambridge University Press 2013) 62.

the principles of sovereignty and territorial integrity, inviolability of borders and independence, as well as countering the proliferation of weapons of mass destruction, related materials and their means of delivery constitute essential elements of that Agreement.[9]

Rhetoric and good intentions aside, the EU's aim of establishing good relations with its neighbours through an attempt to bring about change in its neighbourhood is highly problematic, both when approached through the point of view of its legal-political organization and also when assessed against the aims it was supposed to reach. This opens a Pandora's box of questions about the EU's future engagement with the neighbourhood. The truth is, it seems, that conditionality is poorly suited for the promotion of values – especially when such promotion, as in the case of the ENP, is based on a presumption of commonly shared values between the EU and its partners, a presumption which finds little support in reality. Worse still, in the post-Crimea context of growing hostility in Europe, the ENP seems to be failing not only in terms of legal instruments and starting assumptions, but also at the diplomatic level: the EU's incentives for transformation fade away in the context of Russia's bullying tactic, as the EU is having difficulty with offering support and protection to those ENP partners that choose to adhere to the values it preaches. That strategy is ineffective because it is based on the assumption that the EU is the only actor on the international stage, ignoring any possible competition for the neighbourhood from other actors.[10]

Analyzing some key drawbacks, this chapter scrutinizes the evolution of some key EU instruments, principles, assumptions and approaches which the EU deployed with an eye to bringing about a 'ring of friends' in the Union's neighbourhood, focusing chiefly on the key element of the whole edifice, which is the principle of conditionality. This is done only to find that conditionality – a principle inherited by the EU from the pre-accession context, where it has not worked well[11] – is poorly suited for the promotion of values (democracy, the rule of law, and other fundamental aspects of importance for the EU's ENP agenda), as opposed to the promotion of the concrete rules – the *acquis*.[12] The elephant in the room of the ENP is, obviously, Russia, whose strong opposition to the EU's efforts to Europeanize its neighbourhood is not discussed much in the ENP literature.[13] Yet, EU–Russia relations have an

---

[9] E.g. Art. 2 'Association Agreement between the European Union and its Member States, of the one part, and Ukraine, of the other part' [2014] OJ L161/3 (EU–Ukraine Association Agreement).

[10] It is important to take into account, in this context, that scholars have discovered powerful promotion of own interest behind EU's altruistic claims: the EU emerges as an actor in international relations, which is akin to any other. See, for a vivid example, A. Boute, 'The EU's Shaping of International Law on Energy Efficiency' in D. Kochenov and F. Amtenbrink (eds), *EU's Shaping of the International Legal Order* (Cambridge, Cambridge University Press 2013) 238.

[11] D. Kochenov, *EU Enlargement and the Failure of Conditionality: Pre-Accession Conditionality in the Fields of Democracy and the Rule of Law* (Alphen aan den Rijn, Kluwer Law International 2008).

[12] For more on this distinction, see D. Kochenov, 'The Issue of Values' in Petrov and Van Elsuwege (n 2) 46.

[13] For an exception, see P. Kalinichenko, 'Some Legal Issues of the EU–Russia Relations in the Post-Crimea Era: From Good Neighbourliness to Crisis and Back?' in Kochenov and Basheska (n 7) 334; P. Kalinichenko's chapter in this volume.

important bearing on the success of the EU's ENP efforts, no matter how well the legal instruments behind the ENP are designed.

Discussion of the ENP's legal framework without constantly having this consideration in mind would thus be futile and unhelpful, to which the Russia-sponsored insurgency, coupled with the occupation of part of Ukraine,[14] constant pressure on Moldova[15] and the de facto exclusion of Armenia from the further steps of the ENP process[16] clearly testify. Turning to the Mediterranean dimension of the ENP, a similarly sad picture emerges: with the rise of the Islamic State and instability in the whole region some of the ENP partners de facto no longer exist as sovereign states with a functioning government enjoying control of their territory. War, terrorist attacks and the destruction of effective statehood have caused large flows of migrants towards the EU's borders – a problem which the EU has been remarkably incapable of dealing with.[17] In light of these observations, it would not be an overstatement to claim that the ENP – as an initiative aimed at projecting the EU's influence in the neighbourhood – has failed entirely: the neighbourhood is much worse off now than it was when the ENP was inaugurated. Make no mistake: blaming the ENP for the failure of the neighbours would be an overstatement. Having said this, the failure of the EU's diplomacy and the complete lack of capacity to assess the risks that the ENP would encounter, make it legitimate to lay at least part of the blame on the EU's actions.

Approached against this context – of an all-around deterioration of the situation in the EU's neighbourhood – the design problems undermining the ENP's effectiveness that this chapter discusses are somewhat dwarfed by *Realpolitic*. Yet, such problems still deserve serious consideration since they demonstrate that the ENP was most unlikely to deliver even in an ideal international relations climate. We look at the objective of the 'ring of friends' and then focus on the three key

---

[14] See J. Green, 'Editorial Comment. The Annexation of Crimea: Russia, Passportisation and the Protection of Nationals Revisited' (2014) 1(1) *Journal on the Use of Force and International Law* 3. See also E. Milano, 'The Non-Recognition of Russia's Annexation of Crimea: Three Different Legal Approaches and One Unanswered Question' (2014) 1 *QIL* 35; A. Tancredi, 'The Russian Annexation of the Crimea: Questions Relating to the Use of Force' (2014) 1 *QIL* 5. See also R. Müllersson, 'Ukraine: Victim of Geopolitics' (2014) 13 *Chinese Journal of International Law* 133.

[15] See e.g. P. Fogarty, 'Riding Three Horses: Moldova's Enduring Identity as a Strategy for Survival' in K. Engelbrekt and B. Nygren (eds), *Russia and Europe: Building Bridges, Digging Trenches* (London, Routledge 2010) 230.

[16] See N. Ghazaryan, *The European Neighbourhood Policy and the Democratic Values of the EU: A Legal Analysis* (Oxford, Hart Publishing 2014) Post-scriptum. The Treaty aiming for Armenia's accession to the Eurasian Economic Union was signed on 9 October 2014 and entered into force on 2 January 2015. Available online at www.customs-code.ru/pravovbaza/18429-dogovor-arm (accessed 18 July 2015).

[17] See, in this respect, E. Basheska and D. Kochenov, 'EuroMed, Migration and Frenemy-ship: Pretending to Deepen Cooperation across the Mediterranean' in F. Ippolito and S. Trevisanut (eds), *Migration in Mare Nostrum: Mechanisms of International Co-operation* (Cambridge, Cambridge University Press 2016) 43. See also S. Wolff, *The Mediterranean Dimension of the European Union's Internal Security* (New York, Palgrave MacMillan 2012); M. Ceccorulli and N. Labanca (eds), *The EU, Migration and the Politics of Administrative Detention* (London, Routledge 2014); A. Triandafyllidou and T. Maroukis, *Migrant Smuggling: Irregular Migration from Asia and Africa to Europe* (New York, Palgrave Macmillan 2012).

presumptions underlying the deployment of the principle of conditionality in the context of the ENP: (1) the presumption of shared values; (2) the presumption of effectiveness of the value based conditionality; and (3) the presumption of sufficient incentives. We argue that all three presumptions are untenable, then address the issue of what might be done to solve the outstanding problems.

The ENP should be getting much stricter scrutiny in the post-Crimea world, when the fourth untenable presumption – the presumption that the EU acts in vacuum in a world, with no opposition and disagreement, while doing 'the right thing' – has been undermined so resoundingly.

Article 8 TEU and the 'ring of friends'

Article 8(1) TEU provides that good neighbourliness is based on the foundational values of the Union. In particular, '[T]he Union shall develop a special relationship with neighbouring countries, aiming to establish an area of prosperity and good neighbourliness, founded on the values of the Union and characterised by close and peaceful relations based on cooperation'.[18] As noted by Hillion, the use of the phrase 'shall', stipulates an obligation for the EU to engage with its neighbourhood in the above described way.[19] Yet, several issues come to mind when reading this provision.

First, the substance of the 'special relationship[s]' referred to in the first paragraph is not clear.[20] Similar wording can be found for the Association Agreements based on Art. 217 TFEU, which are said to be 'creating special, privileged links' between the Union and non-member countries. The doubt arises as to the ambiguity of an association which can '[range] from little more than a free trade agreement to a level of integration that comes close to membership'.[21] Closely resembling Art. 217 TFEU, agreements based on Art. 8 TEU can cover all the EU's competences,[22] and a procedural basis can be found in Art. 218 TFEU.[23]

Another question is raised by the countries affected by Art. 8 TEU. Pointing to relations between the EU and its neighbours, the provision in question has been primarily associated with ENP countries, which include not only immediate neighbours, but also states from the wider surroundings.[24] Some scholars go as far

---

[18] Art. 8(1) TEU.
[19] C. Hillion, 'Anatomy of EU Norm Export towards the Neighbourhood' in Petrov and Van Elsuwege (n 2) 13, 16.
[20] Article 8(1) refers to 'a special relationship', while other versions of the Treaty, for instance the German and the French versions, use the plural form referring to 'besondere Beziehungen' and 'des relations privilégiées' respectively.
[21] P. Van Elsuwege, *From Soviet Republics to EU Member States: A Legal and Political Assessment of the Baltic States' Accession to the EU* (Leiden and Boston, Martinus Nijhoff 2008) 131.
[22] In Case 12/86 *Meryem Demirel* v. *Stadt Schwäbisch Gmünd* [1987] ECR 3719, para. 9, the ECJ held that Art. 217 TFEU (then Art. 238 EC Treaty), 'must necessarily empower the Community to guarantee commitments towards non-member countries in all the fields covered by the Treaty.'
[23] M. Cremona, 'The Two (or Three) Treaty Solution: The New Treaty Structure of the EU' in A. Biondi and P. Eeckhout (eds), *EU Law after Lisbon* (Oxford, Oxford University Press 2012) 40, 46.
[24] Armenia and Azerbaijan, for instance, participate in the ENP although not being immediate neighbours of the EU. See, in this respect, European Commission, 'European Neighbourhood Policy Strategy Paper', COM (2004) 373 final (n 3) 10–11.

as to suggest that the new article codifies the ENP and confers a constitutional status on the relationship between the Union and its neighbours.[25] In any event, countries outside the ENP have not been explicitly excluded from the scope of application of Art. 8 TEU. This leaves space for broader interpretation of this provision to also cover other nearby countries such as the European microstates, EEA states, Switzerland and Russia.[26] It has been suggested, however, that the context of relations with the European states enjoying clear prospects of membership would exclude the application of this provision.[27] This can be inferred from the purpose of the agreements concluded under Art. 8(2) TEU, which merely aim to establish 'an area of prosperity and good neighbourliness', rather than to bring non-EU states closer to membership.[28]

Finally, Art. 8 TEU suggests that the EU views good neighbourliness through the prism of its own values, i.e. as being founded on:

> respect for human dignity, freedom, democracy, equality, the rule of law and respect for human rights, including the rights of persons belonging to minorities [which] are common to the Member States in a society in which pluralism, non-discrimination, justice, solidarity and equality between women and men prevail.[29]

EU values are far from unique.[30] In general, they coincide with the fundamental values essential to international relations established by the United Nations Millennium Declaration.[31] The crucial question that arises, however, is whether all

---

[25] E.g. R. Schütze, *European Constitutional Law* (Cambridge, Cambridge University Press 2012) 190; D. Hanf, 'The European Neighbourhood Policy in the Light of the New "Neighbourhood Clause" (Article 8 TEU)' in E. Lannon (ed.), *The European Neighbourhood Policy's Challenges* (New York, P.I.E. Peter Lang 2012) 109.

[26] Such an understanding is also implied by the Declaration on Art. 8 TEU annexed to the Lisbon Treaty, which does not exclude non-ENP states but stipulates that 'the Union will take into account the particular situation of small-sized countries which maintain specific relations of proximity with it' (Declarations annexed to the Final Act of the Intergovernmental Conference which adopted the Treaty of Lisbon [2009] OJ C115/337).

[27] Some scholars go even further, arguing that Art. 8 TEU was introduced to distinguish between countries with accession prospects and states without them. See, in this respect, P. Van Elsuwege and R. Petrov, 'Article 8 TEU: Towards a New Generation of Agreements with the Neighbouring Countries of the European Union?' (2011) 36(5) *ELRev* 688–703, 693, noting that the provision confirms the 'disconnection between ENP and enlargement' through its objectives. See also P.P. Craig and G. de Búrca, *EU Law: Text, Cases and Materials* (5th edn Oxford, Oxford University Press 2011) 324.

[28] Van Elsuwege and Petrov (n 27) 693.

[29] Art. 2 TEU.

[30] See e.g. P. Leino and R. Petrov, 'Between "Common Values" and Competing Universals – The Promotion of the EU's Common Values through the European Neighbourhood Policy' (2009) 15(5) *ELJ* 654.

[31] The fundamental values essential to international relations in the twenty-first century were highlighted in the United Nations Millennium Declaration, UNGA Res 55/2 (8 September 2000) A/Res/55L.2. These include: 'a) Freedom (meaning that) men and women have the right to live their lives and raise their children in dignity, free from hunger and from the fear of violence, oppression

partners in the ENP process equally respect and are committed to the promotion of these values[32] and whether they are rewarded accordingly.

Crucially, although neither Art. 8 TEU, nor any other relevant provision in the Treaties actually makes a direct reference to the principle of conditionality as the driving force of achieving the 'ring of friends', conditionality has emerged as the cornerstone of the ENP edifice. Partly a pre-accession implant,[33] partly a nod in the direction of management and governance approaches to regulation, the principle, like the basis of the ancient world, rests on three groundless assumptions: (1) that the proclaimed values of Art. 8 TEU – as also reflected in other Treaty instruments – are shared by the EU and its partners; (2) that improved adherence to these values can be achieved even in autocratic regimes or in countries which are radically different from EU Member States; and (3) that ensuring compliance with the values the EU is seeking to promote only requires the incentive of a 'stake in the internal market' or a deep and comprehensive free trade agreement. All three will be addressed further, one by one, with yet another failed presumption in mind: that the EU is the only actor in an empty world, where opposition to its external policies is unlikely.

The presumption of shared values

The ENP is largely aimed at uniting the efforts of the EU and ENP partners to create an area of peace and prosperity surrounding the Union that will benefit everyone. One cannot help but wonder what the common ground is that can bridge the many worlds the ENP is concerned with. The numerous countries on the list of ENP partners are not just different; the differences between them seem at times to be absolute. Consequently, the Commission chose to play the old card

---

or injustice. Democratic and participatory governance based on the will of the people best assures these rights; b) Equality (meaning that) no individual and no nation must be denied the opportunity to benefit from development. The equal rights and opportunities of women and men must be assured; c) Solidarity (meaning that) global challenges must be managed in a way that distributes the costs and burdens fairly in accordance with basic principles of equity and social justice. Those who suffer or who benefit least deserve help from those who benefit most; d) Tolerance (meaning that) human beings must respect one other, in all their diversity of belief, culture and language. Differences within and between societies should be neither feared nor repressed, but cherished as a precious asset of humanity. A culture of peace and dialogue among all civilizations should be actively promoted; e) Respect for nature (meaning that) prudence must be shown in the management of all living species and natural resources, in accordance with the precepts of sustainable development [...]; f) Shared responsibility (meaning that) responsibility for managing worldwide economic and social development, as well as threats to international peace and security, must be shared among the nations of the world and should be exercised multilaterally. As the most universal and most representative organization in the world, the United Nations must play the central role.'

[32] This, quite importantly, includes the EU's own Member States, and here the deviations are far from uncommon: J.W. Müller, 'Should the EU Protect Democracy and the Rule of Law Inside the Member States?' (2015) 21 *ELJ* 141; C. Closa and D. Kochenov (eds), *Reinforcement of the Rule of Law Oversight in the European Union* (Cambridge, Cambridge University Press 2015) forthcoming.

[33] Magen (n 2); D. Kochenov, 'The ENP Conditionality: Pre-Accession Mistakes Repeated' in Delcour and Tulmets (n 2) 105.

of 'values'. It had been submitted – and optimistically or reluctantly accepted by the partners – that they share with the EU some values of significant importance.[34] The values approach was deemed to soften the perceived differences between the participants of the ENP and to make possible the move, together, towards certain goals. In practice, this amounts to making the application of conditionality possible, as the shared values provide the starting ground for common engagement: in order to participate in the policy, ENP partners were supposed to subscribe to the values of the Union, which are 'common to the Member States'.[35]

The prescribed values, including democracy, the protection of human rights, the free market economy and the rule of law, are virtually identical to the Copenhagen political criteria applied in the course of the preparation of the eastern enlargement, and are also rooted in the text of Art. 2 TEU and the constitutional traditions of Member States.[36] It is here, in the terrain of values, where a serious drawback in the design of the ENP arises. This is related to the projection of the values of the Union on its partners.

This chapter is not an argument against universalism, especially given that at the purely rhetorical level all states would subscribe to the values outlined. However, the fact that the absolute majority of the ENP partner countries are in fact cooperating with the EU under the auspices of these values – excluding those not actively participating, of course, like Belarus – speaks for the fact that these countries are viewed by the EU as ultimately adhering to these values. Is it so in practice? Doubts are plentiful. It seems unreasonable to dismiss such doubts as unjustified: the meaning of the rule of law, democracy and the protection of human rights in most ENP countries is clearly not to be compared with that in Finland or Spain. Ongoing conflicts aside, the concerns in this respect are numerous. As noted in the most recent Communication on the implementation of the ENP:

> In Egypt, the space for debate in general – and activities by (civil society organisations) in particular – was narrowed through enhanced controls. The democratisation and human rights environment in Azerbaijan worsened over the past year ... In Belarus, the lack of progress on human rights, the rule

---

[34] The Commission formulated these in the following way: 'the Union is founded on the values of respect of human dignity, liberty, democracy, equality, the Rule of Law and respect for human rights. These values are common to the Member States in a society of pluralism, tolerance, justice, solidarity and non-discrimination. The Union's aim is to promote peace, its values and the well-being of its peoples', COM (2004) 373 final (n 3) 7. The earlier formulation of the list of values on which the policy is based, which is contained in fn. 2 to the Commission's Communication on Wider Europe (COM (2003) 104 final (n 3)) was slightly different and included 'democracy, respect for human rights and the rule of law, as set out within the EU in the Charter of Fundamental Rights'.

[35] Art. 2 TEU.

[36] For analysis see C. Hillion, 'The Copenhagen Criteria and Their Progeny' in C. Hillion (ed.), *EU Enlargement: A Legal Approach* (Oxford, Hart Publishing 2004) 19; D. Kochenov, 'Behind the Copenhagen Façade. The Meaning and Structure of the Copenhagen Political Criterion of Democracy and the Rule of Law' (2004) 8 *European Integration Online Papers* 10.

of law and democratic principles persisted. Political developments in Israel and Palestine were significantly influenced by the regional situation, a more conflictual political atmosphere, and hostilities in Gaza. (In respect to) Israel ... there were concerns in 2014 as regards the protection of minority rights, including of Bedouins. In Palestine, key legislation on democratic structures, such as legislation outlining the responsibilities of judicial institutions, still needs to be adopted. Concerns about the respect for human rights remained to be addressed, in particular with regard to the death sentence: it continued to be carried out in Gaza by the *de facto* authorities and executions were resumed in Egypt and Jordan after moratoria had applied in both countries in the years before.[37]

This demonstrates how low the threshold of adherence is. Once it has been agreed that values are the common ground on which the policy is built, the dangers related to the discovery that they are not actually adhered to, or do not even exist, have critical implications for a policy such as the ENP. Connected to the issue of values are the interests that the partners presumably want to pursue together. The presumption of common values thus not only makes the building of the ENP possible, but also affects the expectations of the EU and the ENP partners, trying to respond to the shared problems related to common interests, thus potentially presenting the absence of values in an even more dangerous light. The point that values should ideally be shared de facto, not only de jure, at the level of proclamations, is not a merely rhetorical one: the principle of conditionality, seemingly functioning fine in the context of exporting concrete rules (i.e. in the contexts where the issue of adherence to the values does not arise) is most unworkable in the context of value-export, as will be demonstrated below. The presumption of shared values thus opens the door to the application of conditionality outside of the realm of its effectiveness, threatening to bring about wasted efforts and rampant non-compliance.

The presumption of the effectiveness of values-based conditionality

Notwithstanding the fact that all active ENP partners subscribe to the values of the Union, the only way for the Union to make sure that they actually play an important role on the other side of the EU external border is to regularly monitor their movement towards the realities which these values embody – and to provide partners with positive incentives for change to ensure that they actually embrace the values. Moreover, those partners who are unable or unwilling to move in the stated direction should face the negative consequences of such an unfortunate policy choice. This is, essentially, the core of the idea of conditionality espoused

---

[37] European Commission/High Representative, Joint Communication to the European Parliament, the Council, the European Economic and Social Committee and the Committee of the Regions, 'Implementation of the European Neighbourhood Policy in 2014', JOIN(2015) 9 final, 25 March 2015, 5.

by the Commission in the course of the eastern enlargement preparation.[38] In the eastern enlargement context the EU was faced with a similar task, albeit in a potentially more dangerous form: instead of simply seeking to be surrounded by friends (amid the growing fears of the 'other' beyond the external EU border),[39] the EU had to make sure that in terms of membership accession, going to 'bed with bad guys'[40] would not be the culmination of its eastern enlargement efforts. The warnings sounded by one of us elsewhere about the failure of conditionality in the pre-accession context[41] seem to have materialized: liberal democratic constitutionalism, in a number of the Member States which used to be subject to pre-accession scrutiny by the Union, is experiencing a worrisome meltdown.[42] Klabbers' 'bad guys' are in our bed and it is most unclear what to do with them.[43]

Is values-based conditionality functioning in the ENP context? If ENP partners are reluctant to pursue democratization or adhere to the values outlined by the EU, the incentives on offer should be substantial enough in order to compensate the elites for the losses they suffer and partners must only be rewarded for genuine efforts of compliance. Practically, it is difficult if not impossible to imagine how substantial such incentives should be in order to incite regime change in Belarus or effective protection of human rights in Egypt, for instance. Thus, viewed from a purely practical perspective it seems that the idea of conditionality as entrenched in the ENP is unlikely to promote EU values in all ENP countries.

Quite the contrary, the ENP might have become a vehicle for promoting the EU's 'hard interests' in its tough neighbourhood rather than a values-oriented framework driven by the EU's 'soft power'.[44] To agree with Brummer, '[W]hen

---

[38] For a criticism, see D. Kochenov, 'Overestimating Conditionality' in I. Govaere *et al.* (eds), *The European Union in the World: Essays in Honour of Marc Maresceau* (Leiden, Martinus Nijhoff 2014) 541–556.

[39] Magen (n 2), 398 (calling the fear of the neighbours one of the main motivations behind the formulation of the policy).

[40] J. Klabbers, 'On Babies, Bathwater and the Three Musketeers, or the Beginning of the End of European Integration' in V. Heiskanen and K. Kulovesi (eds), *Function and Future of European Law* (Helsinki, Publications of the Faculty of Law, University of Helsinki 1999).

[41] Kochenov (n 11).

[42] J.W. Müller, 'Safeguarding Democracy inside the EU: Brussels and the Future of the International Legal Order' (2012–2013) 3 *Transatlantic Academy Paper Series*. See also A. von Bogdandy and P. Sonnevend, *Constitutional Crisis in the European Constitutional Area: Theory, Law and Politics in Hungary and Romania* (Oxford, Hart Publishing 2015); M. Bánkuti, G. Halmai and K.L. Scheppele, 'Hungary's Illiberal Turn: Disabling the Constitution' (2012) 23 *Journal of Democracy* 138. See also R. Uitz, 'Can You Tell When an Illiberal Democracy is in the Making? An Appeal to Comparative Constitutional Scholarship from Hungary' (2015) 13 *Int J Constitutional Law* 279; V. Perju, 'The Romanian Double Executive and the 2012 Constitutional Crisis' (2015) 13 *Int J Constitutional Law* 246; M.A. Vachudova, 'Why Improve EU Oversight of the Rule of Law? The Two-Headed Problem of Defending Liberal Democracy and Fighting Corruption' in Closa and Kochenov (n 32), analysing the situation in the Czech Republic.

[43] For an inventory of means, see C. Closa, D. Kochenov and J.H.H. Weiler, 'Reinforcing Rule of Law Oversight in the European Union' (2014/2015) 25 *EUI Working Papers*; J.-W. Müller, 'The EU as a Militant Democracy, or: Are There Limits to Constitutional Mutations within the Member States' (2014) 165 *Revista de Estudios Políticos* 141.

[44] The term 'soft power' is borrowed from J.S. Nye, *Soft Power: The Means to Success in World Politics* (New York, Public Affairs 2004) 86, and designates an 'ability to achieve goals through attraction rather

security and welfare interests are at stake, the EU refrains from adopting sanctions. Conversely, sanctions are only imposed when they entail little cost for the Member States'.[45] The EU leans instead towards a more flexible approach to secure its interests, even if this implies establishing and furthering cooperation with authoritarian regimes.[46] The picture is not the same outside the ENP, where sanctions against Russia following its occupation of Crimea and its support of militants in eastern Ukraine met with a strong response from the Union. Contrary to that, the authorization for and the start of the negotiations of Visa Facilitation and Readmission Agreements with Belarus ('driven by the desire to fill in a gap and conclude a readmission agreement with the only Eastern partner that has not opened negotiations with the EU in this respect')[47] and the maintaining of negotiations with Egypt ('even at a time of a country's serious internal political de-liberalization)'[48] testify to the EU's flexible approach towards some of its neighbours.[49]

Here a theoretical distinction made by Tocci between 'willing' and 'reluctant' partners becomes operational.[50] While countries like Moldova or Georgia might willingly embrace the values that the EU expects them to subscribe to in the context of the ENP, states such as Egypt and Tunisia are rather outside the reach of conditionality policies. Following on from the argument of Magen,[51] Tocci is absolutely right in stating that:

> [I]f democratisation and human rights call for a redistribution of powers, the legal and institutional installation and protection of rights and the enhancement of political participation, it is unclear how EU relations with states whose entire modus operandi often negate these developments, can meaningfully promote these values.[52]

The values-based conditionality is thus non-operational in relations with reluctant ENP partners. This can be clearly demonstrated analytically at a purely theoretical level. In this context, the question about the likely success of conditionality in the EU's relations with 'willing' ENP partner states naturally arises. While functional

---

than coercion. It works by convincing others to follow or getting them to agree to norms and institutions that produce the desired behavior'. See also E. Lazarou, M. Gianniou and G. Tsouropas, 'The Limits of Norm Promotion: The EU in Egypt and Israel/Palestine' (2013) 15(2) *Insight Turkey* 171.

[45] K. Brummer, 'Imposing Sanctions: The Not So "Normative Power Europe"' (2009) 14(2) *European Foreign Affairs Review* 191, 193.
[46] Lazarou, Gianniou and Tsouropas (n 44).
[47] L. Delcour, 'The European Union: Shaping Migration Patterns in Its Neighbourhood and Beyond?' in D. Kochenov and F. Amtenbrink (eds), *The European Union's Shaping of the Legal International Order* (Cambridge, Cambridge University Press 2013) 261, 272.
[48] Lazarou, Gianniou and Tsouropas (n 44), 180.
[49] For the step-by-step evolution of the sanctions regime, see Kalinichenko in Kochenov and Basheska (n 137).
[50] N. Tocci, 'Can the EU Promote Democracy and Human Rights through the ENP? The Case for Refocusing on the Rule of Law' in Cremona and Meloni (n 2) 23, 26–32.
[51] Magen (n 2) 418–419.
[52] Tocci (n 50) 29.

in theory, analogy with the application of values-based conditionality by the EU outside of the ENP setting demonstrates quite clearly that, in the case of willing partners, conditionality is also unlikely to be highly successful. Having failed in the pre-accession,[53] where the candidate countries were overwhelmingly determined to join the Union and could thus be expected to cooperate with the EU in the most wholehearted manner, when transplanted into the ENP setting where the incentives at stake are much more modest,[54] it seems that values-based conditionality when transplanted from the pre-accession context cannot possibly deliver any of the meaningful results expected of it.[55] Such transplantation has only resulted in a 'shadow of enlargement', containing diluted versions of enlargement methodologies applied reflexively by the Commission to the new policy context, with little evidence of regard for their appropriateness.[56] In the words of Cremona and Hillion:

> [T]ransplanting pre-accession routines into a policy otherwise conceived as an alternative to accession and intended to enhance the security of the Union, may ... undermine both its current effectiveness and its longer-term viability, if not its rationale.[57]

Potentially, however, there are no conceptual considerations that would prove the inoperability of conditionality in such a setting – in sharp contrast with the EU's relations with 'reluctant' partners. Conditionality can govern relations with 'willing' partners. This is only possible if the mistakes made by the Commission in the course of the pre-accession application of conditionality are remedied before the transplantation of values-based conditionality regulation into the ENP context.[58]

The presumption of sufficient incentives

The ENP is a clear attempt by the EU to postpone the discussion of the *finalités géographiques* of integration to some unknown time in the future.[59] In this way the ENP, at least when applied to East European partners, is very similar to the

---

[53] For a compelling analysis see Kochenov (n 11).
[54] J. Kelley, 'New Wine in Old Wineskins: Promoting Political Reforms through the New European Neighbourhood Policy', 44 *Journal of Common Market Studies* 2006, 29–55, 32. See also Zaiotti (n 2) 151; G. Meloni, 'Is the Same Toolkit Used during Enlargement Still Applicable to the Countries of the New Neighbourhood? A Problem of Mismatching between Objectives and Instruments' in Cremona and Meloni (eds) (n 2) 97.
[55] For analysis of values-based conditionality in the ENP context as applied also to the 'willing' partners, see D. Kochenov, 'The ENP Conditionality: Pre-Accession Mistakes Repeated' in Delcour and Tulmets (n 2) 105.
[56] Magen (n 2) 390.
[57] Cremona and Hillion (n 2) 26.
[58] Kochenov (n 11) 119.
[59] As initially stated by the European Commission, COM (2003) 104 final (n 3) 5, '[T]he aim of the new Neighbourhood Policy is ... to provide a framework for the development of a new relationship which would not, in the medium-term, include a perspective of membership or a role in the Union's institutions'.

initial ideology behind the European Economic Area (EEA),[60] as well as the initial approach to Eastern Europe preceding the 1993 Copenhagen European Council[61] and the subsequent pre-accession reorientation of the Europe Agreements.[62] While in the pre-accession process full membership was on offer, the ultimate prize in the ENP race is participation in the Neighbourhood Economic Community (NEC), or some watered-down version of it.

The ENP is thus entirely decoupled from the eventual accession prospects of the partner countries and is implemented, in the words of the Commission, 'without prejudging how [the partners'] relationship with the EU may develop in the future'.[63] While it is probably not so important for the ENP partners in the southern Mediterranean, this is bad news for the East European partners and the countries in the Caucasus, since membership of the EU is among their foreign policy priorities. A very positive element of the ENP in this context is the policy of vagueness.[64] While not coupled with the eventual possibility to give accession prospects in the future to those partners who are interested and meet the necessary requirements of Art. 49 EU,[65] it does not mean the closure of the Union's gates to those countries seeking to join. Consequently, good performance in the context of the ENP can be viewed in those countries as the first of a number of steps on the way to future accession of the Union. This has certainly been the case in Ukraine, Moldova and Georgia, three of the most active ENP partner states.[66]

Smaller incentives aside, the jewel in the crown of incentives employed by the Commission in the context of the ENP is the prospective NEC. According to the Commission:

> [T]he Neighbourhood Economic Community would boost trade further among ENP partners via the elimination of both tariffs and non-tariff barriers and by establishing a minimum base for common behind-the-border

---

[60] K.E. Smith, 'The Outsiders: The European Neighbourhood Policy' (2005) 81(4) *International Affairs* 757, 761.

[61] For a concise history of Central and Eastern European countries – EEC relations, see K.E. Smith, *The Making of EU Foreign Policy: The Case of Eastern Europe* (2nd edn, Houndmills and New York, Palgrave Macmillan 2004); F. de la Serre, 'A la recherche d'une Ostpolitik', in F. de la Serre, C. Lequesne and J. Rupnik (eds), *L'Union Européenne: Ouverture à l'Est?* (Paris, Presses Universitaires de France 1994).

[62] K. Inglis, 'The Europe Agreements Compared in the Light of Their Pre-Accession Reorientation' (2000) 37(5) *CML Rev* 117.

[63] COM (2006) 726 final (n 3). Some Member States were severely opposed to such decoupling. Poland, in particular, argued for the necessity of making a link between the neighbourhood policy and an EU membership perspective: P. Kratochvíl, 'New EU Members and the ENP: Different Agendas, Different Strategies', contribution to the forum 'The Neighbourhood Policy of the European Union' (2007) 42(4) *Intereconomics* 191, 193.

[64] It is a positive development, in this respect, that the Commission's Communication on the 'enlargement capacity' does not embrace any strict approach to the EU's future borders. See European Commission (EC), 'Enlargement Strategy and Main Challenges 2006–2007', COM (2006) 649 final.

[65] Kochenov (n 11) Ch. 1.

[66] JOIN(2015) 9 final (n 37) 2.

rules, thereby creating a common regulatory space. This would expand the size of the Common Market, stimulate growth of the ENP partners, and boost productivity through a better exploitation of economies of scale.[67]

Besides the conditional formulation of this blurred perspective, it is also known from the Commission's documents that the creation of such an economic community will depend on the 'partners' willingness to integrate further',[68] which means that both the EU and the ENP partners will have to ascertain their willingness to move in this direction in the future. Ultimately, it means that the NEC is not a real incentive for the partners to continue on the path of the ENP.

Unlike the blurred nature and doubtful attractiveness of the initial promises involving the NEC and a 'stake in the Common Market', the new generation of agreements to be concluded between the EU and those ENP partners which respect and successfully implement the priorities set out in the Action Plans seems to have the potential to become a viable attraction tool. Content-wise, the new agreements are, in the words of the Commission, 'tailor-made deep and comprehensive free trade agreements (DCFTA), including measures to reduce non-tariff barriers through regulatory convergence'[69] and 'cover substantially all trade in goods and services between the [EU] and the ENP partner as well as strong legally-binding provisions on the implementation of trade and economic regulatory issues'.[70] Three such agreements – Association Agreements which include deep and comprehensive free trade areas – were signed in 2014 with Georgia, Moldova and Ukraine,[71] representing 'ENP's core achievements and ... a milestone in the EU's relations with some of its closest partners, upgrading these ties to a significantly higher level'.[72]

The then president of the European Commission, Jose Manuel Barroso, described the Association Agreements as 'the most ambitious document the European Union has entered into so far'.[73] Clearly, partners see these agreements as a step towards membership. Thus, the optimism and active participation of the partner countries can be explained by their future membership aspirations

---

[67] European Commission, Non-Paper Expanding on the Proposals Contained in the Communication to the European Parliament and the Council on 'Strengthening the ENP', COM (2006) 726 final, 4 December 2006, 7.
[68] Ibid. 8.
[69] COM (2007) 774 final (n 3) 4.
[70] Ibid. For broader analysis of the new agreements, see G. Van der Loo, P. Van Elsuwege and R. Petrov, 'The EU–Ukraine Association Agreement: Assessment of an Innovative Legal Instrument' (2014) 9 *EUI working paper*, available at http://cadmus.eui.eu/bitstream/handle/1814/32031/ LAW%20_WP_ 2014_ 9%20.pdf?sequence=1 (accessed 5 July 2015).
[71] Association Agreement between the European Union and the European Atomic Energy Community and their Member States, of the one part, and Georgia, of the other part [2014] OJ L261/4; Association Agreement between the European Union and the European Atomic Energy Community and their Member States, of the one part, and the Republic of Moldova, of the other part [2014] OJ L260/4; EU–Ukraine Association Agreement (n 9).
[72] JOIN(2015) 9 final (n 37) 9.
[73] See http://agenda.ge/news/16836/eng (accessed 31 May 2015).

rather than by the success of the existing ENP framework and attractiveness of its incentives. For instance, Georgia's prime minister, Irakli Garibashvili, stated the following on signing the Association Agreement: 'Unofficially we applied for EU membership today; officially, it depends on the progress that we will make, but I can guarantee you that we will do our best to meet all of the requirements of the European Union'.[74] Similarly, the Ukrainian president, Petro Poroshenko, stated: 'We are ambitious in our plans and our belief, and that's why we declare that within five years we will provide effective implementation of the [EU] association agreement and meet conditions required to apply for membership in the European Union'.[75] These expectations were not particularly welcomed in the EU. As the president of the European Parliament, Martin Schulz, noted most recently, the EU is 'facing a different problem today ... to stabilize the country politically, economically, socially. With a stabilized Ukraine, [there is] a chance to gain stability for the region as a whole'.[76]

The agreements enter fully into force after they are approved by the European Parliament and ratified by EU Member States and the partner country, although large parts can come into force provisionally at an earlier date. The progress of the three countries which have signed these agreements is different, with the implementation of DCFTA being delayed for Ukraine until 31 December 2015 upon a request of Russia,[77] the *cardinal gris* of many an ENP's failure.

The conclusion of an Association Agreement means, first of all, that these are legally binding agreements and have the potential to have direct effect.[78] In other words, the ENP framework, knowing only the purely legal instruments – the European Neighbourhood Instrument (ENI)[79] and its predecessor, the European Neighbourhood Partnership Instrument (ENPI)[80] – besides the foundational bilateral agreements, is moving more and more towards a legal framing of the policy. This means less 'soft law' and more clarity regarding the actual benefits offered to the ENP partners and better articulated rules of compliance.[81] The new agreements will mean a lot for the ENP, since they, unlike all the existing conditionality

[74] See http://www.civil.ge/eng/_print.php?id=27417 (accessed 31 May 2015).
[75] 'Poroshenko: Ukraine Will Be Ready to Join EU Within 5 Years' *VOA News* (27 April 2015).
[76] 'Schulz: Ukraine's EU membership Bid Too Early to Be Discussed' *UNIAN Information Agency* (6 July 2015).
[77] Joint Ministerial Statement on the Implementation of the EU–Ukraine AA/DCFTA (12 September 2014, Brussels).
[78] Case 12/86 *Meryem Demirel v. Stadt Schwäbisch Gmünd* [1987] ECR 3719, para 14. It should not be forgotten, however, that the provisions of the PCAs can also have direct effect: Case C-265/03 *Igor Simutenkov v. Ministerio de Educación y Cultura, Real Federación Española de Fútbol* [2005] ECR I-2579. See Van der Loo, Van Elsuwege and Petrov (n 70), 14, with regard to dispute settlement across sectors.
[79] Regulation (EU) No 232/2014 of the European Parliament and of the Council of 11 March 2014 establishing a European Neighbourhood Instrument [2014] OJ L77/27.
[80] Regulation (EC) No 1638/2006 of the European Parliament and of the Council of 24 October 2006 laying down general provisions establishing a European Neighbourhood and Partnership Instrument [2006] OJ L310/1.
[81] See also L. Delcour and K. Wolczuk, 'Eurasian Economic Integration and Implications for the EU's Policy in the Eastern Neighbourhood' in R. Dragneva and K. Wolczuk (eds), *Eurasian Economic Integration: Law, Policy, and Politics* (London, Edward Elgar 2013) 179, 190.

machinery in place (with the sole exception of ENI), will fall under the scrutiny of the ECJ. This will partly remedy the situation of legal vacuum and over-flexible construct of the policy at the moment.

The funds granted under the EN(P)I also form part of the incentives built into the ENP. The amounts allocated for the implementation of the programmes have grown constantly – while for the period 2007–2013 the ENPI made €11.2 billion available to finance the programme,[82] the budget for the 2014–2020 programme the ENI made available is more than €15.4 billion. Under the previous programmes €8.6 billion was allocated for the period between 2000 and 2006. The developments in financing the ENP could also be considered more significant, since the ENPI was better tuned to guarantee funds' absorption, which was a problem with the previous financing framework. Moreover, a special ENPI 'Governance Facility' was established by the ENPI to reward the best performing ENP partners.[83] Crowning the ENPI system, the Neighbourhood Investment Facility (NIF) was introduced, with a budget of €700 million.[84] The ENI, which replaced the ENPI in 2014, was established:

> with a view to advancing further towards an area of shared prosperity and good neighbourliness involving the Union and the ... partner countries by developing a special relationship founded on cooperation, peace and security, mutual accountability and a shared commitment to the universal values of democracy, the rule of law and respect for human rights in accordance with the TEU.[85]

Discrepancies exist between the perceived needs, as outlined by the Commission,[86] and the funds allocated. Consequently, notwithstanding an increase in the funds allocation, the actual monies available for the implementation of the ENP still fall short of the policy's needs, as outlined by the Commission. According to Balfour and Missiroli, the policy was 'seriously under-funded'[87] almost ten years ago. So it remains today.

Ultimately, the financial assistance side cannot be viewed as the main incentive offered to the ENP partners within the framework of the policy. Given the nature of the majority of the partner countries and their obvious problems with adhering to the values of the ENP, two problems related to the ENPI financial assistance become obvious. First of all, virtually any amount allocated will still not be enough to 'buy' the regime change in the countries concerned, since deep reform touching upon all the spheres of organization of the state is likely to cost the ruling

---

[82] This includes funds for projects in Russia, which is also covered by the ENPI.
[83] The budget of the Governance Facility amounts to €300 million (€43 million per year on average): COM (2006) 726 final (n 3) 12; COM (2007) 774 final (n 3) 10.
[84] COM (2006) 726 final (n 3) 13; COM (2007) 774 final (n 3) 10.
[85] Article 1(1), Regulation (EU) No 232/2014 (n 79).
[86] For the initially ambitious expectations, see Commission Proposal for a Regulation establishing a European Neighbourhood and Partnership Instrument COM (2004) 628 final, 29 September 2004.
[87] Balfour and Missiroli (n 2) 6.

elites infinitely more. Second, all the money allocated (including the money not going to the ENP partner governments directly) still ends up in the economies of the problematic regimes, making them stronger, and does not necessarily result in any change or move to bring such partners closer to the practical realization of the values of democracy, the rule of law or the protection of human rights.

The most important progress has probably been made in the field of mobility. The inability of the EU in its relations with the ENP partners to deliver on the facilitation of people-to-people contacts and the relaxation of visa rules, outlined by the Commission as one of the incentives within the ENP framework, was a particularly weak point.[88] A step forward has been made in this respect with the visa liberalization dialogues, built on Visa Liberalisation Action Plans (VLAPs) which include benchmarks related to document security, border management, migration and asylum, public order and security, and external relations and fundamental rights, and which were launched initially with Georgia, Moldova and Ukraine.[89] Moldova has first successfully implemented all the benchmarks set in its VLAP, which allowed its citizens to enjoy visa-free travel to the Schengen countries as of spring 2014.[90]

That being said, and seeing the low level of attractiveness in terms of the incentives offered by the ENP, the Commission has been seeking to improve the system of instruments and incentives within this policy framework with every revision of the policy. Indeed, this has been recently recognized by the Commission itself: 'There have been calls for a major overhaul of the ENP's toolbox, to enable the EU to respond better to partners' differing aspirations, and more quickly to a fast-changing neighbourhood and broader global trends'.[91] The results so far have been mixed. While some incentives get added, others somehow disappear from the list. The latter is most telling with regard to the four freedoms, which were replaced with the 'stake in the internal market'.[92]

As far as the security dimension of the ENP is concerned, the viable incentives offered to the partners in 2003 have been gradually watered down.[93] All the attempts of the Commission notwithstanding, the incentives on offer still seem inadequate, and this is unlikely to change as the Council gains a more important role to play in governing policy, given its conservatism and the overall negative effects of inter-institutional rivalry.

Add to this the differences existing between the vision of the ENP espoused by each of the 28 Member States and it becomes clear that the unattractiveness of the incentives on offer has systemic explanations.[94] One thing is clear, however: the

---

[88] All Commission Papers mention this incentive.
[89] JOIN(2015) 9 final (n 37) 2.
[90] Ibid.
[91] Ibid.
[92] COM (2004) 373 final (n 3) 3.
[93] Kelley (n 54) 36; Magen (n 2) 413.
[94] For a telling illustration of the differences in the Member States' approaches to the neighbourhood see M. Natorski, 'National Concerns in the EU Neighbourhood: Spanish and Polish Policies on the Southern and Eastern Dimensions' in Delcour and Tulmets (n 2) 57.

current incentives cannot possibly provide effective backing for the deployment of conditionality in dealing with 'reluctant' partners.

Conclusion

All the proactive rhetoric notwithstanding,[95] the EU is not ready to be wholeheartedly engaged with the ENP partners; particularly so, in the context of the growing pressures from the East, where Russia still seems to be approaching some ENP countries as its de facto colonies.[96] Member States have demonstrated with abundant clarity that they are totally unprepared to come up with clearly articulated functional neighbourhood policy in the contemporary context. Pretending that the ENP exists in vacuum is most unhelpful. The policy has failed to pave a way to increased security and prosperity in the neighbourhood. Indeed, the situation has deteriorated dramatically since the ENP was introduced. The neighbourhood is now poorer and unquestionably infinitely less stable than before, which puts the attainment of the goals of the ENP in danger. Clearly, the only viable way to engage with the neighbourhood is to redesign it from scratch. The new design should not start with seeking uniform approaches to all the states that happen to be in the EU's geographic proximity. A tailor-made engagement with the neighbours is needed, starting not only with the EU's security, migration and other concerns, but also with the actual needs of the neighbours. If such an approach is adopted, the Commission will not need the propaganda language of values and 'joint ownership' of the process anymore. There will be no need to pretend that Azerbaijan and Egypt are functional democracies, sharing EU ideals of human rights and the rule of law. The need to change the current approaches applies particularly strongly to the conditionality idea. Depending on the needs of the partner in question, a clear choice needs to be made whether to apply conditionality or not. As has been compellingly demonstrated in the literature, conditionality cannot possibly work when partner states do not wholeheartedly embrace the changes promoted by the EU. This means that playing conditionality games with 'reluctant' partners should stop. With regard to those partners ready to embrace the changes advocated by the Union, conditionality should remain the norm. All in all, a broader move in the direction of *Realpolitic* would definitely be a welcome development, demonstrating the Union's maturity, as it could emerge as an entity prepared to move on from slogans to actions. Indeed, it is actions, not slogans, that are most needed in the contested neighbourhood.

---

[95] See, for instance, W. Wallace, 'Looking after the Neighbourhood: Responsibilities for the EU-25' (2003) 4 *Notre Europe Policy Paper* 7, noting that: 'The European Union has a long record of rhetorical commitments to foreign policy initiatives, not followed through by national governments or by needed agreement to common policies'.

[96] See R. Petrov, 'The Principle of Good Neighbourliness and the European Neighbourhood Policy' in Kochenov and Basheska (n 7) 289; P. Kalinichenko in Kochenov and Basheska (n 7) 334; N. Ghazaryan, '"Good Neighbourliness" and Conflict Resolution in Nagorno-Karabakh: A Rhetoric or Part of the Legal Method of the European Neighbourhood Policy?' in Kochenov and Basheska (n 7) 306; Ghazaryan (n 16).

Bibliography

Attinà, F. and Rossi, R. (2004) *European Neighbourhood Policy: Political, Economic and Social Issues*. Catania: Catania University Press.

Balfour, R. and Missiroli, A. (2007) Reassessing the European Neighbourhood Policy. *EPC*. Paper No. 54.

Bánkuti M., Halmai, G. and Scheppele, K.L. (2012) Hungary's Illiberal Turn: Disabling the Constitution. *Journal of Democracy*. 23(3). pp. 138–146.

Basheska, E. (2015) The Position of the Good Neighbourliness Principle in International and EU Law. In Kochenov, D. and Basheska, E. *Good Neighbourliness in the European Legal Context*. Leiden: Martinus Nijhoff.

Basheska, E. and Kochenov, D. (2016) EuroMed, Migration and Frenemy-ship: Pretending to Deepen Cooperation across the Mediterranean. In Ippolito, F. and Trevisanut, S. *Migration in Mare Nostrum: Mechanisms of International Co-operation*. Cambridge: Cambridge University Press.

Boute, A. (2013) The EU's Shaping of International Law on Energy Efficiency. In Kochenov, D. and Amtenbrink, F. *EU's Shaping of the International Legal Order*. Cambridge: Cambridge University Press.

Brummer, K. (2009) Imposing Sanctions: The Not So 'Normative Power Europe'. *European Foreign Affairs Review*. 14(2). pp. 191–207.

Ceccorulli, M. and Labanca, N. (2014) *The EU, Migration and the Politics of Administrative Detention*. London: Routledge.

Closa, C. and Kochenov, D. (2015) *Reinforcement of the Rule of Law Oversight in the European Union*. Cambridge: Cambridge University Press.

Craig, P. and de Búrca, G. (2011) *EU Law: Text, Cases and Materials*. 5th edition. Oxford: Oxford University Press.

Cremona, M. (2012) The Two (or Three) Treaty Solution: The New Treaty Structure of the EU. In Biondi, A. and Eeckhout, P. *EU Law after Lisbon*. Oxford: Oxford University Press.

Cremona, M. and Hillion, C. (2006) L'Union fait la force? Potential and Limitations of the European Neighbourhood Policy as an Integrated EU Foreign and Security Policy. *EUI Working Paper*. n. 39.

Cremona, M. and Meloni, G. (2007) The European Neighbourhood Policy: A Framework for Modernisation? *EUI Working Paper Law*. n. 21.

Dannreuter, R. (2006) Developing the Alternative to Enlargement: The European Neighbourhood Policy. *European Foreign Affairs Review*. 11(2). pp. 183–201.

Delcour, L. (2013) The European Union: Shaping Migration Patterns in Its Neighbourhood and Beyond? In Kochenov, D. and Amtenbrink, F. *The European Union's Shaping of the Legal International Order*. Cambridge: Cambridge University Press.

Delcour, L. and Tulmets, E. (2008) *Pioneer Europe? Testing EU Foreign Policy in the Neighbourhood*. Baden-Baden: Nomos.

Delcour, L. and Wolczuk, K. (2013) *Eurasian Economic Integration and Implications for the EU's Policy in the Eastern Neighbourhood*. In Dragneva, R. and Wolczuk, K. *Eurasian Economic Integration: Law, Policy, and Politics*. London: Edward Elgar.

Fogarty, P. (2010) Riding Three Horses: Moldova's Enduring Identity as a Strategy for Survival. In Engelbrekt, K. and Nygren, B. (eds), *Russia and Europe: Building Bridges, Digging Trenches*. London: Routledge.

Ghazaryan, N. (2014) *The European Neighbourhood Policy and the Democratic Values of the EU: A Legal Analysis*. Oxford: Hart Publishing.

—(2015) 'Good Neighbourliness' and Conflict Resolution in Nagorno-Karabakh: A Rhetoric or Part of the Legal Method of the European Neighbourhood Policy? In Kochenov, D. and Basheska, E. *Good Neighbourliness in the European Legal Context*. Leiden: Martinus Nijhoff.

Green, J. (2014) Editorial Comment. The Annexation of Crimea: Russia, Passportisation and the Protection of Nationals Revisited. *Journal on the Use of Force and International Law*. 2(1). pp. 1–2.

Hanf, D. (2012) The European Neighbourhood Policy in the Light of the New 'Neighbourhood Clause' (Article 8 TEU). In Lannon, E. *The European Neighbourhood Policy's Challenges*. New York: P.I.E. Peter Lang.

Hillion, C. (2004) The Copenhagen Criteria and Their Progeny. In Hillion, C. *EU Enlargement: A Legal Approach*. Oxford: Hart Publishing.

—(2014) Anatomy of EU Norm Export towards the Neighbourhood. In *Legislative Approximation and Application of EU Law in the Eastern Neighbourhood of the European Union: Towards a Common Regulatory Space?* London: Routledge.

Inglis, K. (2000) The Europe Agreements Compared in the Light of Their Pre-Accession Reorientation. *CML Rev.* 37(5). pp. 1173–1210.

Kalinichenko, P. (2015) Some Legal Issues of the EU–Russia Relations in the Post-Crimea Era: From Good Neighbourliness to Crisis and Back? In Kochenov, D. and Basheska, E. *Good Neighbourliness in the European Legal Context*. Leiden: Martinus Nijhoff.

Kaunert, C. and Léonard, S. (2013) *European Security Governance and the European Neighbourhood after the Lisbon Treaty*. London: Routledge.

Klabbers, J. (1999) On Babies, Bathwater and the Three Musketeers, or the Beginning of the End of European Integration. In Heiskanen, V. and Kulovesi, K. *Function and Future of European Law*. Publications of the Faculty of Law, Helsinki: University of Helsinki.

Kochenov, D. (2004) Behind the Copenhagen Façade. The Meaning and Structure of the Copenhagen Political Criterion of Democracy and the Rule of Law. *European Integration Online Papers*. (8)10. Available online at http://eiop.or.at/eiop/texte/2004-010a.htm (accessed 5 October 2015).

—(2008) The ENP Conditionality: Pre-Accession Mistakes Repeated. In Delcour, L. and Tulmets, E. *Pioneer Europe? Testing EU Foreign Policy in the Neighbourhood*. Baden Baden: Nomos.

—(2008) *EU Enlargement and the Failure of Conditionality: Pre-Accession Conditionality in the Fields of Democracy and the Rule of Law*. Alphen aan den Rijn: Kluwer Law International.

—(2014) The Issue of Values. In Petrov, R. and Van Elsuwege, P. *Legislative Approximation and Application of EU Law in the Eastern Neighbourhood of the European Union: Towards a Common Regulatory Space?* London: Routledge.

—(2014) Overestimating Conditionality. In Govaere, I. *et al. The European Union in the World: Essays in Honour of Marc Maresceau*. Leiden: Martinus Nijhoff.

Kochenov, D. and Closa, C. (2015) *Reinforcement of the Rule of Law Oversight in the European Union*. Cambridge: Cambridge University Press.

Kochenov, D. Closa, C. and Weiler, J.H.H. (2014–2015) Reinforcing Rule of Law Oversight in the European Union. *EUI Working Paper*. n. 25.

Kratochvíl, P. (2007) New EU Members and the ENP: Different Agendas, Different Strategies. *Intereconomics* 42(4), pp. 191–196.

Larik, J. (2013) Shaping the International Order as an EU Objective. In Kochenov, D. and Amtenbrink, F. *European Union's Shaping of the International Legal Order*. Cambridge: Cambridge University Press.

Lazarou, E., Gianniou, M. and Tsouropas, G. (2013) The Limits of Norm Promotion: The EU in Egypt and Israel/Palestine. *Insight Turkey*. 15(2). pp. 171–193.

Magen, A. (2006) The Shadow of Enlargement: Can the European Neighbourhood Policy Achieve Compliance. *Columbia Journal of European Law*. 12(2). pp. 383–428.

Maresceau, M. (2001) The EU Pre-Accession Strategies: A Political and Legal Analysis. In Maresceau, M. and Lannon, E. *The EU's Enlargement and Mediterranean Strategies*. Available online at www.palgraveconnect.com/pc/doifinder/10.1057/9780333977811 (accessed 5 October 2015).

—(2006) Quelques Réflexions sur l'Application des Principes Fondamentaux dans la Stratégie d'Adhésion de l'UE. In *Le droit De l'Union Européenne en Principes: Liber Amicorum en l'Honneur*. LGDJ, pp. 67–97.

Meloni, G. (2007) Is the Same Toolkit Used during Enlargement Still Applicable to the Countries of the New Neighbourhood? A Problem of Mismatching Between Objectives and Instruments. In Cremona, M. and Meloni, G. The European Neighbourhood Policy: A Framework for Modernisation? *EUI Working Paper Law*. n. 21.

Milano, E. (2014) The Non-Recognition of Russia's Annexation of Crimea: Three Different Legal Approaches and One Unanswered Question. *QIL*. 1. pp. 35–55.

Müller, J.W. (2013) Safeguarding Democracy inside the EU: Brussels and the Future of the International Legal Order. *Transatlantic Academy Paper Series*. No. 3.

—(2014) The EU as a Militant Democracy, or: Are There Limits to Constitutional Mutations within the Member States. *Revista de Estudios Políticos*. n. 165. pp. 141–162.

—(2015) Should the EU Protect Democracy and the Rule of Law Inside the Member States? *ELJ*. 21(2). pp. 141–160.

Müllersson, R. (2014) Ukraine: Victim of Geopolitics. *Chinese Journal of International Law*. 3(1). pp. 133–145.

Natorski, M. (2008) National Concerns in the EU Neighbourhood: Spanish and Polish Policies on the Southern and Eastern Dimensions. In Delcour, L. and Tulmets, E. *Pioneer Europe? Testing EU Foreign Policy in the Neighbourhood*. Baden-Baden: Nomos.

Nye, J.S. (2004) *Soft Power: The Means to Success in World Politics*. New York: Public Affairs.

Perju, V. (2015) The Romanian Double Executive and the 2012 Constitutional Crisis. *Int Journal Constitutional Law*. 13(1). pp. 246–278.

Petrov, R. (2015) The Principle of Good Neighbourliness and the European Neighbourhood Policy. In Kochenov, D. and Basheska, E. *Good Neighbourliness in the European Legal Context*. Leiden: Martinus Nijhoff.

Petrov, R. and Leino, P. (2009) Between 'Common Values' and Competing Universals – The Promotion of the EU's Common Values through the European Neighbourhood Policy. *ELJ*. 15(5). pp. 654–671.

Petrov, R. and Van Elsuwege, P. (2011) Article 8 TEU: Towards a New Generation of Agreements with the Neighbouring Countries of the European Union? *ELRev*. 36(5). pp. 688–703.

—(2014), *Legislative Approximation and Application of EU Law in the Eastern Neighbourhood of the European Union: Towards a Common Regulatory Space?* London: Routledge.

Petrov, R., Van der Loo, G. and Van Elsuwege, P. (2014) The EU–Ukraine Association Agreement: Assessment of an Innovative Legal Instrument. *EUI Working Paper*. n. 09.

Pop, I. (1991) *Components of Good Neighbourliness Between States – Its Specific Legal Contents – Some Considerations Concerning the Reports of the Sub-Committee on Good-Neighbourliness Created by the Legal Committee of the General-Assembly of the United Nations*. Editura R.A.I.: Bucharest.

Sasse, G. (2007) 'Conditionality-lite': The European Neighbourhood Policy and the EU's Eastern Neighbours. In Casarini, N. and Musu, C. *European Foreign Policy in an Evolving International System: The Road towards Convergence*. Basingstoke: Palgrave.

Schütze, R. (2012) *European Constitutional Law*. Cambridge: Cambridge University Press.

de la Serre, F.A. (1994) La Recherche d'une Ostpolitik. In de la Serre, F., Lequesne, C. and Rupnik, J. *L'Union Européenne: Ouverture à l'Est?*. Paris: Presses Universitaires de France.

Smith, K.E. (2004) *The Making of EU Foreign Policy: The Case of Eastern Europe*. 2nd edition. Houndmills and New York: Palgrave Macmillan.

—(2005) The Outsiders: The European Neighbourhood Policy. *International Affairs*. 81(4). pp. 757–773.

Tancredi, A. (2014) The Russian Annexation of the Crimea: Questions Relating to the Use of Force. *QIL*. 1. pp. 5–34.

Tocci, N. (2007) Can the EU Promote Democracy and Human Rights through the ENP? The Case for Refocusing on the Rule of Law. In Cremona, M. and Meloni, G. The European Neighbourhood Policy: A Framework for Modernisation? *EUI Working Paper Law*. n. 21.

Triandafyllidou, A. and Maroukis, T. (2012) *Migrant Smuggling: Irregular Migration from Asia and Africa to Europe*. Basingstoke: Palgrave Macmillan.

Uitz, R. (2015) Can You Tell When an Illiberal Democracy is in the Making? An Appeal to Comparative Constitutional Scholarship from Hungary. *Int J Constitutional Law*. 13(1). pp. 279–300.

Vachudova, M.A. (2015) Why Improve EU Oversight of the Rule of Law? The Two-Headed Problem of Defending Liberal Democracy and Fighting Corruption. In Closa, C. and Kochenov, D. *Reinforcement of the Rule of Law Oversight in the European Union*. Cambridge: Cambridge University Press.

Van Elsuwege, P. (2008) *From Soviet Republics to EU Member States: A Legal and Political Assessment of the Baltic States' Accession to the EU*. Leiden and Boston: Martinus Nijhoff.

Van Vooren, B. (2012) *EU External Relations Law and the European Neighbourhood Policy: A Paradigm for Coherence*. London: Routledge.

Von Bogdandy, A. and Sonnevend, P. (2015) *Constitutional Crisis in the European Constitutional Area: Theory, Law and Politics in Hungary and Romania*. Oxford: Hart Publishing.

Wallace, W. (2003) Looking after the Neighbourhood: Responsibilities for the EU-25. *Notre Europe Policy Paper*. No. 4.

Williams, A. (2010) *The Ethos of Europe*. Cambridge: Cambridge University Press.

Wolff, S. (2012) *The Mediterranean Dimension of the European Union's Internal Security*. New York: Palgrave MacMillan.

Zaiotti, R. (2007) Of Friends and Fences: Europe's Neighbourhood Policy and the 'Gated Community Syndrome'. *Journal of European Integration*. 29(2). pp. 143–162.

9 Exporting the rule of law to the EU's eastern neighbours

Reconciling coherence and differentiation

Peter Van Elsuwege and Olga Burlyuk

Introduction

Respect for the rule of law is crucial within the EU legal order. It is not only defined as one of the Union's foundational values, listed in Art. 2 of the Treaty on European Union (TEU), but has also developed into a crucial variable within the context of the EU's external action (Art. 21(2)b TEU), in particular as far as relations with neighbouring countries are concerned (Art. 8 TEU).

This focus on the rule of law is a relatively recent phenomenon. References to the rule of law could hardly be found in EU documents prior to 1992 and the Treaty of Maastricht[1] but became standard practice in various instruments of the Union's internal and external policies,[2] including the European Neighbourhood Policy (ENP).[3] From the outset, it was made clear that the ENP is based on 'mutual

---

[1] Yet, in its famous *Les Verts* ruling of 1986, the European Court of Justice had already concluded that the European Economic Community was '*based on the rule of law, inasmuch as neither its Member States nor its institutions can avoid a review of the question whether the measures adopted by them are in conformity with the basic constitutional charter, the Treaty* (emphasis added).' See Case C-294/83, *Les Verts* ECR [1986] 1339.

[2] On the increasing significance of the rule of law in the policy and academic debate, see e.g. T. Carothers, 'The Rule of Law Revival' (1998) 77(2) *Foreign Affairs* 95; J. Faundez, 'The Rule of Law Enterprise: Promoting a Dialogue between Practitioners and Academics' (2005) 12(4) *Democratization* 567; A. Magen, 'The Rule of Law and Its Promotion Abroad: Three Problems of Scope' (2009) 45 *Stanford Journal of International Law* 51.

[3] This claim is based on the analysis of major ENP and Eastern Partnership policy documents, including: Wider Europe – New Neighbourhood: Proposals from the Swedish Delegation (31 March 2003); Wider Europe – Neighbourhood: A New Framework for Relations with our Eastern and Southern Neighbours, Commission Communication (11 March 2003); European Neighbourhood Policy Strategy Paper, Commission Communication (12 May 2004); On Strengthening the European Neighbourhood Policy, Commission Communication (4 December 2006); A Strong European Neighbourhood Policy, Commission Communication (5 December 2007); Taking Stock of the European Neighbourhood Policy, Commission Communication (12 May 2010); A New Response to the Changing Neighbourhood, Joint Communication (25 May 2011); Delivering on a New European Neighbourhood Policy, Joint Communication (15 May 2012); ENP: Working towards a Stronger Partnership, Joint Communication (20 March 2013); Neighbourhood at the Crossroads, Joint Communication (27 March 2014); Eastern Partnership: A Polish-Swedish Proposal (June 2008); Eastern Partnership, Commission Communication (3 December 2008); Joint Declaration

commitment to common values' involving, inter alia, the rule of law, human rights and good neighbourliness.[4] The first revision of the ENP, launched in 2011 against the background of the Arab Spring, reiterated the importance of respect for the rule of law as one of the fundamental pillars of the EU's partnership with its neighbours and as a constitutive element for the establishment of 'deep and sustainable democracy'.[5] Significantly, the export of the EU's rule of law model is not an objective in itself but an instrument to fight corruption and to create a positive business environment facilitating foreign direct investments and technology transfers, which in turn stimulate innovation and job creation.[6] As such, it is part of a broader strategy which permeates all dimensions of the EU's relations with its neighbours. Or, as Marise Cremona observed, 'the rule of law is not just an aspect of the ENP, but is its foundation or basis.'[7]

Proceeding from this observation, the question arises how the rule of law is to be understood and what mechanisms and instruments are used to ensure its promotion in the framework of the ENP. This chapter will focus specifically on the EU's relations with its East European neighbours, taking into account the increasingly fragmented legal and political relations with the countries concerned. Whereas the EU has concluded far-reaching Association Agreements with Ukraine, Moldova and Georgia, the revision of its bilateral relations with the non-associated eastern neighbours (Armenia, Azerbaijan and Belarus) is still on the agenda. In this context, the relationship between the ambition of policy coherence, on the one hand, and the principle of differentiation, on the other hand, becomes very pertinent.

The tendency towards more 'tailored cooperation', which is reflected in recent ENP policy documents,[8] raises challenges in light of the ambition to provide a coherent regional approach for relations between the EU and its neighbours. In particular, the question arises as to what extent increased differentiation in terms of rule of law export is possible without exposing the EU to accusations of double standards and without undermining the legitimacy, credibility and effectiveness of its efforts. It is often assumed that there is a direct connection between coherence and the effective promotion of values abroad.[9] Specifically, the absence of a

---

of the Prague Eastern Partnership Summit, the Council of the European Union (7 May 2009); and Eastern Partnership Roadmaps to Autumn 2013 Summit, the Bilateral Dimension and the Multilateral Dimension (15 May 2013).

[4] Commission (EC) 'Communication from the Commission European Neighbourhood Policy' (Strategy Paper), COM (2004) 373, 12 May 2004, 3.

[5] European Commission/High Representative 'A New Response to a Changing Neighbourhood', COM (2011) 303, 25 May 2011, 3.

[6] Ibid. 7.

[7] M. Cremona, 'The European Neighbourhood Policy: Legal and Institutional Issues' (2004) 25 *CDDRL Working Papers* 17. Available online at http://iis-db.stanford.edu/pubs/20738/Cremona-ENP_and_the_Rule_of_Law.pdf (accessed 15 September 2015).

[8] European Commission and High Representative, 'Joint Consultation Paper: Towards a New European Neighbourhood Strategy', JOIN (2015) 6, 4 March 2015; Joint Declaration of the Eastern Partnership Summit, Riga, 21–22 May 2015. Available online at www.consilium.europa.eu/en/meetings/international-summit/2015/05/21–22/ (accessed 15 September 2015).

[9] N. Ghazaryan, *The European Neighbourhood Policy and the Democratic Values of the EU: A Legal Analysis* (Oxford, Hart Publishing 2014) 20; P. Koutrakos, 'Primary Law and Policy in EU External Relations: Moving away from the Big Picture' (2008) 33 *European Law Review* 675.

uniform concept of the rule of law, professed by the EU across its external relations, is criticized and problematized in the literature because it is believed to undermine the effectiveness of EU rule of law promotion.[10]

This chapter argues that a certain variation in the EU's approaches towards rule of law export is not necessarily problematic as long as there is a shared understanding of the core meaning and essential components of the concept. After mapping out the conceptual ambiguities surrounding the rule of law as a guiding principle for the EU's external action, the instruments and mechanisms used within the framework of the ENP are critically analyzed. Finally, the connection between coherence and differentiation is addressed in light of the EU's approach to migration and mobility in relation to its East European neighbours. The latter provides an interesting example of how a certain level of policy coherence can be reconciled with differentiated bilateral relations and mechanisms for exporting the rule of law abroad.

The rule of law concept: overcoming conceptual ambiguities

Despite the widespread use of the concept, the meaning and scope of the rule of law as a value to be exported remains somewhat ambiguous. As observed by Laurent Pech, 'EU instruments – and more generally EU policy reports – rarely specify what the rule of law entails and when definitions are offered, they tend to be rather superficial and not perfectly consistent with each other as variable components tend to be referred to.' Consequently, 'the rule of law, as a foreign policy objective, does not impose precise legal obligations but operates as a "soft" ideal.'[11] As is the case with EU values in general, it is relatively easy to agree on the notion at an abstract level. However, the concrete interpretation of the concept depends upon the particular context.[12]

The difficulties surrounding the understanding of the rule of law as an 'export value' of the Union reflect the internal discussion about its interpretation as a 'common value of the EU' in accordance with Art. 2 TEU. This became particularly obvious in light of the rule of law problems in EU Member States such as France, Romania and, most notably, Hungary and Poland.[13] In this context, the

---

[10] L. Pech, 'Rule of Law as a Guiding Principle of the European Union's External Action' (2012) 3 *CLEER Working Papers*; D. Kochenov, 'The EU Rule of Law: Cutting Paths through Confusion' (2009) 2(1) *Erasmus Law Review* 5; P. Leino and R. Petrov, 'Between "Common Values" and Competing Universals – the Promotion of the EU's Common Values through the European Neighbourhood Policy' (2009) 15(5) *European Law Journal* 654; E.O. Wennerström, *The Rule of Law and the European Union* (Uppsala, Iustus Förlag 2007).
[11] Pech (n 10) 47.
[12] Leino and Petrov (n 10) 655.
[13] The discussion surrounding the rule of law problems in those countries and the need for a new rule of law mechanism at the EU level was launched by former EU Justice Commissioner Viviane Reading in September 2013. See V. Reading, 'The EU and the Rule of Law – What Next?', speech at the Centre for European Policy Studies, Brussels, 4 September 2013. Available online at http://europa.eu/rapid/press-release_SPEECH-13-677_nl.htm (accessed 15 September 2015).

European Commission launched a proposal to address so-called systemic deficiencies to the rule of law. The latter are defined as persistent institutional weaknesses undermining the values and principles on which the European legal order rests.[14] Such deficiencies go beyond the 'normal' occasional infringements which can be tackled on the basis of the existing remedies. They do not concern individual cases or miscarriages of justice, but structural issues such as the independence of judges, corruption or lack of transparency, and legal certainty.

Whereas EU institutions are increasingly aware of this problem, the question remains how such structural deficiencies can be effectively tackled without affecting the division of powers between the EU and its Member States. This is clearly illustrated with the ongoing discussion between the European Commission and the Council about which institution should be in charge of supervising rule of law problems in the Union.[15] According to the Council's legal service, the rule of law only applies as an EU value in relation to areas falling within the scope of application of EU law. The observation that neither Art. 2 TEU nor the Charter of Fundamental Rights confer any material competence on the Union but only list certain values that need to be respected by EU institutions and Member States acting within the scope of EU law, leads to the conclusion that 'respect of the values of the Union, including the rule of law, does not as such constitute a Union policy as foreseen by the Treaties.'[16] As a result, a general supervision of the Member States' rule of law commitments is deemed to go beyond the Commission's mandate under the Treaties. The proposed alternative option is a peer review mechanism agreed by Member States on the basis of an intergovernmental agreement. Even though such an arrangement may provide for the participation of the Commission and other EU institutions if necessary, the effectiveness of this approach is highly questionable.[17]

The competence issue has significant implications for the EU's role as a rule of law exporter. First, it means that the precise content of the principles and standards stemming from the rule of law may vary at national level, depending on each Member State's constitutional system. As a result, it appears impossible – and perhaps even undesirable – to apply a strict EU definition of the rule of law in relation to third countries. Rather, it has to be accepted that the rule of law is an essentially multifaceted and abstract concept including certain core principles of which the precise interpretation largely depends on the particular context.[18] Second, it implies that the export of the EU's values differs from the export of the EU's rules

---

[14] See A. Von Bogdandy and M. Ioannidis, 'Systemic Deficiency in the Rule of Law: What It Is, What Has Been Done, What Can Be Done' (2014) 51(1) *Common Market Law Review* 96.

[15] See Editorial Comments 'Safeguarding EU Values in the Member States – Is Something Finally Happening?' (2015) 52(3) *Common Market Law Review* 619; D. Kochenov and L. Pech, 'From Bad to Worse? On the Commission and the Council's Rule of Law Initiatives' *Verfassungsblog*, 20 January 2015. Available online at www.verfassungsblog.de/bad-worse-commission-councils-rule-law-initiatives (accessed 15 September 2015).

[16] Council of the EU, doc. 10296/14, 27 March 2014 (accessed 15 September 2015).

[17] Kochenov and Pech (n 15).

[18] O. Burlyuk, 'Variation in EU External Policies as a Virtue: EU Rule of Law Promotion in the Neighbourhood' (2015) 53(3) *Journal of Common Market Studies* 513.

(commonly referred to as the EU *acquis*).[19] Of course, there is a certain interconnection, in the sense that EU rules on issues such as non-discrimination and transparency contribute to upholding the rule of law in its Member States. However, a comprehensive approach to the rule of law goes beyond the fragmented *acquis*, which is subject to EU competence limitations. The discrepancy between rules and values became particularly clear in respect to the Union's response to the rule of law crisis in Hungary.[20] The European Commission launched infringement proceedings with regard to Hungarian legislation affecting the independence of the national central bank and data protection authorities as well as over measures affecting the judiciary.[21] In all those instances, a violation of the EU *acquis* – not the EU values of Art. 2 TEU as such – allowed the Commission to play its constitutional role as watchdog of the Treaties.[22] Nevertheless, the concerns about the state of the rule of law in Hungary went beyond the formal scope of application of EU law, as observed in the Tavares report of the European Parliament[23] and as acknowledged by (former) Commission President Barroso.[24] After announcing the Commission's infringement procedures, Barroso tellingly stated:

> So much for EU law, now for the rule of law. Hungary will also need to take due account of the opinion that the Council of Europe/Venice Commission will deliver … in full accordance with both European Union and Council of Europe principles, rules and values.

Hence, EU law *sensu stricto* is not sufficient as a yardstick for assessing Member States' compliance with EU values. As a result, the EU's *acquis* is not a sufficiently adequate instrument for exporting the rule of law to neighbouring countries. The work of other organizations, in particular the Council of Europe's Venice Commission, constitutes a key point of reference for determining the full scope of the rule of law concept. This is increasingly recognized by the EU. In a resolution of 12 March 2014, the European Parliament called for increased

---

[19] D. Kochenov, 'The Issue of Values' in P. Van Elsuwege and R. Petrov (eds.), *Legislative Approximation and Application of EU Law in the Eastern Neighbourhood of the European Union: Towards a Common Regulatory Space?* (London, Routledge 2014) 46.

[20] See e.g. B. Bugaric, 'Protecting Democracy and the Rule of Law in the European Union: The Hungarian Challenge' *LEQS Paper* No. 79/2014. Available online at www.lse.ac.uk/europeanInstitute/LEQS/LEQSPaper79.pdf (accessed 15 September 2015).

[21] European Commission, Press Release IP/12/24, 17 January 2012. Available online at http://europa.eu/rapid/press-release_IP-12-24_en.htm (accessed 15 September 2015).

[22] In this context, Arts. 127 (4) and 130 TFEU (with regard to the ECB), Directive 2000/78 on equal treatment in employment and Directive 95/46 on data protection provided the link between the observed infringements to the rule of law and the application of EU law. See Case C-286/12, *Commission v. Hungary*, EU:C:2012:687; Case C-288/12, *Commission v. Hungary*, EU:C:2014:237.

[23] European Parliament, Report on the Situation of Fundamental Rights: Standards and Practices in Hungary, A7-0229/2013, 24 June 2013.

[24] Hungary and the Rule of Law, Statement of the European Commission in the Plenary Debate of the European Parliament, 17 April 2013. Available online at http://europa.eu/rapid/press-release_SPEECH-13-324_nl.htm (accessed 15 September 2015).

cooperation between both organizations.[25] The European Commission even explicitly built upon a Venice Convention's report to identify six key principles constituting the hard core of the rule of law within the EU legal order. This includes the principles of legality and legal certainty, the prohibition of arbitrariness of the executive powers, the existence of independent and impartial courts, guarantees of effective judicial review (including respect for fundamental rights) and equality before the law.[26] Also the EU Council, which is more sceptical about the need for a new rule of law mechanism (see p. 170), agreed that if the Union wants to remain 'the anchor for reforms in the areas of the rule of law and fundamental rights for several third countries,' steps must be taken to develop a more effective monitoring mechanism based upon a common understanding of the concept of the rule of law.[27]

This stocktaking exercise points to a growing consensus about the common elements constituting the pan-European rule of law concept. This is an important evolution and increases the legitimacy and credibility of the EU's values promotion in third countries, most specifically with regard to its European neighbours that are members of the Council of Europe. A shared pre-understanding of the core principles constituting the rule of law ensures a degree of coherence across the EU's internal and external policies, while allowing for a certain variation to take into account the specific circumstances of the Union's relations with particular third countries.[28]

Of course, the instrumental use of the core principles remains challenging. Generally speaking, those principles can either be applied in a formalist or substantive manner. The formalist (or 'thin') approach implies that monitoring of the rule of law in a given country focuses solely on procedural aspects such as the existence of separation of powers in constitutional documents, formal control mechanisms to the functioning of public institutions and a transparent procedure for the adoption of laws. A substantive (or 'thick') approach, on the other hand, presupposes that both the form of the legal system and the actual outcome of the legislative processes and its implications for the rights of citizens are important.[29] Accordingly, the rule of law is inseparable from other values, such as democracy, respect for fundamental values and equal treatment. As observed in a Committee of Permanent Representatives (COREPER) document of May 2013, this second, substantive, understanding of the rule of law should guide the EU's efforts. The alternative, formalist, approach 'allows for a recognition of the rule of law as existing even in countries that are not democracies and that do not recognize individual rights.'[30]

---

[25] European Parliament Resolution of 12 March 2014 on evaluation of justice in relation to criminal justice and the rule of law, A7-0122/2014.
[26] See Annex I to COM (2014) 158, 'A new EU Framework to Strengthen the Rule of Law', 11 March 2014.
[27] Council of the EU, 'Ensuring respect for the Rule of Law', doc. 16862/14, 12 December 2014.
[28] Burlyuk (n 18).
[29] On the distinction between a formalist (or 'thin') and a substantive (or 'thick' approach), see Council of the EU, doc. 10168/13, 29 May 2013 and Pech (n 10) 8 and 26.
[30] Council of the EU, doc. 10168/13, 29 May 2013.

In general, it appears that the EU indeed promotes a substantive, holistic conception of the rule of law in its relations with third countries.[31] However, it has been argued that more could be done to develop a comprehensive framework for EU rule of law activities, including a further operationalization of what the core principles of the rule of law actually entail and how they can be consistently monitored and measured. Despite the so-called legislative mainstreaming of the EU's foundational values, implying that they have been progressively integrated into all aspects of the EU's external policies and actions, the absence of such a comprehensive framework implies that the rule of law export is currently based upon a combination of instruments and mechanisms lacking clear indicators for assessing a particular country's adherence to the rule of law.[32]

The complex toolbox of instruments and mechanisms underlying the EU's 'rule of law export'

The EU uses a variety of instruments and mechanisms to export its values abroad. This includes soft-law instruments (such as Action Plans and Association Agendas)[33] as well as legally binding hard-law instruments (such as 'essential elements clauses' in bilateral agreements). It also involves unilateral (technical and financial assistance), bilateral (framework and sectoral agreements) and multilateral (regional platforms) instruments.[34] Some authors even talk about the existence of an EU 'value diffusion strategy' involving diplomatic instruments and discursive practices such as political dialogue, negotiations and public statements in combination with economic assistance and the institutionalization of the EU's relationship with third countries.[35]

Whatever categorization is used, the bottom line is that the export of values has become an increasingly important aspect of the EU's external action.[36] In line with the spirit of the EU Treaties, in particular Art. 21(3) TEU, the objective of value promotion is not the objective of one single policy but has been integrated into all aspects of the EU's relations with third countries. This is particularly obvious as far as the Union's relations with its neighbouring countries are concerned. In addition to the explicit value dimension of the ENP, the export of values is also part of the EU's trade policy,[37] migration policy[38] and Common Security and Defence Policy (CSDP).[39]

---

[31] Pech (n 10) 47.
[32] Pech (n 10) 48.
[33] On the use of those soft law tools in the ENP, see B. Van Vooren, *EU External Relations Law and the European Neighbourhood Policy. A Paradigm for Coherence* (Routledge, London 2012) 117–224.
[34] For an overview of the instruments used, see e.g. Pech (n 10); M. Cremona, 'Values in EU Foreign Policy' in M. Evans and P. Koutrakos (eds.), *Beyond the Established Orders: Policy Interconnections between the EU and the Rest of the World* (Oxford, Hart Publishing 2011) 275.
[35] A. Haglund-Morresey, 'EU Value Promotion and the European Neighbourhood Policy' (2007) 32 *Southeastern Europe* 39.
[36] Cremona (n 34).
[37] A clear example is the exclusion of Belarus from the EU's General System of Preferences (GSP).
[38] For instance, through the inclusion of rule of law aspects in Visa Liberalisation Action Plans (VLAPs), see *infra*.
[39] For instance, through the organization of EU Rule of Law Missions such as EUJUST THEMIS in Georgia.

Arguably, the EU's efforts all relate to the three interconnected mechanisms of conditionality, differentiation and joint ownership.[40] First, the use of preconditions, incentives and other instruments to ensure that a third country's political, economic and legal development converges with EU values and norms is a key characteristic feature of the EU's external relations. Therefore, it is not surprising that conditionality is a core mechanism in the EU's rule of law export to neighbouring countries. This can either take the form of offering rewards (positive conditionality) or threatening sanctions (negative conditionality).[41] Second, the consistent application of this conditionality approach necessarily implies a certain level of differentiation: the more a country conforms to EU values, the closer it can cooperate with the EU. Third, differentiation cannot be disconnected from the principle of joint ownership or, in particular, from the ambitions of neighbouring countries to engage in deep bilateral relations with the Union. The more a country is interested in closer links with the Union, the more effective the EU's conditionality approach can be, and the more differentiation (in comparison to less ambitious countries) can be expected.

The interconnection between the three principles can be illustrated with the development of the EU's relations with its East European neighbours that are part of the ENP. Whereas they all belong to the same policy framework and are, as such, subject to EU 'rule of law' initiatives, the more far-reaching integration with Ukraine, Moldova and Georgia implies that the Union has more leverage to influence the rule of law developments in those countries. The new generation of Association Agreements (AAs), signed with Ukraine, Moldova and Georgia in June 2014, all include a commitment to establish privileged relations on the basis of 'common values' including, inter alia, respect for democratic principles and the rule of law.[42] More explicitly, those common values are defined as 'essential elements' of the Agreements, implying that a violation of those values may lead to the suspension of the Agreement.[43] Furthermore, reinforcing the rule of law is an explicit objective of the association.[44] For this purpose, the parties established an enhanced political dialogue, including a specific dialogue and cooperation on domestic reform.[45] The Agreements also include a separate 'rule of law' clause.[46] For instance, Art. 14 of the AA with Ukraine provides that:

---

[40] P. Van Elsuwege, 'Variable Geometry in the European Neighbourhood Policy: The Principle of Differentiation and its Consequences' in E. Lannon (ed.), *The European Neighbourhood Policy's Challenges* (Bruxelles, Bern, Berlin, Frankfurt am Main, New York, Oxford, Wien, Peter Lang 2012) 59–84.

[41] See S. Poli's chapter in this book.

[42] G. Van der Loo, P. Van Elsuwege and R. Petrov, 'The EU–Ukraine Association Agreement: Assessment of an Innovative Legal Instrument' *EUI Working Papers, Law* 2014/09.

[43] E.g. Arts. 2 and 478 of the AA with Ukraine. For a critical analysis, see N. Ghazaryan, 'A New Generation of Human Rights Clauses? The Case of Association Agreements in the Eastern Neighbourhood' (2015) 40(3) *European Law Review* 391.

[44] E.g. Art. 2(2)(e) AA with Ukraine.

[45] E.g. Art. 6 AA with Ukraine.

[46] For a comparison between the position of the rule of law in the Association Agreements with southern countries and in those concluded with Ukraine, Moldova and Georgia, see Nariné Ghazaryan's chapter in this book.

[I]n their cooperation on justice, freedom and security, the Parties shall attach particular importance to the consolidation of the rule of law and the reinforcement of institutions at all levels in the areas of administration in general and law enforcement and the administration of justice in particular. Cooperation will, in particular, aim at strengthening the judiciary, improving its efficiency, safeguarding its independence and impartiality, and combating corruption. Respect for human rights and fundamental freedoms will guide all cooperation on justice, freedom and security.

The enhanced political dialogue and the 'rule of law clause' give the Union a mandate to be involved in domestic reforms in the associated countries. The obvious aim is to export the rule of law as understood within the EU legal order and as expressed under Art. 2 TEU. In fact, as discussed above, those values reflect the common constitutional traditions of EU Member States but are also to a large extent based upon the work of the Council of Europe and its Venice Commission. In other words, the 'values are both imported into, and exported from, the EU legal order.'[47] This is also reflected in the Association Agendas, which are adopted by the respective Association Councils to facilitate the implementation of the Association Agreements. For instance, the Association Agenda with Ukraine includes a specific section devoted to 'democracy, rule of law, human rights and fundamental freedoms' with references to the recommendations of the Venice Commission when reform of the judiciary and the constitution is concerned.[48]

The impact of the 'joint ownership' principle was already visible before the conclusion of the Association Agreements. With Ukraine, for instance, the EU Council defined explicit conditions regarding the organization of fair elections, the tackling of so-called problems of selective justice and the implementation of reforms in the field of criminal procedure before the AA could be signed.[49] With regard to Georgia, the EU's involvement with respect to its rule of law developments significantly increased after the establishment of an EU Rule of Law Mission (EUJUST THEMIS) in 2004 at the explicit request of the Georgian authorities.[50] More recently, the EU established an advisory mission for civilian security sector reform in Ukraine which, inter alia, aims to strengthen the rule of law in this country.[51] Significantly, the EU is not the only actor active in promoting rule of law developments in its neighbouring countries. In Moldova, for instance, the Norwegian government launched a mission of

---

[47] Cremona (n 34) 275.
[48] The EU–Ukraine Association Agenda, as endorsed by the EU–Ukraine Association Council on 16 March 2015. Available online at http://eeas.europa.eu/ukraine/docs/st06978_15_en.pdf (accessed 15 September 2015).
[49] Council of the EU, Conclusions on Ukraine, Brussels, 10 December 2012.
[50] Council Joint Action 2004/523/CFSP of 28 June 2004 on the European Union Rule of Law Mission in Georgia, EUJUST THEMIS [2004] OJ L 228/21. For an assessment about this rule of law mission, which was the first under the European Common Foreign and Security Policy, see X. Kurowska, 'EUJust Themis' in G. Grevi, D. Helly and D. Keohane (eds.), *European Security and Defence Policy. The First Ten Years (1999–2009)* (EU Institute for Security Studies 2009) 201.
[51] See www.eeas.europa.eu/csdp/missions-and-operations/euam-ukraine/index_en.htm (accessed 15 September 2015).

rule of law advisors,[52] and the United States runs its own Rule of Law Institutional Strengthening Programme (ROLISP).[53]

Arguably, the EU's rule of law export is much more difficult and, as a result, less developed with regard to its non-associated eastern neighbours. Legal relations with these countries are for the time being still based on largely outdated Partnership and Cooperation Agreements (PCAs). With Belarus, such a framework agreement never even entered into force and no ENP Action Plan has been adopted.[54] Consequently, the Union has not been given a similar mandate to be engaged with domestic rule of law reforms in those countries. This does not mean that no initiatives have been undertaken. On a regular basis, the EU adopts statements expressing its concern about the rule of law in Belarus, Azerbaijan and – to a lesser extent – Armenia. With regard to Armenia and Azerbaijan, the ENP Action Plans refer to the need for judicial reform and initiatives to combat fraud and corruption. However, despite the political rhetoric on paper, the vague and general nature of these references cannot conceal the relatively limited impact of the EU's initiatives in practice.[55] Hence, the question remains how the EU can cope with a situation where neighbouring countries do not necessarily share the same interpretation of its core values. This also relates to the eternal problem of how the Union's values can be reconciled with its (political and economic) interest in having working relations with its direct neighbours. Recent developments in the field of migration and mobility illustrate how this apparent dichotomy is dealt with in practice.

Reconciling coherence and differentiation in the EU's engagement with its East European neighbours: the example of migration and mobility

As argued above, the export of EU values abroad is not the privilege of a single policy but has permeated various aspects of the Union's relations with third countries. This is, for instance, the case with regard to the EU's migration policy, which received a major boost after the adoption of the Global Approach to Migration and Mobility (GAMM) in 2005. In this context, it has been made very clear that:

> Migration and mobility are embedded in the broader political, economic, social and security context. A broad understanding of security means that *irregular migration also needs to be considered in connection with organised crime and lack of the rule of law and justice*, feeding on corruption and inadequate regulation.[56]

---

[52] See www.norlam.md/?l=en (accessed 15 September 2015).
[53] See http://rolisp.org/en/about-rolisp.html (accessed 15 September 2015).
[54] M. Karliuk, 'Legislative Approximation and Application of EU Law in Belarus' in P. Van Elsuwege and R. Petrov (eds.), *Legislative Approximation and Application of EU Law in the Eastern Neighbourhood of the European Union: Towards a Common Regulatory Space?* (London, Routledge 2014) 245.
[55] Ghazaryan (n 9) 148.
[56] European Commission, 'The Global Approach to Migration and Mobility', COM (2011) 743 final, 15, 18 November 2011 (emphasis added).

Proceeding from this approach, supporting the mobility of citizens from partner countries was put high on the agenda of the Eastern Partnership (EaP). In this context, Cecilia Malmström, in her capacity as EU Commissioner for Home Affairs, declared:

> We are sending an important signal that the EU is committed to active cooperation on well-managed and secure mobility with our eastern Partners. *Our engagement to enhance mobility and people-to-people contacts with the countries concerned is guided by the principles of human rights, respect of democracy and the rule of law.* Continuous cooperation based on trust and respect within the EaP is crucial if we are to increase mobility whilst at the same time addressing the challenges, such as trafficking in human beings, organised crime and corruption.[57]

Looking at actual practice, three instruments devoted to migration and mobility can be distinguished. First, the EU has adopted Mobility Partnerships (MPs) with Moldova (2008), Georgia (2009), Armenia (2009), Azerbaijan (2013) and Belarus (2015).[58] The MPs provide a soft-law framework for bilateral cooperation on migratory issues between the partner countries and interested EU Member States. It is a very flexible instrument and includes a wide variety of initiatives, ranging from training and export support to the offer of student and professional exchanges and concrete labour migration programmes. Despite the broad conception of migration under the GAMM and the rhetoric of Commissioner Malmström, the focus of the MPs is almost exclusively on migration management, implying that no concrete efforts to rule of law export could be identified.

Second, the EU has established a network of bilateral visa facilitation and readmission agreements with its eastern neighbours.[59] Both types of agreements are concluded in parallel, implying that a facilitated visa regime is combined with an obligation on countries to take back their nationals as well as third-country nationals and stateless persons who have transited through the country when they do not fulfil the conditions for entry or stay in the territory of the other party. This approach gives the EU an opportunity to pressure countries to reform domestic justice and home affairs.[60] However, in practice the EU's readmission policy is essentially driven by a security logic.[61] It is only after significant pressure

---

[57] European Commission Press Release, IP/11/1075, 27 September 2011 (emphasis added).

[58] Remarkably, Ukraine is the only EaP country without a mobility partnership. This may be related to the country's early conclusion of a visa facilitation agreement with the EU in 2007 and its prioritization of the visa free dialogue (interview with Ukrainian officials, on file with the authors).

[59] Visa facilitation and readmission agreements have been concluded with Ukraine [2007] OJ L 168/11, Moldova [2007] OJ L 168/3, Georgia [2013] OJ L 52/34, Armenia [2013] OJ L 289/2 and Azerbaijan [2014] OJ L 128/49. The visa facilitation agreements with Ukraine and Moldova were amended and upgraded in 2013, OJ L 168/11 and OJ L 168/3.

[60] F. Trauner and I. Kruse, 'EC Visa Facilitation and Readmission Agreements: A New Standard EU Foreign Policy Tool?' (2008) 10(4) *European Journal of Migration and Law* 438.

[61] F. Trauner, I. Kruse and B. Zeilinger, 'Values versus Security in the External Dimension of EU Migration Policy: A Case Study on the Readmission Agreement with Russia' in G. Noutcheva, K. Pomorska and G. Bosse (eds.), *The EU and Its Neighbours: Values vs. Security in European Foreign Policy* (Manchester, Manchester University Press 2012) 217.

from NGOs and the European Parliament that EU readmission agreements now include a standard 'human rights clause'.[62] However, the agreements set out no specific provisions concerning promotion of the rule of law.

Third, the EU launched a process of visa liberalization with three EaP countries (Moldova, Ukraine and Georgia), aiming at the establishment of a visa-free regime.[63] For this purpose, Visa Liberalisation Action Plans (VLAPs) have been adopted and Visa Liberalisation Dialogues established. The VLAPs include four blocks of benchmarks related to: (1) document security; (2) border management, migration and asylum; (3) public order and security; and (4) external relations and fundamental rights. Even though the focus is clearly on security aspects, and none of the benchmarks explicitly deals with the rule of law in the partner countries, the VLAPs include relevant aspects such as the adoption of anti-corruption measures, anti-discrimination legislation and the effectiveness of law enforcement.

In contrast to the MPs and the bilateral agreements on visa facilitation and readmission, the VLAPs are based upon a strict conditionality approach which is borrowed from the EU's pre-accession methodology. This implies, inter alia, regular Commission monitoring. Significantly, the VLAPs include two sets of benchmarks, dealing with the policy framework (legislation and planning) and with the effective and sustainable implementation of relevant measures.[64] Accordingly, the visa liberalization process has two stages. After the fulfilment of all benchmarks, the Commission can make a proposal to the Council and the Parliament for an amendment of Regulation 539/2001 introducing the lifting of short-stay visa obligations for biometric passport holders. Importantly, there is no automaticity in this process and, before submitting its proposal, the Commission shall take into account the overall relations between the EU and the given third country. In other words, there are ample opportunities for influencing the rule of law situation in the partner countries, even beyond the benchmarks that are mentioned in the VLAPs.

Taken together, the MPs, the bilateral agreements on visa facilitation and readmission and the VLAPs lead to a differentiated landscape of bilateral relations with the EU's eastern neighbours. Significantly, the EU's leverage in terms of rule of law export is most developed with regard to the countries that are involved in the process of visa liberalization. Not surprisingly, these are the associated countries, which confirms the identified interconnection between conditionality, joint ownership and differentiation. Accordingly, the rule of law requirements involved

---

[62] For a recent example, see Art. 2 of the readmission agreement between the EU and Azerbaijan [2014] OJ L 128/17.

[63] At the time of writing, only with Moldova a visa-regime for short-term travel had been introduced for holders of biometric passports. See Regulation No 259/2014 of the European Parliament and of the Council of 3 April 2014 amending Council Regulation No 539/2001 listing the third countries whose nationals must be in possession of visas when crossing the external borders and those whose nationals are exempt from that requirement [2014] OJ L 105/9.

[64] See 'Moving towards Visa Liberalisation with Moldova, Ukraine and Georgia'. Available online at http://ec.europa.eu/dgs/home-affairs/what-we-do/policies/international-affairs/eastern-partnership/visa-liberalisation-moldova-ukraine-and-georgia/index_en.htm (accessed 15 September 2015).

Exporting the rule of law 179

in the visa liberalization process coincide with and complement the values dimension of the Association Agreements. Hence, a coherent framework for rule of law export to those countries can be established. For the non-associated countries, their more modest ambition of integration with the EU implies that the Union cannot apply the same pressure but, concomitantly, less far-reaching incentives are offered.

Whereas the EaP thus offers a relatively coherent framework for the development of the EU's relations with its participating eastern neighbours, its credibility also depends upon its approach to other countries. With respect to mobility issues, reference could be made to the EU's southern Mediterranean partners, the Western Balkan countries and the Russian Federation. First, the southern Mediterranean countries are also part of the ENP and, as such, subject to instruments similar to those developed within the EaP. However, it was only in the wake of the so-called Arab Spring and the EU's offer of a Partnership for Democracy and Shared Prosperity that a structured 'dialogue for migration, mobility and security with the southern Mediterranean countries' was set up.[65] In this context, Mobility Partnerships have been concluded with Morocco (2013), Tunisia (2014) and Jordan (2014). With Morocco, the EU opened negotiations on visa facilitation and readmission agreements in January 2015. Hence, the instruments (mobility partnerships, agreements on visa facilitation and readmission) and principles (differentiation, bilateralism, conditionality, monitoring) applicable in relation to the EU's southern neighbours build upon the existing toolbox, as developed with respect to its eastern neighbours. Second, the Western Balkan countries are all recognized as 'potential' EU Member States and, as such, belong to the EU's enlargement policy. Apart from Kosovo, all Western Balkan countries already have a visa-free regime with the EU. This process of visa liberalization followed a pattern largely comparable to the one established for the EaP countries. Even more, the methodology of visa liberalization with Moldova, Ukraine and Georgia is based upon the Western Balkan experience, with some minor differences.[66] Third, certain similarities can be observed with regards to Russia, even though there are also significant differences. The process of visa liberalization, which is currently frozen due to the events in Ukraine, proceeds along the lines of the 'Common Steps towards Visa Free Short-Term Travel of Russian and EU Citizens.'[67] This document was adopted in December 2011 and largely follows the same structure as the VLAPs, with the same four thematic blocks of benchmarks to be fulfilled. However, in contrast to the VLAPs (or 'road maps' used in connection with the Western Balkan countries), the 'Common Steps' document is based on the principle of reciprocity. It does not involve the same unilateral conditionality approach but presupposes that both Russia and the EU need to fulfil certain

---

[65] European Commission, 'A Dialogue for Migration, Mobility and Security with the Southern Mediterranean Countries', COM (2011) 292 final, 24 May 2011.
[66] The key difference is the introduction of two stages for the implementation of the VLAPs.
[67] The text of this document is available online at http://ec.europa.eu/dgs/home-affairs/what-we-do/policies/international-affairs/russia/docs/common_steps_towards_visa_free_short_term_travel_en.pdf (accessed 15 September 2015).

obligations.[68] Even though this distinction may be regarded as largely rhetorical in nature, it has some concrete implications. This is most visible with respect to the fourth block, which addresses external relations. Whereas the VLAPs with the EaP countries are quite explicit in requesting the 'adoption of comprehensive anti-discrimination legislation ... to ensure effective protection against discrimination', the Common Steps document with Russia is less demanding and only requires Russia to 'discuss and cooperate' on the relevant recommendations of international human rights organizations. Obviously, this discrepancy raises questions about the coherence of the EU's approach to visa liberalization – and, indirectly, about the export of its values to its eastern neighbours.[69] It seems, therefore, to be no coincidence that the EU Council has been very reluctant to release the content of the Common Steps with Russia because it could have an adverse effect on the climate of trust between the EU and the EaP countries.[70]

Conclusions

The rule of law is an essentially contested concept. As a result, its export raises a number of practical difficulties. First, references to the rule of law are frequently used in political discourse and official documents. However, without a further operationalization of what the concept means, the actual impact of such references is fairly limited. Second, the rule of law cannot be easily reduced to the EU *acquis*. Whereas certain EU Regulations and Directives certainly contribute to important aspects of the rule of law, such as the principles of non-discrimination and transparency, a mere export of EU rules is not sufficient to change the rule of law culture in third countries. Third, there is no EU competence to develop a comprehensive rule of law policy internally. As a result, the Union cannot merely export its own policy abroad but rather is dependent upon the work of other relevant actors, in the first place the Council of Europe and its Venice Commission.

Despite the identified conceptual challenges, the EU has developed a wide variety of instruments and mechanisms supporting the export of the rule of law abroad. The key challenge for the EU is to ensure a certain level of coherence in its rule of law export while, at the same time, allowing for a certain level of differentiation in the development of its bilateral relations. This is particularly the case in the EU's eastern neighbourhood, where several countries with a questionable track record in the rule of law have increasingly differentiated bilateral relations with the EU. A key distinction can be made between the EU's associated countries, which are subject to a strict conditionality approach, and the non-association countries, where the Union has less leverage to influence the domestic situation. Arguably, this variation is not necessarily to be interpreted as a sign of incoherence, as long as the

---

[68] P. Van Elsuwege, J. Fomina, O. Korneev *et al.* 'EU–Russia Visa Facilitation and Liberalisation. State of Play and Prospects for the Future' (2013) *EU–Russia Civil Society Forum* 49.

[69] P. Van Elsuwege, 'Coherent Approach Needed on Visa Liberalisation' Euractiv.com, 8 April 2013 (accessed 15 September 2015).

[70] Van Elsuwege, Fomina, Korneev *et al.* (n 68) 36.

approach vis-à-vis each particular country (or group of countries) is based upon a clear and consistent operationalization of the rule of law requirements.

Bibliography

Bugaric, B. (2014) Protecting Democracy and the Rule of Law in the European Union: The Hungarian Challenge. *LEQS Paper*. n. 79. pp. 1–44. Available online at www.lse.ac.uk/europeanInstitute/LEQS/LEQSPaper79.pdf (accessed 15 September 2015).

Burlyuk, O. (2015) Variation in EU External Policies as a Virtue: EU Rule of Law Promotion in the Neighbourhood. *Journal of Common Market Studies*. 53(3). pp. 509–523.

Carothers, T. (1998) The Rule of Law Revival. *Foreign Affairs*. 6 October 2015. Available online at www.foreignaffairs.com/articles/1998-03-01/rule-law-revival&gt (accessed 15 September 2015).

Cremona, M. (2004) The European Neighbourhood Policy: Legal and Institutional Issues. *CDDRL Working Papers*. n. 25. pp. 1–27. Available online at http://iis-db.stanford.edu/pubs/20738/Cremona-ENP_and_the_Rule_of_Law.pdf (accessed 15 September 2015).

—(2011) Values in EU Foreign Policy. In Evans, M. and Koutrakos, P. *Beyond the Established Orders: Policy Interconnections Between the EU and the Rest of the World*. Oxford: Hart Publishing.

Editorial Comments (2015) Safeguarding EU Values in the Member States – Is Something Finally Happening? *Common Market Law Review*. 52(3). pp. 619–628.

Faundez, J. (2005) The Rule of Law Enterprise: Promoting a Dialogue Between Practitioners and Academics. *Democratization*. 12(4). pp. 567–586.

Ghazaryan, N. (2014) *The European Neighbourhood Policy and the Democratic Values of the EU: A Legal Analysis*. Oxford: Hart Publishing.

—(2015) A New Generation of Human Rights Clauses? The Case of Association Agreements in the Eastern Neighbourhood. *European Law Review*. 40(3). pp. 391–410.

Haglund-Morresey, A. (2007) EU Value Promotion and the European Neighbourhood Policy. *Southeastern Europe*. 31–32. pp. 39–59.

Karliuk, M. (2014) Legislative Approximation and Application of EU Law in Belarus. In Van Elsuwege, P. and Petrov, R. *Legislative Approximation and Application of EU Law in the Eastern Neighbourhood of the European Union: Towards a Common Regulatory Space?* London: Routledge.

Kochenov, D. (2009) The EU Rule of Law: Cutting Paths Through Confusion. *Erasmus Law Review*. 2(1). pp. 5–24.

—(2014) The Issue of Values. In Van Elsuwege, P. and Petrov, R. *Legislative Approximation and Application of EU Law in the Eastern Neighbourhood of the European Union: Towards a Common Regulatory Space?* London: Routledge.

Kochenov, D. and Pech, L. (2015) From Bad to Worse? On the Commission and the Council's Rule of Law Initiatives. *Verfassungsblog*. 20 January 2015. Available online at www.verfassungsblog.de/bad-worse-commission-councils-rule-law-initiatives (accessed 15 September 2015).

Koutrakos, P. (2008) Primary Law and Policy in EU External Relations: Moving Away from the Big Picture. *European Law Review*. 33(5). pp. 666–686.

Kurowska, X. (2009) EUJust Themis. In Grevi, G., Helly, D. and Keohane, D. *European Security and Defence Policy. The First Ten Years (1999–2009)*. Paris: EU Institute for Security Studies. pp. 201–209.

Leino, P. and Petrov, R. (2009) Between 'Common Values' and Competing Universals – the Promotion of the EU's Common Values Through the European Neighbourhood Policy. *European Law Journal*. (15)5. pp. 654–671.

Magen, A. (2009) The Rule of Law and Its Promotion Abroad: Three Problems of Scope. *Stanford Journal of International Law*. 45. pp. 51–115.

Pech, L. (2012) Rule of Law as a Guiding Principle of the European Union's External Action. *CLEER Working Papers*. 3. Available online at www.asser.nl/upload/documents/2102012_33322cleer2012-3web.pdf (accessed 15 September 2015).

Reading, V. (2013) The EU and the Rule of Law – What Next? Speech at the Centre for European Policy Studies, Brussels. 4 September 2013. Available online at http://europa.eu/rapid/press-release_SPEECH-13-677_nl.htm (accessed 15 September 2015).

Trauner, F. and Kruse, I. (2008) EC Visa Facilitation and Readmission Agreements: A New Standard EU Foreign Policy Tool? *European Journal of Migration and Law*. 10(4). pp. 411–438.

Trauner, F., Kruse, I. and Zeilinger, B. (2012) Values Versus Security in the External Dimension of EU Migration Policy: A Case Study on the Readmission Agreement with Russia. In Noutcheva, G., Pomorska K. and Bosse G. *The EU and Its Neighbours: Values vs. Security in European Foreign Policy*. Manchester: Manchester University Press.

Van der Loo, G., Van Elsuwege, P. and Petrov, R. (2014) The EU–Ukraine Association Agreement: Assessment of an Innovative Legal Instrument. *EUI Working Papers, Law*. n. 09.

Van Elsuwege, P. (2012) Variable Geometry in the European Neighbourhood Policy: The Principle of Differentiation and its Consequences. In Lannon, E. *The European Neighbourhood Policy's Challenges*. Bruxelles, Bern, Berlin, Frankfurt am Main, New York, Oxford, Wien: Peter Lang.

—(2013) Coherent Approach Needed on Visa Liberalisation. Euractiv.com. 8 April 2013. Available online at www.euractiv.com/europes-east/visa-liberalisation-eastern-neig-analysis-518893 (accessed 15 September 2015).

Van Elsuwege, P., Fomina J., Korneev, O. *et al*. (2013). EU–Russia Visa Facilitation and Liberalisation: State of Play and Prospects for the Future. *EU–Russia Civil Society Forum 2013*. September 2013. pp. 1–47. Available online at http://eu-russia-csf.org/fileadmin/Policy_Papers/Others/Visa_Report_eng.pdf (accessed 15 September 2015).

Van Vooren, B. (2012) *EU External Relations Law and the European Neighbourhood Policy: A Paradigm for Coherence*. London: Routledge.

Von Bogdandy, A. and Ioannidis, M. (2014) Systemic Deficiency in the Rule of Law: What It Is, What Has Been Done, What Can Be Done. *Common Market Law Review*. 51(1). pp. 59–96.

Wennerström, E.O. (2007) *The Rule of Law and the European Union*. Uppsala: Iustus Förlag.

Index

References to footnotes consist of the page number followed by the letter 'n' followed by the number of the note, e.g. 52n124 refers to note no. 124 on page 52.

9/11 terrorist attacks 133, 138

Abkhazia: EU response to conflict 69, 108; and EU restrictive measures 54
acquis: and Association Agreements (AAs) 68, 101, 104–6; within EU–Russia sectoral cooperation 118; and principles of homogeneity/legal certainty 70; and rule of law 170–1, 180; v. values 62, 63, 147, 153, 170–1
Action Plans (APs) of ENP: and action against corruption 92; and democratic values 15, 62; and EU values 13, 14, 15–16, 18, 35, 58; and joint ownership principle 75; and rule of law export 173, 176; and support for EU sanction regimes 95–6; and WMD clauses 86–7; *see also* Association Agreements (AAs); *separate countries*
Albania: EU macro-financial assistance 44; Stabilisation and Association Agreement 24n78, 27n94; support for EU sanctions against Syria 96
Alexander I, tsar of Russia 131
Alexy II, Patriarch of Moscow 134, 137
Algeria, Euro-Med Agreement 24n74, 25n84, 28n101
Al Matri, Fahed 49n105, 93
Al Tabbaa, Mazen 126
Anti-Ballistic Missile Treaty (ABMT) 138
Arab countries: rise of political Islam 65; and Russia under Putin 140
Arab Spring: and deep democracy 35; and emancipation from the West 72; and EU mobility for southern Mediterranean countries 179; and EU restrictive measures 49, 51; and EU's connivance with authoritarian regimes 70; EU's response to 19–20, 22, 58, 64, 71; and rule of law in ENP 168
Armenia: and Collective Security Treaty Organization (CSTO) 140; ENP Action Plan 15, 16, 95–6; ENP participation 149n24; and ENP process and Russia 148; EU macro-financial assistance 45–6; and Eurasian Economic Union 73, 148n16; Mobility Partnership (MP) 177; Nagorno–Karabakh conflict and EU response 69; Partnership and Cooperation Agreement (PCA) 25; and rule of law in ENP 168, 176; support for EU sanctions against Burma 96; visa facilitation and readmission agreement 177n59
arms: Arms Trade Treaty (ATT) 88–9; EU Code of Conduct on Arms Exports 91; small arms and light weapons (SALW) 88; *see also* weapons of mass destruction (WMD)
Association Agreements (AAs): and *acquis* 68, 101, 104–6; and action against corruption 92; and Art. 217 TFEU 149; and CJEU case law 106–7; and EU 'common values' 100; and Eurasian projects 116–17; and EU values 13, 63; and human rights in Eastern v. Euro-Mediterranean AAs 23–9; and ICC, references to 87; and international legal norms 91; and rule of law 24–6, 173; and WMD clauses 86; *see also* Action Plans (APs) of ENP; EU values in Association Agreements with Ukraine, Moldova and Georgia (Roman Petrov); *separate countries*

Austria, critic of EU sanctions against Russia 128
Azerbaijan: ENP Action Plan 15, 16, 87, 95; ENP participation 149n24; and Eurasian Economic Union 73; human rights violations and maintenance of EU-Azerbaijani relations 30–40; and Islamic law (sharia) 65; Mobility Partnership 177; Nagorno–Karabakh conflict and EU response 69; Partnership and Cooperation Agreement (PCA) 25; and rule of law in ENP 168, 176; and shared values 152; visa facilitation and readmission agreement 177n59, 178n62

Balfour, R. 160
Barcelona Process 17, 19
Barroso, José Manuel 127n79, 158, 171
Basheska, Elena 6–7; *see also* values-based conditionality and ENP (Elena Basheska and Dimitry Kochenov)
Bedouins 153
Belarus: and Collective Security Treaty Organization (CSTO) 140; and Eurasian Customs Union 139; and Eurasian Economic Union 73; EU restrictive measures against 49, 50–1, 52; and General System of Preferences (GSP) 173n37; Mobility Partnership 177; and rule of law in ENP 168, 176; and shared values 152–3; Visa Facilitation and Readmission Agreements negotiations 155
Ben Ali, Zine El Abidine 49n105, 51n120, 93
Berdyaev, Nikolai 130
Berezovskij, Boris 138
bilateral relations: and conditionality 71; EU–Switzerland bilateralism 70; v. regional economic integration 64–5
Björkdahl, A. 60n10
Bosnia-Herzegovina: Eastern Partnership / CSDP mission in 97; EU macro-financial assistance 44, 45n69; EU restrictive measures 53n135
Bosse, G. 62, 71
Brazil, and EU's 'normative' identity 65
breakaway regions, and EU restrictive measures 54
BRICS: and EU's 'normative' identity 65; and ties with Russia 127, 140
British Bank v. the Svyatoslav Fyodorov 'Eye Microsurgery' clinic case (Russia) 120

Brummer, K. 154–5
Bulgaria, EU macro-financial assistance 44
Burlyuk, Olga 7–8; *see also* rule of law and EU's Eastern neighbourhood (Peter van Elsuwege and Olga Burlyuk)
Burma, EU restrictive measures/sanctions against 51, 96
Bush, George W. 138

Central African Republic, EUFOR RCA 96
Central America, Association Agreement 87n29
CFSP (Common Foreign and Security Policy) 41, 43n59, 93–4, 95, 126
chapter overview 2–8
Charter of Fundamental Rights of the European Union (2010) 13, 29, 62, 63, 94, 170
Charter of Paris for a New Europe (Paris Charter) 28, 102, 118
Chechen conflict 133, 138
China: and Eurasian Economic Union 73; and EU's 'normative' identity 65
civil liberties, in ENP's Wider Europe Communication document (2003) 14
civil society: and Eastern Partnership (EaP) 18–19; and Partnership for Democracy and Shared Prosperity with the Southern Mediterranean (PDSP) 20; and review of ENP 22; Southern Neighbourhood Civil Society Forum 20; and Union for the Mediterranean (UfM) 19
Clima East and South projects 91
coherence: principle of 2; and rule of law export 168–9, 180–1
Collective Security Treaty Organization (CSTO) 140
coloured revolutions 133, 138
Commission on Security and Cooperation in Europe's (CSCE), Bonn document 27
Common Foreign and Security Policy (CFSP) 25, 41, 43n59, 93–4, 95, 126
Common Security and Defence Policy (CSDP) 69, 96–7, 108, 173
'common values' 61, 63, 65, 67, 70, 100, 102–3, 115, 153
conditionality: and *acquis* export 62; and bilateral relations 71; common values conditionality 63; criticism of 12; and democracy 22, 42–3; effectiveness of values-based conditionality, presumption of 153–6; enhanced

conditionality 102; in ENI regulation 41–3; ENP underpinning principle 2, 33, 151; and EU v. Russian values 72; *Ex ante / Ex post* conditionality 67; and integration-oriented agreements 101–2; market access conditionality 66, 68, 103–4; negative v. positive 67; political conditionality 19, 44–8, 74, 75; pre-accession conditionality model 35; and promotion of EU values 61; and regional economic integration 64–5; and rule of law export 174; and Union for the Mediterranean 19; and VLAPs 178; *see also* values-based conditionality and ENP (Elena Basheska and Dimitry Kochenov)
conflict resolution: and ENI / IPA II regulations 41; and EU 69–70, 83, 91, 96
consistency principle 43n59, 64, 70
constitutionalism, liberal democratic constitutionalism 154
contestation of values in ENP (Sieglinde Gstöhl): chapter overview 3–4; background and issues 58–60; ambiguity of values 61–2; conflict potential of values 63–5; emergence/re-emergence of competing values, 65–6; export of values, contestation of 66–7; lack of capacity and/or willingness in ENP countries 67–9; lack of capacity and/or willingness in EU 69–71; normative (market) power rivalry 72–3; summary and conclusions: ENP's conceptual flaws 73–5
Copenhagen European Council (1993) 157
Copenhagen political criteria 152
corruption, anti-corruption measures 90, 92–4
Cossacks 137
Côte d'Ivoire, EU restrictive measures 52n124
Council of Europe: collaboration with EU 91–2; Criminal Law Convention on Corruption 92, 94; Group of States against Corruption (GRECO) 92; human rights conventions 62; protection of personal data instruments 90; and rule of law 170; Venice Commission and rule of law 171–2, 175, 180
Court of Justice of the European Union (CJEU): case law of and Association Agreements 106–7; *Les Verts* ruling (1986) 167n1

Cremona, Marise 4, 33n1, 60, 156, 168, 175n47; *see also* multilateralism and ENP (Marise Cremona)
Crimea: EU sanctions/restrictive measures re. annexation of 96, 109; post-Crimea context and ENP 147–8, 149; proclamation of Autonomous Republic of Crimea 52; Russian annexation of 26, 38, 53, 71, 109, 123, 139, 140, 148; shutdown of Tatar-language media outlets, EU response to 37–8
Criminal Law Convention on Corruption (Council of Europe) 92, 94
crisis prevention/management, and EU 91, 96
CSDP (Common Security and Defence Policy) 69, 96–7, 108, 173

Damro, C. 59, 66
Deep and Comprehensive Free Trade Areas (DCFTAs): and EU values 61, 63, 66, 68, 70, 71, 72–3, 151; and implementation of EU law 91; as incentives 158; and integration-oriented agreements 101, 105, 106, 107; and Ukraine 159
deep and sustainable democracy 21–2, 23, 35, 42, 43, 63, 168
deep economic integration 63, 70
Delcour, L. 68n53, 73n76, 155n47
Del Sarto, R. 36
democracy: and action against corruption 92; and civil society 20; and conditionality principle 22, 42–3; deep and sustainable democracy 21–2, 23, 35, 42, 43, 63, 168; and Eastern Partnership 18, 19; and economic interests, conflict with 63–4, 70; and ENP reform 55; in ENP's 2004 Strategy Paper 14; and ENP's Action Plans 15, 62; in ENP's Wider Europe Communication document (2003) 13, 14; and EU macro-financial assistance 45–8; EU promotion of 70–1, 72; and EU restrictive measures 50, 51–2; as EU value 1, 12, 59; liberal democratic constitutionalism 154; and Partnership for Democracy and Shared Prosperity with the Southern Mediterranean (PDSP) 19–20; and security / stability 35–6; and Union for the Mediterranean 19
differentiation: ENP underpinning principle 2, 75; and regional economic integration 64–5; and rule of law export 168–9, 174, 180–1

186 *Index*

diffusion: of EU norm 66; value diffusion strategy 173
disability, UN Disability Convention 91
dispute settlements 68
Donetsk, People's Republic of, and EU restrictive measures 53, 56, 109–10
Dugin, Aleksandr 132, 134
dumping, anti-dumping initiatives 122
Dundovich, Elena 5–6; *see also* Russia's 'new values' (Elena Dundovich)

Eastern enlargement of EU 63, 152, 154
Eastern European countries: and ENP 156–7; *see also* post-Soviet countries
Eastern neighbours: and ENP 12–13, 23, 69; and ENP's Action Plans 15–16; and ENP's Action Plans and human rights 23–9; EU and competition with Russia over Eastern Neighbourhood 58, 60; and EU's 'normative' identity 65; and Wider Europe Communication document (2003) 14, 15; *see also* EU values and southern / eastern neighbours (N. Ghazaryan); post-Soviet countries; rule of law and EU's Eastern neighbourhood (Peter van Elsuwege and Olga Burlyuk)
Eastern Partnership (EaP): creation 11, 74, 83; CSDP cooperation panel 96–7; and deep and sustainable democracy 22; description of and values 16–19, 23; and Eurasian Economic Union 71, 73; and mobility 177, 179, 180; and Russia 18, 139; Summit Declaration (Prague, May 2009) 18; Summit Declaration (Riga, May 2015) 100
Ecofin Council, Genval Criteria 45
economic integration: and EU accession process 63; regional economic integration 64–5; *see also* pre-accession process
economic interests/values, and political values, conflict with 63–4, 70
EEA (European Economic Area) 70, 106, 150, 157
EFTA (European Free Trade Association) states, support for EU sanctions re. annexation of Crimea 96
Egypt: anti-terrorism law, EU response to 37n22; ENP Action Plan 15, 16; ENP conditionality and overthrow of President Morsi 22; ENP 'reluctant' partner 155; and ENP shared values 152, 153; EU restrictive measures/ sanctions 49, 50, 51, 52, 56, 92, 93–4; Euro-Med Agreement 24n77, 25n84, 28n101; EU's flexible approach towards 155; rebellion against Western-backed authoritarian rulers 72; repressive measures, European Parliament's condemnation of 38n28, 39; repressive measures, EU's mild criticism of 38–9
Ekho Moskvy (Russian radio station) 138
Elsuwege, Peter van 7–8, 149n21, 150n27; *see also* rule of law and EU's Eastern neighbourhood (Peter van Elsuwege and Olga Burlyuk)
emerging economies, and EU's 'normative' identity 65
energy, EU Third Energy Package 122
essential elements clauses 17, 23–9, 63, 86, 102, 103, 108, 173, 174
'The EU and Its Values: Contestation and Consistency' (University of Pisa, 2014) 8
EUBAMs (European Union Border Assistance Missions) 69–70, 108
EUFORs (European Union Forces): Libya 70; RCA (Central African Republic) 96
Eurasian Customs Union 139
Eurasian Economic Commission 123
Eurasian Economic Community 116
Eurasian Economic Union (EAEU) 71, 73, 100n3, 116, 148n16
Eurasism 130, 131; Eurasist Movement (2001) 134; neo-Eurasism 132, 133
Euratom 85
Euro-Mediterranean Associations Agreements (AAs) 13; and human rights compared with Eastern AAs 23–9
Euronest parliamentary cooperation framework 18
Europe Agreements 157
European Commission: Communication on strengthening the ENP (206) 15; ENP driven by 74; and rule of law 170, 172; Wider Europe Communication (2003) 13–14, 15, 61–2, 145, 152n34
European Common Aviation Area (ECAA) 106
European Convention on Human Rights and Fundamental Freedoms (ECHR) 14, 24, 28, 43n61, 54, 90, 91–2, 94, 102, 103
European Economic Area (EEA) 70, 106, 150, 157
European External Action Service (EEAS) 37, 74
European Free Trade Association (EFTA) states, support for EU sanctions re. annexation of Crimea 96

European Instrument for Democracy and Human Rights 92
European Neighbourhood Instrument (ENI) 33, 40–3, 83, 92, 159–60
European Neighbourhood Partnership Instrument (ENPI) 41, 42n54, 159–61
European Neighbourhood Policy (ENP): aims and vision 1–2, 58; conceptual flaws 74–5; and Eastern European countries 156–7; and Eastern neighbours 12–13, 23, 69; enlargement methodology without membership option 69; and EU accession prospects 157–9; Eurocentric approach 75; European Commission Communication on strengthening the ENP (206) 15; and EU values, exporting of 11–13; EU values as set out in ENP documents and Action Plan 13–16; EU values-based approach, rationale and criticism of 33–40; funding allocation for 160–1; 'Implementation of the European Neighbourhood Policy in 2014' 152–3; incentives issue 156–62; and migrants, large flows of 148; reviews of 20–3, 55–6, 63, 71, 75, 168; and Russia 72, 116, 139, 147–8, 149, 150; Strategy Paper (2004) 14–15, 16, 62; Wider Europe Communication document (2003) 13–14, 15, 61–2, 152n34; 'willing' v. 'reluctant' partners 155–6, 162; *see also* Action Plans (APs) of ENP; Association Agreements (AAs); coherence; conditionality; contestation of values in ENP (Sieglinde Gstöhl); differentiation; Eastern Partnership (EaP); multilateralism and ENP (Marise Cremona); Union for the Mediterranean (UfM); values-based conditionality and ENP (Elena Basheska and Dimitry Kochenov)
European Parliament: condemnation of anti-human rights legislation 38; condemnation of Egypt's repressive measures 38n28, 39; on EU-Russia relations 117; Resolution (2013/2081(INI) on Common Foreign and Security Policy 35; and suspension of assistance under ENI 43; Tavares report on Hungary 171
European Security Strategy (ESS) 71; and multilateralism 81, 84
European Union (EU): 2004 enlargement 12; accession prospects and ENP 157–9; accession to and economic reform agenda 63; community of values 1; competition with Russia over Eastern Neighbourhood 58, 60; and conflict resolution 69–70, 83, 91, 96; and Council of Europe, collaboration with 91–2; as democratizer 71; Eastern enlargement 63, 152, 154; and Eurasian Economic Union 73; lack of capacity and/or willingness and value export 69–71; 'market power Europe' concept 59–60; and multilateralism 81–4, 88–9; 'normative' identity of 36, 59, 65; outside perception of 65; soft power of 37, 154; and United Nations Security Council (UNSC) Resolutions 43; *see also* EU-Russia relations and shared values (Paul Kalinichenko); pre-accession process
European Union Basic Anti-Dumping Regulation (2009) 122
European Union Border Assistance Missions (EUBAMs) 69–70, 108
European Union Code of Conduct on Arms Exports 91
European Union Forces (EUFORs): Libya 70; RCA (Central African Republic) 96
European Union Monitoring Mission (EUMM) 69
European Union Multinational Tactical Battle Groups 97
Euroscepticism, and Islamist parties 64
EU-Russia relations and shared values (Paul Kalinichenko): chapter overview 5; introduction 115–17; legal aspects of modern confrontation in EU-Russia relations 123–7; legal background of EU-Russia relations 117–21; trade disputes between EU and Russia within WTO 121–3; conclusions 127–8
EU values: v. *acquis* 62, 63, 147, 153, 170–1; economic v. political values 63–4, 70; export of 2, 11–13, 36–7, 55–6, 61–2, 66–71, 73; list of 1, 12, 34, 60; value diffusion strategy 173; *see also* contestation of values in ENP (Sieglinde Gstöhl); EU values and financial instruments / restrictive measures (S. Poli); EU values and southern / eastern neighbours (N. Ghazaryan); EU values in Association Agreements with Ukraine, Moldova and Georgia (Roman Petrov); values; values-based conditionality and ENP (Elena Basheska and Dimitry Kochenov)

188 *Index*

EU values and financial instruments / restrictive measures (S. Poli): chapter overview 3; background and issues 33–4; EU values-based approach to ENP, rationale and criticism of 34–40; importance of EU values and principle of conditionality in ENI regulation 40–3; macrofinancial assistance and political conditionality 44–8; restrictive measures in context of ENP 48–55; strategy for reforming ENP and EU values 55–6; summary and conclusions 56

EU values and southern / eastern neighbours (N. Ghazaryan): chapter overview 2–3; ENP and export of EU values 11–13; EU values as set out in ENP documents and Action Plan 13–16; geographic split of neighbourhood policies and projection of EU values after Arab Spring 16–23; human rights clauses in Eastern v. Euro-Mediterranean Association Agreements 23–9; summary and conclusions 29

EU values in Association Agreements with Ukraine, Moldova and Georgia (Roman Petrov): chapter overview 4–5; introduction 99–100; agreements' objectives and specific features 100–2; enhanced conditionality 102–4; EU values and countries' legal systems 104–7; EU values and restrictive measures 107–10; concluding remarks 110

Ex ante / Ex post conditionality 67
Ezz, Ahmed Abdelaziz 93–4

finalités géographiques 156
Financial Action Task Force (FATF) 90
financial instruments *see* EU values and financial instruments / restrictive measures (S. Poli)
Finland, critic of EU sanctions against Russia 128
formalist (or 'thin') approach, v. substantive (or 'thick') approach 172
France: rule of law problems 169; and Union for the Mediterranean (UfM) 19
freedom: EU value 1, 12; fundamental freedoms and ENP's Action Plans (APs) 15
Füle, S. 18n39
Fyodorov, Svyatoslav 120

Garibashvili, Irakli 159
Gaza: and ENP shared values 153; European Union Border Assistance Mission (EUBAM) 69; *see also* Palestine
General System of Preferences (GSP) 173n37
Genval Criteria 45
Georgia: 2008 war with Russia 18, 46, 71, 108, 137, 139; Abkhazia conflict 54, 69, 108; agreement re. EU crisis management operations 96; ENP Action Plan 15, 16, 87, 95–6; ENP Association Agreement ('common values' 100; 'common values' conditionality 102–3; enhanced conditionality 102; EU security agenda 95; EU values 13, 23, 25n85, 26, 27, 28–9; EU values and national legal system 104–7; EU values and restrictive measures 107–10; human rights 24; ICC references 87n30; international standards 24–5; legislative approximation mechanisms 68; 'market access' conditionality 103–4; objectives and specific features 100–2; ratification of 99; rule of law 168, 174–5; as a step towards EU membership 158–9; WMD clause 86; ENP participation and accession prospects 157, 158–9; and ENP's value export 73; EUFOR RCA (Central African Republic) mission 96; EUJUST THEMIS 173n39, 175; EU macro-financial assistance 45–6; EU response to conflicts in 69; European Union Monitoring Mission (EUMM) 69; EU sanctions, support for 96; EU Training Mission in Mali 96; Mobility Partnership 177; Partnership and Cooperation Agreement) 25; South Ossetia conflict 38, 54, 69, 109; visa facilitation and readmission agreement 177n59; Visa Liberalisation Action Plan 161, 178, 179; as 'willing' ENP partners 155

Ghazaryan, Nariné 2–3, 62; *see also* EU values and southern / eastern neighbours (N. Ghazaryan)
Gianniou, M. 155n48
Gillespie, R. 20
Global Approach to Migration and Mobility (GAMM) 176, 177
good governance: and Eastern Partnership 18, 19; in ENP's 2004 Strategy Paper 14
GOST technical standards 72–3

Greece, critic of EU sanctions against Russia 128
Group of States against Corruption (GRECO) 92
Gstöhl, Sieglinde 3–4; *see also* contestation of values in ENP (Sieglinde Gstöhl)
Gulag 135
Gusinskij, Vladimir 138

Hague Conference on Private International Law 91
Hahn, Johannes 1
Hariri, Rafiq 48n94, 50
Haukkala, H. 72
Helsinki Final Act (1975) 28, 102, 118
Hillion, C. 149, 156
Hoffmeister, F. 28n105
homogeneity, principle of 70
human rights: and admission agreements 178; and deep democracy 21–2; and Eastern v. Euro-Mediterranean Association Agreements 23–9; and economic interests, conflict with 63–4, 70; and ENI regulation 40–1; in ENP's 2004 Strategy Paper 14; and ENP's Action Plans 15; in ENP's Wider Europe Communication document (2003) 13, 14; European Convention on Human Rights and Fundamental Freedoms (ECHR) 14, 24, 28, 43n61, 54, 90, 91–2, 94, 102, 103; European Instrument for Democracy and Human Rights 92; European Parliament's condemnation of anti-human rights legislation 38; EU value 1, 12, 59; international conventions 62; Russian elite's and Western understanding of human rights 66; United Nations Universal Declaration of Human Rights (UDHR) 15, 24, 27, 28, 102, 103; violation of by Azerbaijan and maintenance of EU-Azerbaijani relations 30–40; violation of by Israel and upgrading of EU-Israel relations 39; violations of and EU restrictive measures 50
Hungary, rule of law problems 169, 171

ICC (International Criminal Court) 14, 15, 87; Rome Statute of 87, 90
ILO Conventions 91
Ilyin, Ivan 130
incentives: incentive-based approach 42, 43n58; presumption of sufficient incentives 156–62

India, and EU's 'normative' identity 65
institution-building 22
Instrument for Development Cooperation 42n55
Instrument of Pre-Accession Assistance II (IPA II) 40, 41, 41n50, 42n55, 92n55
integration: *finalités géographiques* of 156; *see also* economic integration; pre-accession process
integration-oriented agreements: concept 101; and Deep and Comprehensive Free Trade Areas (DCFTAs) 101, 105, 106, 107
intellectual property, international treaties on 91
International Atomic Energy Agency (IAEA): Additional Protocols 85; and EU Decisions on nuclear security 87
international commitments, implementation and enforcement of 90–1
International Criminal Court (ICC) 14, 15, 87; Rome Statute of 87, 90
international institutions, support for 87
international law: and ENI regulation 43; and ENP 146; and EU multilateralism 82, 90; and EU values 35; Hague Conference on Private International Law 91; humanitarian law 35, 39; intellectual property 91; violations of by ENP countries and EU response 38; violations of by ENP countries and EU restrictive measures 50, 52–3; violations of by Russia and EU response 40
International Monetary Fund 44
international order, rule-based 81, 84
international standards: and Association Agreements 24–5, 27–9; in ENP's 2004 Strategy Paper 14–15; and 'shared values' 61–2
IPA II (Instrument of Pre-Accession Assistance II) 40, 41, 41n50, 42n55, 92n55
Islam, rise of political Islam 65, 72
Islamic law (sharia) 65
Islamic State 148
Islamic terrorism 133, 138
Islamist parties, and Euroscepticism 64
Israel: ENP Action Plan 16; Euro-Med Agreement 24n77, 28n100, 29; human rights violations and upgrading of EU-Israel relations 39; Israel-Palestine conflict, EU response to 69; and 'shared values' 153

190   *Index*

Italy, critic of EU sanctions against Russia 128
Ivan the Terrible, tsar of Russia 134
Izborsk Club 134

Janukovich (or Yanukovych), Viktor 52, 100
joint ownership, principle of 70, 75, 162, 174, 175
Jordan: cosmetic domestic reforms 72; ENP Action Plan 15, 16, 87, 95, 96; EU macro-financial assistance 46–7; Euro-Med Agreement 24n77, 25n84, 28n101; mobility partnership 179; and 'shared values' 153

Kalinichenko, Paul 5; *see also* EU-Russia relations and shared values (Paul Kalinichenko)
Kazakhstan: and Collective Security Treaty Organization 140; and Eurasian Customs Union 139; and Eurasian Economic Union 73
Klabbers, J. 154
Kochenov, Dimitry 6–7, 62; *see also* values-based conditionality and ENP (Elena Basheska and Dimitry Kochenov)
Kolchak, Aleksandr 134
Korosteleva, E. 37, 66
Kratochvíl, P. 66
Kurki, M. 71
Kyoto Protocol 91
Kyrgyztan: and Collective Security Treaty Organization 140; EU macro-financial assistance 47–8; and Eurasian Economic Union 73

labour standards: in ENP's 2004 Strategy Paper 14; in ENP's Wider Europe Communication document (2003) 14; ILO Conventions 91
law *see* international law; rule of law; rule of law and EU's Eastern neighbourhood (Peter van Elsuwege and Olga Burlyuk)
Lazarou, E. 155n48
Lebanon: ENP Action Plan 15, 16, 87; EU restrictive measures 48, 49, 50; Euro-Med Agreement 25n84; and Islamic law (sharia) 65
legal certainty, principle of 70
legal systems, and EU values 104–7
legislative approximation 62, 66, 68, 102, 103–5, 118

Leino, P. 61, 66n38, 68n51, 72n72
Lenin, Vladimir 131, 136
Leonard, M. 72
Leont'ev, Konstantin 130
liberal democratic constitutionalism 154
Libya: EUFOR Libya 70; EU response to conflict 69; EU restrictive measures 48, 49, 50; European Union Border Assistance Mission (EUBAM) 69–70; rebellion against Western-backed authoritarian rulers 72
Liechtenstein, support for EU sanctions against Syria 96
Luhansk People's Republic, and EU restrictive measures 52–3, 109–10

Macedonia: Eastern Partnership / CSDP mission in 97; EU macro-financial assistance 44–5; support for EU sanctions against Syria 96
macro-financial assistance (MFA) 33, 44–8
Magen, A. 154n39, 155–6
Malaysia Airlines Flight 17 (MH17), shooting down of 109
Mali, EU Training Mission in 96
Malmström, Cecilia 177
Manners, I. 59, 66
market access conditionality 66, 68, 103–4
market economy principle: and ENI regulation 41; and EU Charter of Fundamental Rights 63; and EU macro-financial assistance 45; and EU-Russia Partnership and Cooperation Agreement 118; as EU value 26–7, 35, 59; and human rights/democratic principles 63–4; and IPA II Regulation 41n50
'market power Europe' concept 59–60
Memorial Association (Russia), Center for Research and Information (NITs) 135
migration policy 176–9; Global Approach to Migration and Mobility (GAMM) 176, 177; *see also* mobility
minority rights 1, 12, 14, 34, 35, 37–8, 41n47
Missiroli, A. 160
mobility: and Eastern Partnership 177, 179, 180; Global Approach to Migration and Mobility (GAMM) 176, 177; as incentive 161; Mobility Partnerships (MPs) 177, 178; and Southern Mediterranean countries 179
Mogherini, Federica 1, 35–6, 55, 117

Moldova: agreement re. EU crisis management operations 96; ENP Action Plan 15, 16, 87, 95–6; ENP Association Agreement (collaboration with Council of Europe 92; 'common values' 100; 'common values' conditionality 102–3; enhanced conditionality 102; EU security agenda 95; EU values 13, 23, 25n85, 26, 27, 28–9; EU values and national legal system 104–7; EU values and restrictive measures 107–10; human rights 24; ICC references 87n30; legislative approximation mechanisms 68; 'market access' conditionality 103–4; objectives and specific features 100–2; ratification of 99; rule of law 168, 174–6; as a step towards EU membership 158–9; WMD clause 86; ENP participation and accession prospects 157, 158–9; and ENP's value export 73; EU macro-financial assistance 45; European Union Border Assistance Mission (EUBAM) 69; EU sanctions, support for 96; and EU Training Mission in Mali 96; Mobility Partnership 177; Partnership and Cooperation Agreement 27n94; and Russia 148; Transnistria breakaway region 48–9, 50, 54, 69, 108, 137; visa facilitation and readmission agreement 177n59; Visa Liberalisation Action Plan 161, 178, 179; as 'willing' ENP partners 155
money laundering, and Financial Action Task Force (FATF) 90
Montenegro, support for EU sanctions against Syria 96
'more for more' principle 46, 55, 71, 75
Morocco: cosmetic domestic reforms 72; ENP Action Plan 15, 16; EU membership rejection (1987) 12; Euro-Med Agreement 25n84, 28n101; mobility partnership 179
Morsi, Mohamed 22
multilateralism and ENP (Marise Cremona): chapter overview 4; introduction: multilateralism as principle of EU external policy 81–4; common problems and multilateral solutions 84 (promoting ratification of multilateral conventions 84–7; support for international institutions 87; support for the EU's own multilateral agenda 88–9; effective enforcement of the law and collaboration 90; collaboration with Council of Europe 91–2; EU sanctions regimes for anti-corruption investigations 92–4; implementation/enforcement of international commitments 90–1; ENP states and EU's security agenda 94–5; EU-led missions 96–7; EU sanctions regimes 95–6; summary and conclusions 97–8
multivectoralism 139

Nagorno-Karabakh, EU response to conflict 69
Naši (Russian youth organization) 137
nationalism, v. patriotism (Russian context) 133–4
NATO, Putin on 138
Neighbourhood Economic Community (NEC) 157–8
Neighbourhood Investment Facility (NIF) 160
Nicholas II, tsar of Russia 136
'normative' identity of Europe 36, 59, 65
norms, definition 60
North Africa, Arab Spring and EU reaction to 64
Norway: rule of law advisors mission in Moldova 175–6; support for EU sanctions against Syria 96
Nye, J. S. 154n44

Olympic Games (Sochi) 137
Operation Atlanta (anti-piracy mission) 97
Organization for Security and Co-operation in Europe (OSCE) 15, 17, 24, 50–1, 62
organized crime, Palermo Convention (UN Convention against Transnational Organized Crime) 89, 90
ORT (Russian TV channel) 138

Pace, M. 65, 67n48
Palermo Convention (UN Convention against Transnational Organized Crime) 89, 90
Palestine: ENP Action Plan 16, 29; Israel-Palestine conflict, EU response to 69; and 'shared values' 153; *see also* Gaza
Panebianco, S. 63–4
Paris Charter (Charter of Paris for a New Europe) 28, 102, 118

192 *Index*

parliamentary cooperation: Euronest parliamentary cooperation framework 18; and Union for the Mediterranean 19
Partnership and Cooperation Agreements (PCAs) 17, 25, 26–7, 176; EU-Russia PCA 117, 118, 119–21, 126
Partnership for Democracy and Shared Prosperity with the Southern Mediterranean (PDSP) 19–20, 22, 179
patriotism, v. nationalism (Russian context) 133–4
Patten, Chris 145n1
Pech, L. 26n88, 169
personal data, protection of personal data instruments 90
Peter the Great, tsar of Russia 130, 131, 134
Petrov, Roman 4–5, 61, 66n38, 68n51, 72n72, 150n27; *see also* EU values in Association Agreements with Ukraine, Moldova and Georgia (Roman Petrov)
piracy, Operation Atlanta (anti-piracy mission) 97
pluralism: in ENP's Wider Europe Communication document (2003) 14; and Union for the Mediterranean 19
Poland: and Eastern Partnership (EaP) 18n33; on ENP and EU membership perspective 157n63
Poli, Sara 3; *see also* EU values and financial instruments / restrictive measures (S. Poli)
political conditionality 19, 44–8, 74, 75
political values, and economic values, conflict with 63–4, 70
Poroshenko, Petro 100, 159
post-Soviet countries: and Eurasian Economic Union 73; and Russian values 72; and Western values 37, 65–6; *see also* Eastern European countries
pre-accession process: conditionality 35; market access conditionality 66; *see also* Instrument of Pre-Accession Assistance II (IPA II)
Pridnestrovian Moldovan Republic *see* Transnistria breakaway region (Moldova)
Pussy Riot 135
Putin, Vladimir: and 9/11 terrorist attacks 133, 138; attitudes towards the West 133–5; EU sanctions against 'acquaintances of' 53; and foreign policy 138–40; and 'Great Russia' image 130; KGB past 136; on mass media and oligarchs 137–8; and patriotism 133, 134; on Russian history 135; and Russian Orthodox Church 134–5, 137; and 'traditional' v. 'new' European values 135; *see also* Russia's 'new values' (Elena Dundovich)

Reading, Viviane 169n13
readmission agreements 177–8, 179
regional economic integration, v. bilateral relations 64–5
regionalism, and multilateralism 83
restrictive measures/sanctions: in context of ENP 33, 34, 48–55; EU sanctions regimes 92–4, 95–6, 154–5; and integration-oriented agreements (Ukraine, Moldova, Georgia) 107–10; against Russia 48–9, 50–1, 52–3, 55, 56, 109–10, 123–7, 128, 139–40, 155; *see also* EU values and financial instruments / restrictive measures (S. Poli)
'ring of friends' notion 94–5, 145–6, 147, 148, 151
ROLISP (Rule of Law Institutional Strengthening Programme) 176
Romania: EU macro-financial assistance 44; rule of law problems 169
Rompuy, Herman van 100n4
Rosneft case (Russia) 126
rule-based international order 81, 84
rule of law 1, 12, 13, 14, 15, 21, 24–6, 35; *see also* rule of law and EU's Eastern neighbourhood (Peter van Elsuwege and Olga Burlyuk)
rule of law and EU's Eastern neighbourhood (Peter van Elsuwege and Olga Burlyuk): chapter overview 7–8; introduction 167–9; concept of rule of law 169–73; EU's 'rule of law export': instruments and mechanisms 173–6; reconciling coherence and differentiation: migration/mobility example 176–80; conclusions 180–1
Russia: 1993 Constitution 115, 119–20; and 2004 EU enlargement 12; and Arab countries 140; and Armenia 148; and BRICS 127, 140; Chechen conflict 133, 138; and Collective Security Treaty Organization 140; competition with EU over Eastern Neighbourhood 58, 60; Cossacks 137; and Crimea, annexation of 26, 38, 53, 71, 109, 123, 139, 140, 148; and Eastern Partnership 18, 139; and ENI regulation 40;

and ENP 72, 116, 139, 147–8, 149, 150; and ENP countries 162; and Eurasian Economic Community 116; and Eurasian Economic Union 71, 73, 100n3; EU restrictive measures/sanctions against 48–9, 50–1, 52–3, 55, 56, 109–10, 123–7, 128, 139–40, 155; EU–Russia Common Spaces 118; EU-Russia Partnership and Cooperation Agreement 117, 118, 119–21, 126; and EU's 'normative' identity 65; and EU values export 55–6; Fyodorov's Eye Microsurgery clinic case 120; Georgia war (2008) 18, 46, 71, 108, 137, 139; Gulag and historical memory 135; international law violation, EU response to 40; and Malaysia Airlines Flight 17 (MH17), shooting down of 109; and mass media 137–8; and mobility 179–80; and Moldova 148; Naši (youth organization) 137; New Basic Agreement negotiations 121; Olympic Games (Sochi) 137; Pussy Riot case 135; Rosneft case 126; Russian elite's and Western understanding of human rights 66; and Shanghai Cooperation Organization 140; Simutenkov case 120; and South Ossetia, treaty with 38; Ternavsky case 126–7; Topol case 120; and Transnistria breakaway region (Moldova) 108, 137; and Ukraine's DCFTA, delayed implementation of 159; and United States 138–9, 140; and Wider Europe Communication document (2003) 14; WTO accession 121; Young Guards 137; YUKOS case 120; *see also* EU-Russia relations and shared values (Paul Kalinichenko); Russia's 'new values' (Elena Dundovich)
Russian Orthodox Church 134–5, 137
Russia's 'new values' (Elena Dundovich): chapter overview 5–6; 'Great Russia' new image 130; origin of Russian identity 130–2; Putin's attitudes towards the West 133–5; question of historical memory 135–6; rituals and symbols 136–8; Russia's foreign policy under Putin 138–40

sanctions *see* restrictive measures/sanctions
Schengen countries, and Visa Liberalisation Action Plans 161
Schulz, Martin 159

security: and democracy 35–6; and ENP states 94–5; European Security Strategy (ESS) 71, 81, 84; nuclear security 87; participation in EU-led missions 96–7; and support for EU sanctions regimes 95–6; UN and EU security agenda 84
Segodnya (Russian newspaper) 138
Serbia: Stabilisation and Association Agreement 27n94; support for EU sanctions against Syria 96
Shanghai Cooperation Organization (SCO) 140
'shared values' 13, 14, 34–5, 61–2, 65, 75, 84, 151–3; *see also* EU-Russia relations and shared values (Paul Kalinichenko)
sharia (Islamic law) 65
Simutenkov case (Russia) 120
Slavophilism 131
small arms and light weapons (SALW) 88
soft power 37, 154
Solana, Javier 145n1
solidarity, as goal of EU external action 63
South Africa, and EU's 'normative' identity 65
Southern Neighbourhood Civil Society Forum 20
Southern neighbours: and ENP 17, 23; and ENP's Action Plans 15, 16; and EU's 'normative' identity 65; and mobility 179; and Partnership for Democracy and Shared Prosperity with the Southern Mediterranean (PDSP) 19–20; and Wider Europe Communication document (2003) 14; *see also* Euro-Mediterranean Associations Agreements (AAs); EU values and southern / eastern neighbours (N. Ghazaryan)
South Ossetia: EU response to conflict 38, 69, 109; and EU restrictive measures 54
Spain, critic of EU sanctions against Russia 128
Stabilisation and Association Agreements (SAAs) 24n78, 25, 26–7; with the Western Balkans 61, 102
stability, and democracy 35–6
Stalin, Josef 132, 134, 135, 136
Stolypin, Pyotr 134
substantive (or 'thick') approach, v. formalist (or 'thin') approach 172
Sudan, EU restrictive measures 54n137
supranationality, v. national autonomy 70
Switzerland: and ENP 150; EU–Switzerland bilateralism 70

Index

Syria: EU response to conflict 69; EU restrictive measures/sanctions 49, 50, 96; Euro-Med Agreement 25n87; rebellion against Western-backed authoritarian rulers 72

Tajikistan, and Collective Security Treaty Organization 140
Tavares, Rui, report on Hungary 171
Ternavsky case (Russia) 126–7
terrorism: 9/11 terrorist attacks 133, 138; EU response's to Egypt's anti-terrorism law 37n22; United Nations Global Counter-Terrorism Strategy 90
'thin' (or formalist) approach, v. 'thick' (or substantive) approach 172
Third Energy Package 122
Tjutčev (or Tyutchev), F. I. 130n1
Tocci, N. 155
Tömmel, I. 36n13
Topol case (Russia) 120
tout court approach 27–8
Transatlantic Trade and Investment Partnership (TTIP) 139
Transnistria breakaway region (Moldova) 48–9, 50, 54, 69, 108, 137
Trans-Pacific Partnership (TPP) 139
Treaty of Lisbon 21, 43, 59, 60, 73, 83, 150n26
Treaty of Maastricht 167
Treaty of the European Union (TEU): Art. 2 (EU values) 1, 12, 34, 35, 59, 146n4, 150n29, 152, 167, 169, 170–1, 175; Art. 3 146n4; Art. 3(1) 63; Art. 3(3) 63; Art. 3(5) 36, 59, 82, 95, 146; Art. 6 34n7; Art. 8 21, 35, 56, 82, 84, 149–51, 167; Art. 8(1) 60, 149, 152n35; Art. 8(2) 150; Art. 13 36–7; Art. 21 64, 81n1; Art. 21(1) 27, 34n7, 61, 63, 82, 83, 146; Art. 21(2) 83–4, 90, 95; Art. 21(2)(a) 37; Art. 21(2)(b) 94, 167; Art. 21(2)(c) 27; Art. 21(2)(d) 94; Art. 21(3) 173; Art. 31(1) 101; Art. 37 101; Art. 49 12, 59; Art. 308 44n62; Preamble 34n6
Treaty on Eurasian Economic Union (EAEU) 116
Treaty on the Functioning of the European Union (TFEU): Art. 212 44n62, 46, 47n88; Art. 213 47n88; Art. 217 101, 149; Art. 218 149; Art. 352 45
TRIPS (Trade-Related Aspects of Intellectual Property Rights) 91
Tsouropas, G. 155n48

TTIP (Transatlantic Trade and Investment Partnership) 139
Tunisia: corruption 92–3; ENP Action Plan 15, 16, 95, 96; EU macro-financial assistance 46–7; EU restrictive measures/sanctions 49, 50, 51, 52, 56, 92–3; Euro-Med Agreement 25n84, 28n100; mobility partnership 179; rebellion against Western-backed authoritarian rulers 72; as 'reluctant' ENP partner 155
Turkey: and collaboration between EU and Council of Europe 92; EU–Turkey customs union 70; rise of political Islam 65
Tyutchev (or Tjutčev), F. I. 130n1

Ukraine: agreement re. EU crisis management operations 96; corruption 92, 94; DCFTA, delayed implementation of 159; and Eastern Partnership / CSDP missions 97; ENP Action Plan 15, 16; ENP Association Agreement (Arms Trade Treaty 89; collaboration with Council of Europe 92; 'common values' 100; 'common values' conditionality 102–3; CSDP cooperation 97; enhanced conditionality 102; EU security agenda 95; EU values 13, 23, 25n85, 26, 27, 28–9; EU values and national legal system 104–7; EU values and restrictive measures 96, 107–10; good neighbourly relations 146–7; human rights 24; ICC references 87; international commitments 90–1; legislative approximation mechanisms 68; 'market access' conditionality 103–4; objectives and specific features 100–2; ratification of 73, 99–100; rule of law 168, 174–5; as a step towards EU membership 158–9; WMD clause 86; ENP participation and accession prospects 157, 158–9; and ENP's value export 73; EU macro-financial assistance 45, 46–7; EU restrictive measures/sanctions 49, 50, 52–3, 56, 92, 94, 110; EuroMaidan revolution 73, 100, 123; European Union Border Assistance Mission 69; and EU-Russian relations 116–17; EU sanctions, support for 51, 96; and Malaysia Airlines Flight 17 (MH17), shooting down of 109; and mobility 177n58; Partnership and

Cooperation Agreement 27n94; visa facilitation and readmission agreement 177n59; Visa Liberalisation Action Plan 161, 178, 179; war in Easter Ukraine 71, 110, 137; *see also* Crimea; Donetsk, People's Republic of; Luhansk People's Republic
Union for the Mediterranean (UfM) 11, 17, 19, 23, 74, 83; Paris Summit for the Mediterranean Joint Declaration (13 July 2008) 19
United Nations: and EU-led peacekeeping missions 96; and EU multilateralism 81; and EU restrictive measures 48; and EU's Arms Trade Treaty 88–9; and EU security agenda 84; human rights conventions 14, 62; and Russia's annexation of Crimea 53, 109
United Nations Charter 14, 24, 82, 146
United Nations Convention against Corruption 90, 92, 93, 94
United Nations Convention against Transnational Organized Crime (Palermo Convention) 89, 90
United Nations Disability Convention 91
United Nations Framework Convention on Climate Change, Kyoto Protocol 91
United Nations Global Counter-Terrorism Strategy 90
United Nations Millennium Declaration 150
United Nations Office for the Coordination of Humanitarian Affairs 70
United Nations Refugee Convention 90
United Nations Security Council (UNSC): and EU 43; Resolution 1373 (2001) 90; Resolution 1540 (2004) 87, 89; and Ukraine's Association Agreement 90
United Nations Universal Declaration of Human Rights (UDHR) 15, 24, 27, 28, 102, 103
United States: Rule of Law Institutional Strengthening Programme (ROLISP) 176; and Russia under Putin 138–9, 140
universal values 37, 40, 61, 65, 75, 152
University of Pisa, 'The EU and Its Values: Contestation and Consistency' (2014) 8

values: 'common values' 61, 63, 65, 67, 70, 100, 102–3, 115, 153; 'shared values' 13, 14, 34–5, 61–2, 65, 75, 84, 151–3; in United Nations Millennium Declaration 150n31; universal values 37, 40, 61, 65, 75, 152; Western values 35, 37, 65–6, 72; *see also* EU values
values-based conditionality and ENP (Elena Basheska and Dimitry Kochenov): chapter overview 6–7; introduction 145–9; Article 8 TEU and 'ring of friends' 149–51; presumption of effectiveness of values-based conditionality 153–6; presumption of shared values 151–3; presumption of sufficient incentives 156–62; conclusion 162; *see also* conditionality
Van Elsuwege , P. *see* Elsuwege, Peter van
Venice Commission (Council of Europe) 171–2, 175, 180
visa facilitation and readmission agreements 155, 177–8, 179
Visa Liberalisation Action Plans (VLAPs) 161, 173n38, 178, 179–80

weapons of mass destruction (WMD) 25, 84–7, 90
Western Balkan countries: and collaboration between EU and Council of Europe 92; and mobility 179; Stabilisation and Association Agreement with 61, 102
Western Newly Independent States (WNIS), and Wider Europe Communication document (2003) 14
Western Sahara, EU response to conflict 69
Western values 35, 37, 65–6, 72
Wider Europe Communication (2003) 13–14, 15, 61–2, 145, 152n34
Wolczuk, K. 68n53, 73n76
World Trade Organization (WTO) 63, 73, 118, 121–3; Anti-Dumping Code 122

Yanukovych (or Janukovich), Viktor 52, 100
Yeltsin, Boris 133
Young Guards (United Russia Party) 137
YUKOS case (Russia) 120

Zimbabwe, EU restrictive measures 51